MW00618268

Nahum, Habakkuk, and Zephaniah

Lights in the Valley

Yaakov Beasley

נחום חבקוק
צפניה

Nahum, Habakkuk, and Zephaniah

Lights in the Valley

Maggid Books

Nahum, Habakkuk, and Zephaniah
Lights in the Valley

First Edition, 2020

Maggid Books
An imprint of Koren Publishers Jerusalem Ltd.

POB 8531, New Milford, CT 06776-8531, USA
& POB 4044, Jerusalem 9104001, Israel
www.maggidbooks.com

Cover images: www.shutterstock.com
by Denis Belitsky and Kamira

The publication of this book was made possible
through the generous support of the *Jewish Book Trust*.

ISBN 978-1-59264-521-3, *hardcover*

A CIP catalogue record for this title is
available from the British Library

Printed and bound in the United States

In Loving Memory of

Mr. Albert Allen, a"h

אברהם בן סלחא

Contents

HABAKKUK

ZEPHANIAH

Introduction

Studying Prophets

> There were many [prophets], as it is taught in a *baraita*: Numerous prophets arose for the Jewish people – double the amount [of Israelites] as left Egypt [1.2 million].... Prophecies that were relevant for future generations were recorded [in the Bible]; otherwise they were not recorded. (Megilla 14a)

> The Torah is the supreme prophetic vision, yet it is completely foreign to us. Not only are we baffled by most of its commandments and prohibitions, we don't even recognize the world it portrays. It is filled with descriptions of miracles and the appearance of God in the world.... Prophecy is a complement to miracle and worship – all involve an awareness of a direct relationship with the Creator. We lack this awareness. The consistency of worship in the ancient world and the existence of prophecy in the past indicate to us that the nature of awareness has a history.[1]

1. Jeremy Kagan, *The Jewish Self: Recovering Spirituality in the Modern World* (Jerusalem: Feldheim Publishers, 1998), 25–26.

In this study of the books of Nahum, Habakkuk, and Zephaniah, the seventh, eighth, and ninth books of the Twelve Minor Prophets, or *Trei Asar* in Hebrew, we attempt to decipher the timeless meaning of these sacred words. These words are more than inspired poetry – they are part of a divine message that is still meaningful and relevant for us today.[2] Nonetheless, whenever I teach these works I encounter students asking at least one of these questions: How does one read the books of the Prophets? Given the countless interpretations that have arisen over the years, can one claim to have arrived at a "correct" reading? Aren't all the prophets essentially saying the same thing? Once our greatest sages have offered an interpretation, isn't it enough to then study their writings instead rather than study the text of the Tanakh? Why turn to secular sources, whether academic biblical scholarship, history, or archaeology – what do they know anyway? Most importantly, why do these books matter? The answers to these questions form the underlying premises and principles that guide this commentary, and as such, I wish to address them at the beginning.

Our first and fundamental premise is that although "only those prophecies that were relevant for future generations were recorded" (Megilla 14b), the timelessness of their messages does not remove those messages from having been originally said in a specific time and place. To fully appreciate the prophet's lesson, the reader first has to have a basic understanding of the historical setting and situation that are the

---

2. Discussing the distinction between the prophetic texts (*Nevi'im*) and the written texts (*Ketuvim*) in Maimonides's thought, Rabbi Yaakov Weinberg writes:

> Rambam's choice (in his commentary on the mishna in Sanhedrin 10:1) of the term "prophecy" rather than "inspiration" is significant: Prophecy is defined as the reality of man receiving a direct and clear message from God.... Those contemporary thinkers who believe that the Torah was not given through direct communication with the Almighty, that the words of Torah are not His exact words but merely divinely inspired words of men, do humanity a great disservice. Since a person is easily inspired by a message he wants to hear, a law built upon inspiration obviously will not command the respect and authority necessary to bind man; it will become malleable in his hands. Such a Torah would cease to be the source of life from Above, and would instead become a mere product and target for human manipulation. (Yaakov Weinberg, *Fundamentals and Faith* [Jerusalem: Targum Press, 1991], 69–70)

background to his message. No prophet spoke in a vacuum; he spoke to live people who faced real concerns and challenges. The reader must identify those challenges and distill what message the prophet wished to convey to his immediate listeners. Only then should the reader attempt to draw parallels to his own situation. Not every empire is Babylon and not every metropolis is Nineveh. The idolatry that Isaiah faced was vastly different from that faced by Zephaniah. Isaiah spoke to a prosperous Judah, whose prosperity and wealth led them to worship "their own handiwork" (see Is. 2:11, 17). Zephaniah's Judah was immensely different, having lived under Assyrian oppression for so long that they doubted that God even heard their cries anymore. Lack of familiarity with the historical context often leads readers to conflate two separate messages, while understanding of the historical setting of each prophet enables us to distill what is truly unique about each message. To help facilitate this understanding, this study includes brief overviews that introduce each prophet and his background before delving into the textual analysis, as well as a separate historical overview of the time period in which Nahum, Habakkuk, and Zephaniah spoke, covering both general and Jewish history as necessary.

Second, we attempt to read the words of the prophets as a dynamic dialogue. Each sentence spoken by a prophet was intended either to evoke a reaction from his listeners, address potential concerns, or refute a mistaken belief that prevented the prophet's message from penetrating the hearts of his listeners. Though the texts generally record only the prophet's words,[3] prophecy, like all communication, has two components[4] – the explicit communication, and the response of the people that the prophet is addressing. I have tried to be sensitive to this in my commentary. The prologue and epilogue attempt to reflect the situation the prophet was facing, and how his words may have been received. Additionally, the prophet does not always identify the target audience or the message that his prophecy wishes to convey at its beginning. Understanding the

3. On occasion, however, the prophet does record his debate with the people, giving them a voice even while disagreeing with their message (cf. Ezek. 18:1–5, Mal. 1–3).
4. For a summary of the role of communication theory in understanding prophetic interactions, see Gary Smith, *The Prophets as Preachers* (Nashville: Holman Bible Publishers, 1994), 6–13.

prophet's words as discourse means that if the words spoken were at first equivocal, and the implied listener would attribute multiple meanings to the prophet's words, then these meanings must be identified at that point in the text, even if the prophet later clarifies his intentions.

As these three books are smaller works, ranging between forty-seven and fifty-six verses, I have chosen to relate to them as unified wholes, with each prophet delivering one central message.[5] To deliver this message, however, the prophet sometimes divides his discourse into sections. We must plot and track the connection between them, and demonstrate how the sections combine to prove his thesis. Because of the fluid nature of the written word and interpretation, the criteria by which sections are delineated may differ from book to book, and sometimes even within a book. Each study begins with a suggested explanation of the book's overall structure as a guide to following the development of its lessons and ideas. While the reader may discern a new section due to a change in subject matter, it is often actually a literary marker that separates one section from another. Habakkuk introduces his third chapter with the statement that what follows is a psalm. With other prophets, the flow from one part to another may be so smooth that the end of one section and the beginning of another is almost indiscernible. In Nahum, the study tracks his alternating usage of masculine and feminine language when addressing the people, a distinction not noticeable in a standard English translation. With Zephaniah, the written text is split based on the addressee and the subject matter.

The first resources when approaching these texts are the traditional sources and commentaries that have guided us throughout the generations and continue to guide us today. This work does not provide a comprehensive guide to everything that the traditional biblical commentaries – including Rashi, Ibn Ezra, Radak, Abarbanel, and Malbim – say on these verses, but it does attempt to summarize the main issues and approaches that these commentaries discuss. Additionally, this book draws upon knowledge from outside sources when

---

5. This is the case with the book of Zephaniah as well, even though his prophecy is understood as spanning several decades and different kings.

they are necessary to enrich our understanding of the text, without compromising the belief in the Bible's status as divine message. Arriving in the Land of Israel in 1263, Nahmanides was handed an authentic coin used in the Temple hundreds of years previously as a *maḥatzit hashekel.* Close investigation led him to realize that his previously written commentary regarding his understanding of the coin had been mistaken, and he immediately wrote to his students to correct his error.[6] We hope that our efforts to "hear the truth from whoever says it"[7] lead only to a greater understanding of these words.

Another important tool for understanding the texts is sensitivity to the fact that these prophets drew heavily on their predecessors in formulating their message. Not only did this enable the prophet to find a shared common language with his listeners, but he was able to utilize the messages of his predecessors in creative ways to maximize the rhetoric effect of his message. Recognizing quotations and allusions in these books is imperative, and this project attempts to do so.

Finally, these works are poetry. Ignoring that fact can lead to misreading them entirely.[8] Just as the historical background is important to fully understand a text, so too is an awareness of the form and genre of that text. The prophecies here are unlike the narratives in the historical books (Joshua through Kings), which generally contain straightforward and non-cryptic messages of punishment and salvation. These prophecies are characterized by more extensive use of poetic imagery and metaphors, unconventional syntax, parallelism, and wordplay. These literary

6. Nahmanides, *Commentary to the Torah*, vol. 2 (Jerusalem: Mossad HaRav Kook, 1988), 507.
7. From Maimonides's introduction to *Pirkei Avot* (*Shemoneh Perakim*), as cited by Rabbi Hayyim Angel in his excellent discussion of the issues modern yeshiva students face when studying Tanakh seriously. See additional sources in his essay "From Black Fire to White Fire," in *Revealed Texts, Hidden Meanings: Finding the Religious Significance in Tanakh* (Jersey City: Ktav Publishing, 2009), 16nn11–12.
8. Robert Alter writes, "For a reader to attend to these elements as literary art is not merely an exercise in appreciation but a discipline in understanding: the literary vehicle is so much the necessary medium through which the Hebrew writers realized their meanings that we will grasp the meanings at best imperfectly if we ignore their articulations as literature" (*The Literary Guide to the Bible* [Cambridge: Harvard University, 1987], 21).

tools and devices not only frame and help convey the message, at times they become the message. As Leland Ryken concludes his work on the Bible's literary features:

> We should read the Bible expecting to encounter religious and moral truth. More often than not, that truth will come to us in a literary form – in stories, poems, proverbs, and visions, for example. To understand the Bible, therefore, we need to understand how these literary genres work. Our enjoyment of the Bible will be enhanced if we have developed the capacity to perceive its artistry and beauty. In short, the Bible is not an occasionally literary book – it is mainly a work of literature.[9]

To help appreciate how the literary artistry of the prophets assists and conveys their message, we will highlight the relevant poetic devices as they appear throughout the commentary.

* * *

It is with both tremendous trepidation and gratitude to Hashem that I present this volume on the biblical books of Nahum, Habakkuk, and Zephaniah. I emphasize trepidation, because one should not flippantly claim an understanding of the biblical word, especially when dealing with works that have not been studied widely. These three books suffer from relative obscurity: they are small in size, not part of the traditional *haftara* cycle, and the Tanakh's prophetic works tend to be less familiar generally. Yet, they all contain important and pertinent messages for our time. Very little material of quality exists for the discriminating reader who wishes to study the Latter Prophets in English and the challenges in reading them are numerous. The terse and cryptic style of biblical prose makes reading it difficult, even with the myriad of translations available today, and this issue is even more striking regarding the prophetic works in particular. They are written in semi-poetic form, often relying upon the

9. Leland Ryken, *Words of Delight: A Literary Introduction to the Bible* (Michigan: Baker Academic), 355.

reader to recognize the many allusions within their words and unpack the full import of their meaning. There is much we don't know about the exact time, place, or circumstances in which the prophet spoke, we aren't familiar with the nature or appeal of the idolatrous practices that the prophets decry, and we view the words of reproof against abusing widows and orphans as belonging to a different time.

Yet, these words are meant for us. Rabbinic thought teaches (Megilla 14a) that only prophecies that contain an eternal message were preserved for the generations. We live in amazing times. The image in Zechariah's vision of redemption, of boys and girls playing in Jerusalem's streets (8:5), has come to pass before our eyes, and his message of the importance of pursuing social justice, to "execute true judgment and perform loving-kindness and mercy" (7:9), is as relevant as ever. Thus it behooves us to revisit these words to discover their message for us. Therefore, my trepidation is accompanied by a tremendous feeling of gratitude to the *Ribbono shel Olam* for affording me this opportunity to share with the world, in a very small way, His ideas as transmitted by the prophets and hopefully in doing so, helping make it a better place.

* * *

This work is not the work of a single person. Though I bear sole responsibility for the material presented within, this book would not have come to fruition without the support and encouragement of many people along the way, and I wish to acknowledge as many of them as possible. First and foremost, I would like to thank the publisher of Koren Publishers and Maggid Books, Matthew Miller, and his wonderful and professional team, whose dedication to producing intelligent and thought-provoking Torah literature in English is unparalleled. I am especially grateful to Rabbi Reuven Ziegler, editor in chief, who has not only pushed me forward professionally at many key junctures in my life, encouraging me to place words on paper for several outlets, including *Tradition* magazine and Yeshivat Har Etzion's Israel Koschitzky Virtual Beit Midrash (VBM), but has also been there as a friend and colleague as well. Special thanks also to Ita Olesker, Sara Henna Dahan, Yonatan Shai Freedman, and Debbie Ismailoff.

Though this book was written in Israel, it really began in a small town in Canada many years ago, where children on outdoor ice rinks dream of Gretzky and Sittler, not ancient prophets. Despite living in a small town with an anti-Semitic past, which at one time had grouped dogs and Jews together on a sign forbidding both parties to bathe on the beach, I grew up with tremendous pride in my heritage. My parents and grandparents on both sides provided me with unconditional love, a thirst for knowledge, and a healthy dose of curiosity, paving the way for my interest in Tanakh. All of my teachers – from Rabbi Larry Englander in Mississauga, my first teacher, to all the teachers at the Community Hebrew Academy of Toronto, including Rabbis Pachino, Saknowitz, Levine, Kapustin, Bloomberg, Gurvitz, and Feldman – showed tremendous patience for an energetic, small-town student. I would like to make a special mention of the former head of Toronto's Board of Jewish Education, Rabbi Yitzchak Witty *zt"l*, his wife Rebbetzin Shulamit Witty, and his family. His home was a paradigm of scholarship and generosity, and I am privileged to still count his family among my close friends today.

I began to study Tanakh extensively for the first time at Yeshiva University under Rabbis Allen Schwartz and Mitchell Orlian. When I moved to Israel and eventually to the community of Alon Shvut, I was exposed to the new style of learning Tanakh, with its emphasis on its literary aspects and with the understanding that behind it lay real historical events that needed to be placed into their proper context. Special mention goes to those who became my guides: Rabbis Menachem Leibtag, Yaakov Medan, and Yoel Bin-Nun. At Bar-Ilan University, where I am continuing Tanakh studies on the doctoral level, I wish to thank Professors Elie Assis, James Kugel, Esther Eshel, and Michael Avioz.

Many of the ideas in this book in particular, and the underlying approach to Tanakh on which they are based, have been battle-tested in the classroom over time by excellent students whose insights and questions have often forced me to sharpen and revise my thoughts. These exchanges spanned several years that I spent teaching at Yeshivot Shaarei Mevaseret Zion, Darchei Noam, and Machon Gold, in communities in Minnesota and Toronto, at Yeshivat AMIT Nachshon under Rav Noam Krigman and Avi Dadon, and especially at Yeshivat Lev HaTorah, where several years ago Rabbis Boaz Mori and Michael Cytrin hired me as Tanakh coordinator with the mandate to teach as much Tanakh as possible. To them, and all my students, many of whom I remain in touch with until today, I remain grateful.

Several talented scholars generously donated of their time to read, edit, and critique this manuscript. Because of the efforts and insights of Rabbi Yitz Etshalom, Dr. Yael Ziegler, Rabbanit Shani Taragin, and especially Rabbanit Mali Brofsky, this book is a much better product. Thank you.

Most importantly, I wish to thank from the bottom of my heart all my family members, whose unstinting support provided me with the strength to persevere and complete this work. To my in-laws Alberto and Matilde Nowosiolski, I wish you many years of enjoyment from your grandchildren. To my mother and her husband, Adela and Zwi Zur, I can only hope for many more years of health and happiness in each other's company. To my children, Mordechai, Shabtai, Michaya, Yair, and Yoshiyahu, and my amazing daughters-in-law, Noa and Tamar, I wish that Hashem will fulfill all the requests of your hearts – so ask for the sky! To the Katchalski and Fuld families, I wish nothing but shared happiness, and may the memory of Tamar's father, Ari Fuld *Hy"d,* be a source of blessing to all.

Finally, to my wife, Devorah – without your love and faith, this book would never have come into being. I only hope that I continue to be worthy of being together with you and deserving of your love for many decades to come.

Prologue

In the year 658 BCE, ten miles south of Jerusalem, a teenage shepherd named Amos carefully leads his sheep through a steep and winding path in a valley near Tekoa. He thinks about the famous prophet whose name he bore, a legend who walked those very hills a century before. His parents called him Amos after the prophet Amos; they told him that bearing the name of a man of God would bring him fortune. Amos knew their real reason, though. Using the name of a prophet who stood down tyrants and injustice was their quiet protest against Manasseh, the wicked king who ruled the Kingdom of Judah (the Southern Kingdom). They could never say so, or at least never out loud. Spies lurked everywhere; people advanced their position in the regime by slandering their neighbors. But Amos could discern his parents' contempt for Manasseh, and Amos knew why they held this contempt.

Judah, with Jerusalem as its capital, was a proud, independent kingdom a mere hundred years earlier. To its north lay the Kingdom of Israel (the Northern Kingdom), even more prosperous and powerful, with Samaria as its capital. While the people of Judah were strong in their monotheistic belief and faithful in their worship of the God of Israel, the northerners were wayward in their beliefs. God commanded Amos the prophet to leave Tekoa to deliver a blunt prophecy to Israel:

Change your corrupt ways, or disappear and never rise again (Amos 5:2). Israel ignored Amos; the dangerous Assyrian Empire, though always a threat, was far away, and besides, they reasoned, didn't Israel's prosperity signify God's approval? But then came the earthquake of 760 BCE.

The earthquake devastated the northern kingdom.[1] Israel's economic prosperity disappeared and the ruling dynasty of Jehu soon collapsed. Ambitious princes who tried to rule in its wake were soon assassinated by even more aggressive officers. Politically, the country was divided over whether to continue to pay the yearly tribute to Assyria instituted by Jehu or to rebel and join the Aramean coalition that promised to push the Assyrians back to the Euphrates. Israel became fragmented and impoverished. By the time the Assyrian armies invaded, the Northern Kingdom was barely a whisper of its former glory. Sargon II overran Samaria in 722 BCE, exiling the remaining population far from Israel.

In the south, with vast hordes of Assyrians perched on his border, King Ahaz of Judah capitulated and became a vassal to Assyria. He even placed an altar for offerings to Assyria's idols in Solomon's Temple. Though his son Hezekiah, who remained faithful to God, valiantly tried to remove the Assyrian yoke, his insurgency led to Judah's near destruction. God performed a miracle and decimated Sennacherib's armies outside of Jerusalem, but it was a Pyrrhic victory. As the remnant of the Assyrian army retreated to its homeland in 701 BCE, Judah was by then

1. The earthquake was so powerful that hundreds of years later, the prophet Zechariah could taunt his listeners with the words: "You shall flee as you fled from the earthquake in the days of Uzziah, king of Judah" (Zech. 14:5), secure in the knowledge that they would be daunted by his threat. Josephus records a tradition that an earthquake shook the land when Uzziah entered the Holy of Holies (*Antiquities of the Jews* IX:10:4). Archaeological excavations at Hazor, Samaria, and other places reveal leaning and crooked walls, displaced rows of stones, and broken debris lying around, evidence of a violent earthquake (between 7.8 and 8.2 on the Richter scale) that occurred around 760 BCE. Y. Yadin et al., *Hazor II: An Account of the Second Season of Excavations* (Jerusalem: Magnus Press, 1956), 24, 26, 36–37; Philip J. King, *Amos, Hosea, Micah: An Archaeological Commentary* (Philadelphia: Westminster Press, 1988), 21; S. A. Austin, G. W. Franz, and E. G. Frost, "Amos' Earthquake: An Extraordinary Middle East Seismic Event of 750 B.C," *International Geology Review* 42 (2002): 657–71.

largely a smoldering ruin, with forty-six of its largest cities destroyed. On his walks, shepherding his herds, Amos could see these ruins, a series of black scars that dotted the landscape for miles.

Following Hezekiah's death in 696 BCE, his young son Manasseh decided that it was in Judah's interest to reassume the status of being Assyria's loyal vassal. He surrendered the independence for which his father had fought and reintroduced Assyrian rites into the Temple. In the process, he brutally suppressed dissent, and Jerusalem's golden-colored stone streets ran red with the blood of prophets. According to rabbinic tradition, Manasseh did not spare even his father-in-law, the great prophet Isaiah; his soldiers slaughtered him with axes.[2] He ruled as king of Judah for decades with an iron fist, supported by the rehabilitated and now invincible Assyrian Empire. It was during this period that Egyptian refugees and slaves began to appear in the markets for the first time, as even Egypt's once impregnable capital, No-Amon (Thebes), fell to the Assyrians in 663 BCE.

Most of Judah's inhabitants acclimated themselves to life under Assyrian rule. The God of Amos, Micah, and Isaiah, who spoke of social justice and mercy, appeared to have abandoned His people, possibly defeated by the Assyrian deities worshipped by their empire's overlords. Amos the shepherd could merely wonder: Would prophets who spoke in God's name ever be heard again?

---

2. There are two accounts in the Talmud that claim that Manasseh killed Isaiah. Yevamot 49b states:

> Manasseh said to Isaiah, "Moses, your master, said, 'For man shall not see Me and live' (Ex. 33:20), but you said, 'I saw the Lord seated upon [His] throne' (Is. 6:1)." ... [He continued to point out other contradictions and] Isaiah thought: I know that he will not accept my explanations; why should I increase his guilt? He then uttered a divine name, a cedar tree opened, and Isaiah disappeared within it. However, Manasseh ordered the cedar to be sawed open, and when the saw reached his mouth Isaiah died. So he was punished for having said, "I dwell in the midst of a people of unclean lips" (Is. 6:5).

A somewhat different version of this legend appears in the Jerusalem Talmud (Y. Sanhedrin 10), where Isaiah hides himself in a cedar tree but is discovered by the fringes of his garment. This second legend about the martyrdom of Isaiah became the kernel of the Christian Apocryphal work *The Ascension of Isaiah*.

Historical Background

To begin our study of and to fully appreciate the messages of Nahum, Habakkuk, and Zephaniah, we shall quickly summarize the reigns of the kings of Assyria, also called the Assyrian Empire, and of the Neo-Babylonian Empire, the superpowers of the time, as well as the kings of Judah who ruled in each period, also taking into account major historical events.

Table 1 – Time Line of Kings of Judah, Kings of Assyria, and Prophets[1]

Year	King of Judah	King of Assyria	Prophet	Historical Events
770 BCE	Uzziah* (794–742 BCE)		**Amos**	

1. For simplicity's sake, we have followed the accepted conventional historical dating system, and do not address the discrepancies with the midrashic chronology suggested by *Seder Olam*.

Year	King of Judah	King of Assyria	Prophet	Historical Events
760 BCE				760 BCE – A major earthquake devastates Israel
	Jotham (752–736 BCE)			
750 BCE		Tiglath-Pileser III (745–727 BCE)	**Isaiah**	
740 BCE	Ahaz (742–726 BCE)		**Micah**	
730 BCE			**Hosea**	
	Hezekiah (726–697 BCE)	Shalmanesser V (726–722 BCE)		721 BCE – Downfall of Samaria and exile of ten tribes
720 BCE		Sargon II (722–705 BCE)		
710 BCE				
700 BCE		Sennacherib (705–681 BCE)		701 BCE – Assyrian invasion of Judah, siege of Jerusalem and defeat of Sennacherib
	Manasseh (696–641 BCE)			
690 BCE				

Year	King of Judah	King of Assyria	Prophet	Historical Events
680 BCE		Esarhaddon (681–669 BCE)		681 BCE – Assassination of Sennacherib
670 BCE		Ashurbanipal (668–626 BCE)		
				663 BCE – The Egyptian capital No-Amon (Thebes) falls to Assyria
660 BCE				
				652 BCE – Assyrian civil war
650 BCE			**Nahum**	650–648 BCE – Manasseh arrested after rebellion
640 BCE	Josiah** (639–608 BCE)			
			Zefaniah	
630 BCE				
		Civil War, Downfall of Assyria	**Habakkuk**	626 BCE – Nabopolassar takes power in Babylon, attains independence, and begins to wage war on Assyria

Year	King of Judah	King of Assyria	Prophet	Historical Events
620 BCE			**Jeremiah**	612 BCE – Fall of Nineveh
610 BCE				609 BCE – Death of Josiah; Nebuchadnezzar takes throne in Babylon
	Jehoiakim*** (608–597 BCE)			605 BCE – Battle of Carchemish, final defeat of Assyria
600 BCE				598 BCE – Nebuchadnezzar invades Judah, first exile to Babylon.

* It is widely believed that Uzziah's final years and Jotham's early years overlap, as Uzziah retired after contracting leprosy (II Chr. 26:21).

** Josiah was briefly preceded by his father, Amon, who ruled from 641 to 639 BCE.

*** Jehoiakim was briefly preceded by his brother, Jehoahaz, who ruled for three months before being exiled to Egypt in 609 BCE, and was followed by his son Jehoiachin, who also ruled briefly for three months in 598 BCE before being exiled to Babylonia.

THE ASSYRIAN EMPIRE

Though the roots of the Assyrian Empire began in the third millennium BCE, the entity that would dominate the ancient Near East, including Israel and Judah, began in 966 BCE with the reign of Tiglath-Pileser II and lasted until its final defeat in 605 BCE at the hands of the Babylonians. The Assyrian Empire was the most technologically advanced empire of its era, among the first to mass-produce iron weaponry, while most other nations still relied on bronze.[2] At the height of their power and influence, they dominated the ancient Near East, conquering and enslaving entire nations,[3] as seen on the map below:

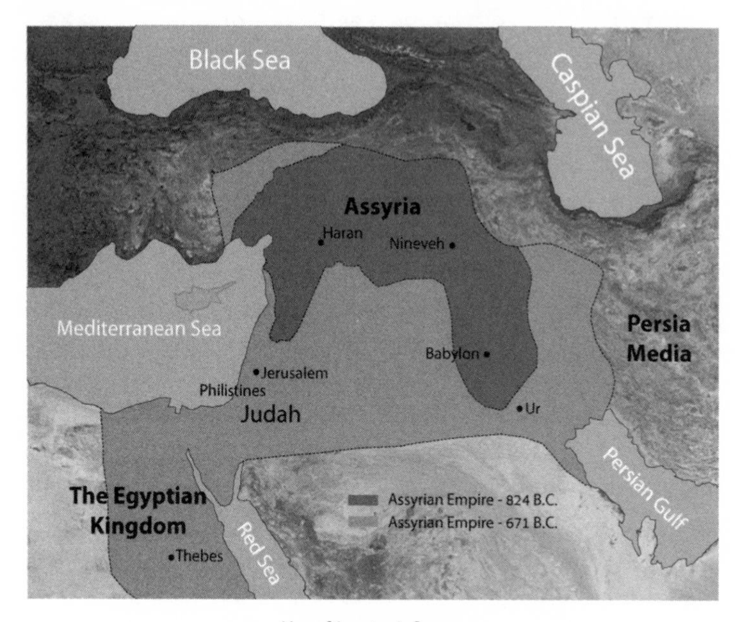

Map of Assyrian Influence

The first surviving record of an Assyrian ruler that had direct contact with Israel is that of Shalmanesser III (859–824 BCE). In his royal annals (the Kurkh Monolith, a stele found near the Tigris River in Turkey), Shalmanesser III records the events of his campaign to Qarqar in 853 BCE. There, he fought a coalition of kings that included King Ahab of Israel

2. Simon Anglim et al., *Fighting Techniques of the Ancient World 3000 BCE–500 CE* (London: Amber Books, 2013), 12.
3. Paul Kriwaczek writes that "Assyria must surely have among the worst press notices of any state in history. Babylon may be a byname for corruption, decadence and sin but the Assyrians and their famous rulers, with terrifying names like Shalmanesser, Tiglath-Pileser, Sennacherib, Esarhaddon and Ashurbanipal, rate in the popular imagination just below Adolf Hitler and Genghis Khan for cruelty, violence, and sheer murderous savagery." Paul Kriwaczek, *Babylon: Mesopotamia and the Birth of Civilization* (New York: Thomas Dunne Books, 2010), 208.

and Hadad-Ezer of Damascus (possibly Ben Hadad of I Kings 20). He would return twelve years later, this time receiving tribute from King Jehu of Israel. He recorded that the Israelite king prostrated himself on the Black Obelisk, on display today at the British Museum.

Five weaker kings followed Shalmanesser III on the Assyrian throne, and the people of Israel and Judah were able to live in relative tranquility for over a century. This period of calm ended in 745 BCE with the ascension of Tiglath-Pileser III (745–727 BCE). The new Assyrian monarch reverted to pursuing aggressive expansionist policies in the west, expanding Assyria until the empire reached Israel's borders. The Assyrians then applied unrelenting pressure on the Northern Kingdom, waging war on Israel's border towns and slowly depleting the countryside.[4] The next Assyrian king, Shalmanesser V (726–722 BCE), besieged Samaria, the capital of Judah, for three years, beginning in 722 BCE.[5] When he died suddenly, his general Sargon II (722–705 BCE) took the reins, defeating and exiling Israel, and bringing thousands of foreigners to repopulate the now empty lands.[6] At home, Sargon II moved the capital of the empire to Dur Sharrukin, but after his untimely death in battle, his successor Sennacherib moved it to Nineveh. In 701 BCE, Sennacherib (705–681 BCE) campaigned against Hezekiah and nearly destroyed Judah, until his armies were decimated almost overnight outside of Jerusalem's walls.[7] Despite the defeat, Sennacherib continued to rule the Assyrian Empire with an iron fist. He waged war against Elam and Babylonia for years, and this war culminated in the destruction of Babylonian temples and shrines in 689 BCE. He was ultimately murdered by his eldest children in 681 BCE (II Kings 19:37).

Though Sargon II established Nineveh as the new Assyrian capital, it was Sennacherib who was responsible for transforming the ancient metropolis into a truly great city. The name Nineveh is generally assumed to have meant "Place of Fish" (the cuneiform symbol for Nineveh was a

4. II Kings 15:29, II Kings 16, I Chr. 5:26, II Chr. 28:20.
5. II Kings 17:3, 18:9.
6. II Kings 17, Is. 20:1. Some estimate that in total, the Assyrians were responsible for moving as many as 4.5 million people between 745 BCE and 612 BCE. Cline and Graham, *Ancient Empires: From Mesopotamia to the Rise of Islam* (Cambridge: Cambridge University Press, 2011), 50.
7. II Kings 18–19, II Chr. 32, Is. 36–37.

fish within a house, from the Aramaic *nuna*, "fish"). Others understand Nineveh to mean either "the city of Nin" (the Babylonian version of Hercules), or "the city of Inanna" (Inanna was the name of an ancient Sumerian goddess, associated with both love and beauty as well as war and power). Genesis 10:8 credits Nimrod with founding Nineveh, attesting to its antiquity. Sennacherib devoted almost twenty-five years of his reign to enlarging Nineveh,[8] adding palaces, aqueducts, temples, ramparts, and palace gardens.[9] The streets were lined with stone carvings that boasted of Sennacherib's military conquests, and according to uncovered ruins, the boulevards were almost twenty feet wide. Population estimates from that time range from 100,000 to 150,000 residents, making Nineveh among the largest cities in the Middle East. By the end of Sennacherib's reign, the words Assyria and Nineveh had become interchangeable.[10]

His successor Esarhaddon (681–669 BCE; mentioned in II Kings 19:37, Ezra 4:2, and Is. 37:38) maintained the empire's strength and managed to keep the restless Babylonians, also known as Chaldeans, at bay.[11]

---

8. According to Nelson's *Illustrated Bible Dictionary* (Nashville, TN: Thomas Nelson, 1986), 760: "In Sennacherib's day the wall around Nineveh was 40 to 50 feet high. It extended for 4 kilometers along the Tigris River and for 13 kilometers around the inner city. The city wall had fifteen main gates, five of which have been excavated. Each of the gates was guarded by stone bull statues. Both inside and outside the walls, Sennacherib created parks, a botanical garden, and a zoo. He built a water-system containing the oldest aqueduct in history at Jerwan, across the Gomel River [65 kilometers away]."
9. According to British Assyriologist Stephanie Dalley, these were the famous Hanging Gardens, one of the ancient Seven Wonders of the World. Though later writers placed them at Babylon, extensive research has failed to find any trace of them, and Sennacherib's account of the palace gardens he built matches accounts of the Hanging Gardens in several significant details. Christopher Scarre and Brian M. Fagan, *Ancient Civilizations* (New Jersey: Prentice Hall, 2007), 231.
10. Nahum uses the term "Nineveh" to refer to both the capital city and to the entire empire. This is not uncommon in the Bible, when prominent cities represent their countries (the city of Samaria become synonymous with the northern Kingdom of Israel; today we talk of news from Jerusalem or Washington meaning Israel or the United States). This is an example of metonymy, when a writer uses the name of one thing for that of another associated with or suggested by it.
11. Historically, the Chaldeans lived in southern Babylonia, in an area about four hundred miles long and one hundred miles wide alongside the Tigris and Euphrates Rivers (today's southern Iraq). In the Bible, the term Chaldeans generally refers to

He successfully handed over the flourishing empire to his son, Ashurbanipal (668–626 BCE). Ashurbanipal reigned successfully for many decades, continuing to extend Assyrian control until it reached Persia in the east, Arabia in the south, and Egypt in the southwest. The capture of its arch-rival, Egypt's capital No-Amon (Thebes), in 663 BCE represented the zenith of Assyrian imperialism. Though Ashurbanipal had to fight an insurrection led by his brother (whom he had appointed governor of Babylonia) between 652 and 648 BCE, Ashurbanipal's reign was generally unchallenged. Due to the complete control that they exercised over the ancient Near East, this era has been termed the *Pax Assyriaca*, the "Assyrian peace."

As rulers, the Assyrian kings acquired a well-deserved reputation for brutality. Cruelty has been a constant in warfare since the beginning of time, but few bragged about it as much as the Assyrian monarchs. They would meticulously document and record their exploits on tablets, obelisks, reliefs, and carvings. Dismemberment, impaling, flaying, and beheading of the captured, whether soldier or civilian, were common. Among Ashurbanipal's boasts we find the following:

> I flayed as many nobles as had rebelled against me [and] draped their skins over the pile [of corpses]; some I spread out within the pile, some I erected on stakes upon the pile.... I felled three

---

Babylonians in general, but can refer to the tribes from that specific area. Gen. 11:28 speaks of Abraham's father Terah, who was from "Ur of the Chaldeans," the specific tribe or people known as the Chaldeans. Similarly, God called Abraham a Chaldean in Gen. 11:31 and Gen. 15:7.

The kings of Babylon came from Chaldean stock: Ukinzer, a Chaldean, became king of Babylon in 731 BCE for a brief period; Merodach-Baladan, also a Chaldean, became king over Babylon a few years later (King Hezekiah is mentioned as meeting his envoys in II Kings 20). With the rise of Nabopolassar, another Chaldean, to the throne of Babylon and the severing of ties with Assyria, the words Chaldean and Babylonian became synonymous with each other (see Is. 13:19, 47:1, 5, 48:14, 20).

After the Persian conquest of Babylon in 538 BCE, the Bible uses the term Chaldeans to refer to wise men rather than a separate people. They influenced Nebuchadnezzar's decision to throw Shadrach, Meshach, and Abednego into the fiery furnace (Dan. 3:8) and appear throughout the book of Daniel as wise men and astrologers (Dan. 1:4, 2:10, 4:7, 5:7, 11).

> thousand of their fighting men with the sword... I captured many troops alive: I cut off of some their arms [and] hands; I cut off of others their noses, ears, [and] extremities. I gouged out the eyes of many troops. I made one pile of the living [and] one of heads. I hung their heads on trees around the city... I slew two hundred and sixty fighting men; I cut off their heads and made pyramids thereof. I slew one of every two. I built a wall before the great gates of the city; I flayed the chief men of the rebels, and I covered the wall with their skins. Some of them were enclosed alive in the bricks of the wall, some of them were crucified on stakes along the wall; I caused a great multitude of them to be flayed in my presence, and I covered the wall with their skins. I gathered together the heads in the form of crowns, and their pierced bodies in the form of garlands.[12]

It is no wonder that one historian concluded that "it is tempting to see the Assyrian Empire... as a historical forebear of Nazi Germany: an aggressive, murderously vindictive regime supported by a magnificent and successful war machine."[13]

The mid-640s BCE was a period of transition for the Assyrians. After the bloody civil war with his brother, Ashurbanipal turned away from further military adventures, concentrating instead on building projects, religious pursuits, and cultivating the arts. By the final decade of Ashurbanipal's reign, signs of weakness began to surface. The empire's coffers were empty and there was not enough manpower to garrison the border posts facing the Scythians in the north and the Medes to the east. Some sources suggest that even Ashurbanipal himself degenerated into slothfulness and laziness, preferring poetry to the

12. Albert Kirk Grayson, *Assyrian Royal Inscriptions, Part 2: From Tiglath-pileser I to Ashur-nasir-apli II* (Wiesbaden: Otto Harrassowitz, 1976), 124, 126.

13. Anglim, *Fighting Techniques*, 12. Assyriologist H. W. F. Saggs takes an alternative view, arguing that the Assyrian Empire was actually a stabilizing force for progress in the ancient Near East, enabling transportation and hence innovation. He argues that their reputation for cruelty is vastly exaggerated. His main work on the empire is *The Might That Was Assyria* (London: Sidgwick and Jackson, 1984).

burdens of rule.[14] And with his death in 627 BCE, Assyrian fortunes underwent a rapid decline.

Following Ashurbanipal's death, his many children each claimed the right to succeed their father. Their ill-timed squabble led to a civil war, enabling Babylon to regain its independence under the aggressive leadership of an officer named Nabopolassar. Allying himself with the neighboring Medes and other countries in the region chafing for independence, Nabopolassar began to slowly but systematically reduce Assyrian control over the area between the Euphrates and Tigris Rivers. Much of the information that we have about this period comes from accounts in the Babylonian Chronicles (tablet ABC 2),[15] which describe a long, twelve-year struggle between the two historical rivals and enemies. In 614 BCE, Nabopolassar conquered the ancient political and religious center of Ashur; by 612 BCE, he laid siege to the great imperial capital of Nineveh. The Assyrian king Sinsharishkun was killed during the siege, and in August, the last remaining defenses finally broke down and Nineveh was razed.[16] A new king, Ashuruballit II, managed to fight his way out of Nineveh, reorganizing his forces at Harran. However, though there would be several more battles between the Babylonians and the Assyrians, the battle for Nineveh was the turning point in the war. Harran fell in 608 BCE, and Nabopolassar's son Nebuchadnezzar delivered the final blow at the battle of Carchemish, defeating the remnants of the Assyrian army and their Egyptian allies in 605 BCE. Assyria would never rise again.

The devastation of Nineveh was so total and complete that within two generations no one even knew where the city once lay. For the next two millennia its ruins were covered by sand; many rejected the biblical

14. H. W. F. Saggs writes: "It was a defect of Ashurbanipal as a king that he had nothing in him of the great strategist, statesman, or soldier. He was as barren in political insight as he was rich in vindictiveness. It was his misfortune that he was called to be king when by inclination he was a scholastic." *The Might That Was Assyria*, 116.

15. The Babylonian Chronicles are a series of inscribed clay tablets, held at the British Museum, which are the primary historical record of and source for many major events in Babylonian and Mesopotamian history.

16. According to some historical sources, the Medes were responsible for the actual destruction of Nineveh. "Indeed, the Babylonians were very careful in their records to distance themselves from the general looting of the city and especially the temples of this great city." Tremper Longman III and Raymond B. Dillard, *An Introduction to the Old Testament*, 2nd ed. (Grand Rapids: Zondervan, 2006), 459.

descriptions of Nineveh as belonging to the realm of myth, not history.[17] This was the case until the nineteenth century, when archaeologists and scholars, trying to corroborate the biblical narratives with historical evidence, began to scour present-day Iraq, Syria, and Turkey. In 1847, Sir Austen Layard discovered the ruins of Nineveh at the Kuyunjik Mound, opposite the present-day Iraqi city of Mosul. He unearthed a city that was 4 miles by 2 miles in area,[18] and in 1849 uncovered Sennacherib's "palace without a rival." He also found Ashurbanipal's library, containing 22,000 inscribed clay tablets. These discoveries not only reveal the extent of the wealth and glory of ancient Assyria, but also help to confirm and complete the historical record of the Bible.

THE NEO-BABYLONIAN EMPIRE: BEGINNINGS

Babylonia has a long, ancient history; archaeological digs at the site of ancient Ur reveal remnants of civilization dating back to the fourth millennium BCE. The most famous city in ancient Mesopotamia was Babylon, whose ruins today lie in modern-day Iraq, ninety-four kilometers southwest of Baghdad. The city's name is derived from *bav-il* or *bav-ilim*, which means "gate of god" or "gate of the gods" in Akkadian.[19] Babylon

---

17. Will Durant writes about the extent of Nineveh's destruction:

> Nineveh was laid waste as ruthlessly and completely as her kings had once ravaged Susa and Babylon; the city was put to the torch, the population was slaughtered or enslaved, and the palace so recently built by Ashurbanipal was sacked and destroyed. At one blow Assyria disappeared from history.... In a little while all but the mightiest of the Great Kings were forgotten, and all their royal palaces were in ruins under the drifting sands. Two hundred years after its capture, Xenophon's Ten Thousand marched over the mounds that had been Nineveh, and never suspected that these were the site of the ancient metropolis that had ruled half the world. Not a stone remained visible of all the temples with which Assyria's pious warriors had sought to beautify their greatest capital. (*The Story of Civilizations: Our Oriental Heritage* [New York: Simon & Schuster, 1983], 283–84)

18. Additional excavations revealed that suburbs extended for miles outside the wall. This could explain why Jonah required three days to traverse the city while delivering his warning (see Jonah 3:3).
19. The story of the Tower of Babel, told in Genesis, chapter 11, states that the city was named for the confusion that ensued after God caused the people to begin speaking in different languages (in Hebrew, the root *bavel* means "confusion").

was celebrated for its impressive buildings and its reputation as a great seat of learning and culture. Its most well-known ruler, Hammurabi (1792–1750 BCE), transformed it into the most powerful and influential city in Mesopotamia. Famous for the extensive law codes that bear his name, Hammurabi was both a great administrator and a masterful conqueror. By 1755 BCE, he had united the entire region under Babylon's rule.

Hammurabi's successors were unable to maintain his dominion and his empire quickly crumbled. Many different people ruled over Babylonia in the ensuing centuries until the rise and expansion of the neo-Assyrian Empire. As Babylonia was too independent to assimilate into the Assyrian Empire, Assyrian kings attempted to incorporate it instead. However, Babylonia rejected the Assyrian advances and desire for unity. The Babylonians rebelled twice under Mardukaplaiddin (known as Merodach-Baladan in II Kings 20), from 721 BCE until 710 BCE and in 703 BCE. After the second revolt, the Assyrian king Sennacherib sacked and razed Babylon and its temples as a lesson to others. But his display of brutality and irreverence backfired, and Sennacherib was soon after assassinated by his sons. His successor Esarhaddon rebuilt Babylon as an act of penance, but did not manage to remove the tension between the two empires. Esarhaddon's son Assurbanipal (668–631 BCE) tried a different approach to solve Assyria's Babylonian problem. He appointed his brother Shamash-Shumukin as viceroy and granted Babylonia some independence. However, during a campaign in the west, his brother, hoping to achieve complete independence for Babylonia, rebelled against him. It took Assurbanipal several years to restore Assyrian rule over the area (648 BCE). Upon his death, a Babylonian soldier named Nabopolassar expelled the Assyrian governors and declared independence from Assyria. According to the Babylonian chronicle known as ABC 2, he was recognized as king on November 23, 626 BCE. This date signifies the beginning of the Neo-Babylonian Empire.

Sensing weakness, Nabopolassar continued to challenge Assyria, who received support and assistance from Egypt. Despite the Egyptian support, the Babylonians made steady advances into Assyrian territory, defeating an Assyrian force on the banks of the Euphrates, south of Harran. A year later, they invaded the Assyrian heartland and laid siege to Assur, Assyria's religious capital. With the help of soldiers from neighboring

Medes, Assur fell in 615 BCE. Three years later, an alliance of Babylonians and Medes conquered the Assyrian capital Nineveh in July of 612 BCE.

The final campaigns against Assyria took place near the city of Harran. By this time, the Assyrians were fighting with their last forces, supported by the Egyptian army led by Pharaoh Neco II. Then–crown prince Nebuchadnezzar defeated the Assyrian-Egyptian coalition in 605 BCE, near Carchemish, on the banks of the Euphrates. The Babylonian Empire ruled unopposed. Ascending the throne after his father's death, Nebuchadnezzar continued the policy of westward expansion, conquering former Assyrian possessions. He captured Jerusalem in 597 BCE, exiling many of the inhabitants to Babylonia, including the newly crowned King Jehoiachin. He installed Zedekiah as a puppet king, hoping that would preserve the peace. However, when Zedekiah rebelled, Nebuchadnezzar returned to fight Judah one last time, overwhelming the kingdom in 586 BCE, and burning Jerusalem and the Temple to the ground.

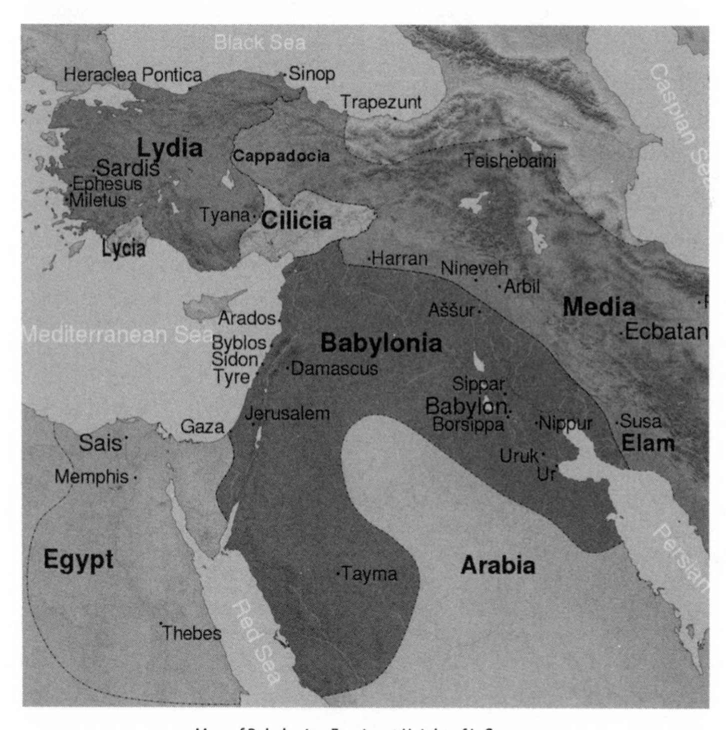

Map of Babylonian Empire at Height of Influence

THE KINGS OF JUDAH DURING THE SEVENTH CENTURY BCE

1. Hezekiah (725–696 BCE)

The last days of the righteous king Hezekiah on the throne of Judah were at the beginning of the seventh century. Unlike his father, Ahaz, who submitted to Assyrian dominance and forsook the Torah, Hezekiah led the people in a tremendous religious revival that removed idolatry from the country. Below is a comparison of the verses in II Kings that describe the reign of Ahaz and Hezekiah, respectively:

Ahaz	Hezekiah
Ahaz was twenty years old when he began to reign, and he reigned for sixteen years in Jerusalem. He did not do what pleased the Lord his God, [in contrast to] his ancestor David. He followed in the footsteps of the kings of Israel. He passed his son through the fire, a horrible sin practiced by the nations whom the Lord drove out from before the Israelites (II Kings 16:2–3).	He did what the Lord approved, just as his ancestor David had done. He eliminated the high places, smashed the sacred pillars to bits, and cut down the *asherim*. He also demolished the bronze serpent that Moses had made, for up to that time the Israelites had been offering incense to it; it was called Nehushtan. He trusted in the Lord God of Israel; in this regard there was none like him among the kings of Judah either before or after. He was loyal to the Lord and did not abandon him. He obeyed the commandments that the Lord had given to Moses (II Kings 18:3–6).

The defining moment of Hezekiah's leadership was the public celebration of the Passover offering and the renewal of the covenant between God and his people in a manner that had not been seen for centuries. Hundreds of years later, Hezekiah would be remembered as one who facilitated a historic unification of his people; even the few Jews who remained in the north after the Assyrian destruction of Samaria came to Jerusalem to participate in the ceremony (see II Chr. 30:10–11, 18). Hezekiah's defiance of Assyria did not go unnoticed. Toward the end of his reign, in 701 BCE, Assyria invaded Judah, torching most of the country and besieging Jerusalem. The situation was dire until the miraculous destruction of the Assyrian army overnight, when 185,000 soldiers died suddenly, and the survivors beat an ignoble retreat back to Assyria (I Kings 19, II Chr. 32).[20] However, by this point the land was in ruins, and Hezekiah died five years later.

The Bible holds up Hezekiah as a living example of one who had complete faith in God (see II Kings 18:5–6). Indeed, the Talmud relates that when he lay mortally ill on his deathbed, the prophet Isaiah told him that the decree of his death was irrevocable and advised him to prepare his affairs. Hezekiah spurned Isaiah's advice and chose to pray for mercy instead. God granted his request and extended his life for fifteen years (see Berakhot 10a). Chapter 21 of II Kings concludes the narration of his reign with the story of Hezekiah's one grave error, that of displaying the Temple riches to Babylonian envoys, possibly in an effort to convince them to join him in an anti-Assyrian alliance. Isaiah rebukes Hezekiah for this foolish act, telling him that after his death it would be the Babylonians who would conquer Jerusalem and plunder the city (see II Kings 20:16–19). Nonetheless,

---

20. As Rabbi Alex Israel notes in his commentary on II Kings:

> The Greek historian Herodotus (485–425 BCE) reported…[that] field mice invaded the Assyrian camp and gnawed the quivers, bow strings, and leather shield handles, thus disarming the military force…Josephus too reports the miracle of Jerusalem's reprieve in the days of Hezekiah, ascribing the death of the Assyrian troops to a devastating plague (*Antiquities* X:21–23). (www.etzion.org.il, English, "Shiur no. 23: Chapters 18–19: Sancheriv's Siege of Jerusalem")

The Talmud chides Hezekiah for not offering praise to God for this miracle, as prescribed by Isaiah, chapter 12 (Sanhedrin 94a). In Hezekiah's defense, we can suggest that surviving the Assyrian onslaught and invasion was the ancient world's equivalent of emerging from a concrete bunker after the detonation of a nuclear device aboveground. Isaiah's poetic depiction of the devastation gives an idea of the scope of the destruction:

> Your country is desolate, your cities are burned with fire: your land, strangers devour it in your presence, and it is desolate, as overthrown by strangers. And the daughter of Zion is left as a cottage in a vineyard, as a lodge in a garden of cucumbers, as a besieged city. Except the Lord of hosts had left unto us a very small remnant, we should have been as Sodom, and we should have been like unto Gomorrah. (Is. 1:7–9)

the overall picture of Hezekiah in the Bible, both as a person and as a king, remains overwhelmingly positive.

2. Manasseh (696–641 BCE)

Unfortunately, Hezekiah's righteousness did not extend to his young son Manasseh, who replaced his father as king at the tender age of twelve:

> He did evil before the Lord and committed the same horrible sins practiced by the nations whom the Lord drove out from before the Israelites. He rebuilt the high places that his father Hezekiah had destroyed; he set up altars for Baal and made an *ashera* just like King Ahab of Israel had done. He bowed down to all the stars in the sky and worshipped them. He built altars in the Lord's Temple.... He passed his son through the fire and practiced divination and omen reading. He set up a pit to conjure up underworld spirits, and appointed magicians to supervise it. He did a great amount of evil before the Lord and angered Him. (II Kings 21:2–6)

Despite his evil behavior, Manasseh maintained his rule over Israel for fifty-five years, the longest reign of any king of Israel or Judah. Under Manasseh, Judah reached its lowest spiritual point ever, with the situation so bleak that II Kings points to his reign as the time when God finally decreed Judah's destruction:

> King Manasseh of Judah has committed horrible sins. He has sinned more than the Amorites before him.... Therefore the Lord God of Israel said, 'I am about to bring disaster on Jerusalem and Judah. The news will reverberate in the ears of those who hear about it. I will destroy Jerusalem the same way I did Samaria and the dynasty of Ahab. I will wipe Jerusalem clean, just as one wipes a plate on both sides. I will abandon this last remaining tribe among My people and hand them over to their enemies; they will be plundered and robbed by all their enemies. (II Kings 21:11–14)

Politically, however, Manasseh's rule was characterized by relative peace and prosperity until the final years of his rule, when he attempted to exploit a civil war between Ashurbanipal and his brother in order to attempt to remove Judah from its vassal state. In 648 BCE he was taken in chains to Babylon, where he repented. Although Manasseh did undergo spiritual transformation and attempted to repair the spiritual damage he had wrought, his repentance did not have a strong influence on Judah. True spiritual reform did not occur until the reign of his grandson Josiah (639–608 BCE). The following verses in II Chronicles recount the story of Manasseh's capture and repentance, and its lack of influence on the kingdom:

> So the Lord brought against them the commanders of the army of the king of Assyria. They seized Manasseh, put hooks in his nose, bound him with bronze chains, and carried him away to Babylon. In his pain Manasseh asked the Lord his God for mercy and truly humbled himself before the God of his ancestors. When he prayed to the Lord, the Lord responded to him and answered favorably his cry for mercy. The Lord brought him back to Jerusalem to his kingdom. Then Manasseh realized that the Lord is the true God. After this Manasseh built up the outer wall of the City of David ... he placed army officers in all the fortified cities in Judah. He removed the foreign gods and images from the Lord's Temple ... he threw them outside the city. He erected the altar of the Lord and offered on it peace offerings and thanks offerings. He told the people of Judah to serve the Lord God of Israel. The people continued to offer sacrifices at the high places, but only to the Lord their God. (II Chr. 33:11–17)

3. *Josiah (639–608 BCE)*

Manasseh's son Amon (641–639 BCE) reigned for only two years before being assassinated by his servants. In his stead, Amon's eight-year-old son Josiah was placed on the throne. The Bible remembers Josiah as one of the best kings ever to reign in Judah. At the time of Josiah's reign, Assyria's power and influence had begun to wane, and Babylonia was still not yet a major force in the world. With no superpower to oppose him, Josiah was able to expand Judah's borders until the kingdom encompassed much of what once was the Northern Kingdom. Now he could legitimately claim to be the first monarch to rule over twelve tribes (or remnants thereof) since Solomon. Additionally, his northward movement to Megiddo meant that he controlled the crucial roadways that connected Assyria to the north with Egypt to the south. He utilized this opportunity to reform the people's religious behavior and to renew their covenant with God – efforts that in retrospect represented the nation's last opportunity to remain an independent entity before ultimately succumbing to Babylonia in 586 BCE.

The Bible doesn't relate much about Josiah's early spiritual development and what caused him to turn away from the path of his wicked father and grandfather. One could speculate that a repentant Manasseh planted the seed within him, warning Josiah to make different choices than those that he himself made. Perhaps Zephaniah, who prophesied during his reign, was a hidden influence on Josiah in his early, formative years. What we do know is that when Josiah turned sixteen, he had already begun to purposefully seek the Lord (II Chr. 34:3), and by age twenty, he began the process of cleansing Judah of the all-pervasive idolatry into which it had fallen:

> In the eighth year of his reign, while he was still young, he began to seek the God of his ancestor David. In his twelfth year he began ridding Judah and Jerusalem of the high places, *asherim*, idols, and images. He ordered the altars of the Baals to be torn down, and broke the incense altars that were above them. He smashed the *asherim*, idols, and images, crushed them up and sprinkled the dust over the tombs of those who had sacrificed to them. He burned the bones of the priests on their altars; he purified Judah and Jerusalem. In the cities of Manasseh, Ephraim, and Simeon, as far as Naphtali, and in the ruins around them, he tore down the altars and *asherim*, demolished the idols, and smashed all the incense altars throughout the Land of Israel. Then he returned to Jerusalem. (II Chr. 34:3–7)

With his actions, Josiah fulfilled the prophecy given to Jeroboam centuries earlier:

> And he called [in prophecy] about the altar at the command of the Lord, and he said: "Altar, altar," so said the Lord: "Behold a son will be born to the House of David, Josiah will be his name, and upon you he will slaughter all the priests of the high places who offer sacrifices on you, and human bones will they burn upon you." (I Kings 13:2)

At this time in history, religious reform and political reform were inexorably linked together. Removing idolatry from Judah was also an act of rebellion against the Assyrians. However, the crumbling Assyrian Empire was too occupied elsewhere to pay much attention to Israel. As noted above, this enabled Josiah to extend his rule to portions of northern Israel that had been in Assyrian hands since 721 BCE. Emboldened by his successes, Josiah then began his most ambitious reform yet: he ordered that the Temple undergo repair and refurbishing. During these renovations, a workman made a dramatic discovery:

> When they took out the silver that had been brought to the Lord's Temple, Hilkiah the priest found the law scroll the Lord had given to Moses. Hilkiah informed Shaphan the scribe, "I found the law scroll in the Lord's temple." Hilkiah gave the scroll to Shaphan. Shaphan brought the scroll to the king and reported, "Your servants are doing everything assigned to them. They melted down the silver in the Lord's Temple and handed it over to the supervisors of the construction foremen." Then Shaphan the scribe told the king, "Hilkiah the priest has given me a scroll." Shaphan read it out loud before the king. When the king heard the words of the law scroll, he tore his clothes. The king ordered Hilkiah, Ahikam son of Shaphan, Abdon son of Micah, Shaphan the scribe, and Asaiah the king's servant, "Go, seek an oracle from the Lord for me and those who remain in Israel and Judah. Find out about the words of this scroll that has been discovered. For the Lord's fury has been ignited against us, because our ancestors have not obeyed the word of the Lord by doing all that this scroll instructs!" (II Chr. 34:14–21)

When the prophetess Huldah verified the accuracy of the findings, Josiah gathered the people together in Jerusalem to renew the covenant, and then intensified his program of eradicating idolatry in the country. He systematically destroyed the pagan shrines, temples, and objects used in the rituals, eliminated practices instituted by Manasseh, deposed the priests of Baal and other deities (see II Kings 23:5), abolished the outlying shrines at Bethel and Samaria that had always been a source of Baal worship, and actively promoted centralized worship in Jerusalem.

How successful was Josiah? How deeply Josiah's attempts to reform society penetrated the people's hearts is unknown. From the prophet Jeremiah's perspective, the effects of Josiah's reforms were only superficial (Jeremiah 4 describes the prophet's indignation with the people's insincerity).[21] Josiah's own life would end prematurely. When Pharaoh Neco decided to assist the remnants of the Assyrian army in defeating the upstart Babylonians, his army went through the coastal road then controlled by Judah. Josiah attempted to prevent the Egyptian march, but to no avail:

> After this ... Pharaoh Neco came up to fight at Carchemish by the Euphrates, and [Josiah] came up to meet him militarily at the Megiddo Valley. And the archers shot King Josiah ... and he was brought to Jerusalem and he died there ... and all of Judah and Jerusalem mourned over Josiah. (II Chr. 35:19–24)

21. According to rabbinic tradition, Josiah was unaware that his efforts changed the people on only a superficial level. The Midrash (Lamentations Rabba 1:53) describes how Josiah would send inspectors to check for idolatry in people's houses. They wouldn't find any when entering the houses, because the Jews would set it up so the idol was painted on the back of two doors - when the doors opened, it wasn't visible, but when they were closed the painted image formed an idol. The Talmud (Taanit 22b) suggests that it was this misplaced confidence that Josiah had in both his and his people's righteousness that encouraged him to challenge Pharaoh Neco in battle in Megiddo in 609 BCE:

> "For the sword [the alarm is sounded]." Our Rabbis taught: "[Regarding] the sword of which they spoke, it is not necessary to mention a sword that is not of peace but even a sword of peace. For you do not have a sword more peaceful than [that of] Pharaoh Neco, and even so King Josiah came to grief on account of it ... [Josiah] said: "Since he [Pharaoh] trusts in idolatry, I can [defeat] him".... But [Josiah] did not know that his generation was not worthy [of receiving the blessings of security mentioned in Lev. 26].

4. Josiah's Children (608–586 BCE)

With Josiah's death, the country fell into the hands of his children, who lacked his wisdom and character. Jehoahaz (609 BCE) succeeded his father, but was removed by Pharaoh Neco after only three months, replaced by his older brother Jehoiakim (608–597 BCE). Neco preferred a puppet king in Jerusalem, loyal to Egypt, who would provide a buffer between Egypt and Babylon. For the next four years, between 609 and 605 BCE, Judah enjoyed a brief respite from war while the major powers fought decisive battles a thousand miles away. Secure under Egyptian patronage, Jehoiakim abandoned his father's ways, making himself wealthy at the expense of the impoverished population, earning Jeremiah's unrelenting scorn and wrath:

> Woe unto him that builds his house by unrighteousness, and his chambers by injustice; that uses his neighbor's service without wages, and gives him not his hire; that says, "I will build me a wide house and spacious chambers," and cuts himself windows, and it is ceiled with cedar, and painted with vermilion. Shall you reign, because you strive to excel in cedar? Did not your father eat and drink, and do justice and righteousness? Then it was well with him. He judged the cause of the poor and needy; then it was well. Is not this to know Me? says the Lord. But your eyes and your heart are not but for your covetousness, and for shedding innocent blood, and for oppression, and for violence, to do it. Therefore, so says the Lord concerning Jehoiakim the son of Josiah, king of Judah: They shall not lament for him: "Ah, my brother!" or: "Ah, sister!" They shall not lament for him: "Ah, Lord!" or: "Ah, his glory!" A donkey's burial shall he be buried, dragged and tossed past the gates of Jerusalem. (Jer. 22:13–19)

In 605 BCE, the Babylonian army defeated Neco's forces and the remaining remnants of the Assyrian Empire at Carchamish. They pursued the Egyptians back to Egypt, and in 604 BCE the Babylonians reached the Philistine coastal territory southwest of Judah. Jehoiakim immediately switched allegiance to Nebuchadnezzar, and Judah began to pay tribute to Babylon, functionally becoming a vassal state. However, in 601 BCE the

Babylonians left Egypt and returned to Babylon to deal with minor rebellions on the eastern side of their empire. Ignoring Jeremiah and expecting renewed Egyptian assistance, Jehoiakim decided to renounce his allegiance from the Babylonians (II Kings 24:1). It was a fatal miscalculation, and in late 598 BCE Nebuchadnezzar sent his army to reestablish control over Judah. When Jehoiakim suddenly died due to uncertain circumstances,[22] his son Jehoiachin, or Jeconiah (598 BCE), took the throne of Judah at the age of eighteen, and within three months surrendered to the invaders. As a result, Nebuchadnezzar exiled to Babylon along with him several thousand members of the Judahite upper class, hoping that this act would weaken Judah enough to discourage the remaining inhabitants from rebelling.[23] Jehoiachin languished in prison for thirty-seven years, until a later Babylonian king, Evil-Merodach (in Babylonian, *Amel-marduk*) released him from prison and gave him a seat at the Babylonian palace.[24]

The Babylonians appointed a new king to replace Jehoiachin, his uncle Zedekiah. They hoped that Zedekiah would be a loyal vassal. However, there was strong pressure from his populace to revolt against

22. According to II Kings 24:5–6, the king died peacefully, and the same is reported in the Septuagint version of II Chr. 36. However, the Hebrew version of II Chr. 36:6 describes Jehoiakim being taken in chains to Babylon. Jeremiah promised that no one would lament the passing of the corrupt, despised king. Instead, "A donkey's burial shall he be buried, dragged and tossed past the gates of Jerusalem" (Jer. 22:19). In Jer. 36, the prophet reacts to Jehoiakim's burning of the scroll that Jeremiah had written warning the people of their eventual destruction if they continued to forsake God's ways by declaring that "his corpse shall be cast to the heat by day and to the frost at night" (36:30–31). Josephus also suggests a similar grisly death, stating that "the Babylonians put Jehoiakim to death, and his body was cast in front of the walls of Jerusalem, with no burial" (*Antiquities* X:7). Rashi in II Kings tries to reconcile the text with the II Chronicles version, suggesting that "Nebuchadnezzar bound him with copper chains to take him to Babylon, and they were dragging him, and he died in their hands." An excellent summary of the issues can be found in Oded Lipschits's article "Jehoiakim Slept with his Fathers – Did He?" available online at http://www.jhsonline.org/Articles/article_23.htm#_ednref26.
23. In his vision of two baskets of figs, Jeremiah describes how the people who remained behind misunderstood the divine message. Believing that God exiled only sinners, they viewed the fact that they were not forced to leave their homes as a sign of divine favor, and did not appreciate the precarious situation they were in.
24. II Kings 25:27–30.

the Babylonians. Surrounding nations and Egypt promised assistance, and false prophets like Hananiah promised victory and an end to the exile.[25] Only Jeremiah advocated for continued submission, writing letters to the exiles to convince them that the exile would last for seventy years.[26] Despite Jeremiah's warning, Zedekiah bowed to the public pressure and began a revolt.

Within a few months, the Babylonian armies arrived in Judah and crushed the uprising. By 588 BCE, only Jerusalem and the fortresses of Lachish and Azekah were still standing. When the outposts fell, Jerusalem came under siege as it had under the Assyrians in 701 BCE. However, no miracle awaited the inhabitants this time. The Babylonians breached the walls in the winter of 587 BCE. Zedekiah attempted to flee, but was captured and taken to Nebuchadnezzar, who forced the fugitive king to watch his sons' execution before blinding him. He was then taken captive to Babylon where he died.[27] His death was the final demise of the Davidic dynasty that had ruled for over four centuries. Jerusalem and the Temple were burned to the ground, and Nebuchadnezzar exiled to Babylonia the few remaining survivors of Jerusalem. A small remnant of people who inhabited the surrounding hills were allowed to remain; however, the assassination of the appointed governor, Gedaliah son of Ahikam, caused the remaining populace to flee in fear to Egypt (Jer. 40–42). The destruction of Judah, the Southern Kingdom, which had existed since the time of David, was complete.

25. Jer. 28.

26. Ibid. 29.

27. II Kings 25:5–7, Jer. 52:11.

Nahum

Introduction

The seventh book of *Trei Asar*, the Twelve Minor Prophets, opens by identifying its author, Nahum, and its subject, Nineveh.[1] The name Nahum means comfort or consolation, but for Nineveh, Nahum's prophecy is anything but consoling. Nahum uses some of the Bible's harshest yet most imaginative poetry to describe the terrifying and violent end that awaits Nineveh, at a time when even imagining that Assyria could be defeated would have made him seem insane. His imagery is dramatic and disturbing; his message of vengeance is frightening.[2] Unlike other

1. In the Septuagint's ordering of the Twelve Minor Prophets, Nahum immediately follows Jonah. This ordering is thematically appropriate: Jonah and Nahum are linked by the common subjects of the Assyrian Empire, and in particular the empire's capital city, Nineveh. In Jonah, though, God accepts Nineveh's repentance and grants them a reprieve, while in Nahum, God personally leads the invading armies that will raze the city to its foundations. Jonah struggles to comprehend why Nineveh's existence is not a slight on God's righteousness and justice, while for Nahum, God's attributes of righteousness and justice require that Nineveh must cease to exist. In their opening remarks, both the *Targum Yonatan* and Rashi (commentary on 1:1) understand Nahum as reacting to Jonah's prophecy.
2. Nahum's message is so strikingly unforgiving and violent that for many Christian commentaries, Nahum became the prime example of these commentaries' claim of the moral inferiority of the Old Testament. Typical of this view are the words of

prophets, Nahum does not ask anything of the Jewish people. There is no call for repentance or listing of failings; there is just the promise that their suffering will end and that a horrible fate awaits their oppressors.[3]

Among the books of the prophets, Nahum is short, only forty-seven verses in length, and his words never found their way into the liturgy or readings.[4] Beginning to read Nahum, we see why the book was shunted aside. Nahum portrays God primarily as an angry God, filled with outrage and seeking vengeance, preparing to destroy and humiliate

---

G. A. Smith in 1903: "Such is the sheer religion of... [the] Book of Nahum – thoroughly Oriental in its sense of God's method and resources of destruction; very Jewish... in the bursting of its long pent up hopes of revenge... we [the Christian West] should not attribute so much personal passion to the Avenger. With our keener sense of law, we should emphasize the slowness of the process" (quoted in Julia M. O'Brien, *Nahum, Habakkuk, Zephaniah, Haggai, Zechariah, Malachi*, Abingdon Old Testament Commentaries [Nashville: Abingdon Press, 2004], 27).

Among modern scholars, Elizabeth Achtemeier's words reflect this unease with the book's tone: "We often wish Nahum were not in the canon, and the book has almost been totally ignored" (*Nahum–Malachi*, Interpretation: A Bible Commentary for Teaching and Preaching [Nashville: John Knox, 1986], 5). See additional sources in O'Brien, *Nahum*, 106.

3. Due to the absence of a call for repentance or any demand for moral improvement in the book of Nahum, R. H. Pfeiffer argues that

> Nahum was not a prophet – neither a reforming prophet like his contemporary Jeremiah nor an optimistic "false prophet" like Hananiah (see Jer. 28). He was a poet... there is nothing specifically religious in this exultant outburst of joy over the inevitable downfall of the Assyrian Empire. (*Introduction to the Old Testament* [New York: Harper, 1941], 595)

4. There are two exceptions: According to the ancient custom of the Land of Israel, when the Torah was read publicly on a triannual cycle, Nahum 1:12–2:6 was read as the *haftara* to Genesis 34, the story of the rape of Dinah. Additionally, several verses of Nahum were appended to the end of Micah as the *haftara* to Exodus 11, which describes the upcoming obliteration of the Egyptians in the final plague.

Among the Dead Sea Scrolls discovered in 1952 in cave 4 of Qumran was a fragment of a work known as the Nahum Commentary, *Pesher Naḥum* (4Q169). Here, the writer alternates between verses from the book of Nahum and his interpretation, in which he calls for divine vengeance against those whom he viewed as deviants and sinners in the first century before the Common Era. Comparing this fragment to our text, we are able to see that "the consonantal text of the Hebrew Bible has been handed down with amazing accuracy for almost 2000 years" (Kevin J. Cathcart, *Nahum in the Light of Northwest Semitic* [Rome: Biblical Institute Press, 1973], 13).

the mighty Assyria and its capital, Nineveh. Yet a careful reading demonstrates that the message of the book of Nahum is not a shallow cry for revenge. At a time of national humiliation for Judah, Nahum thoughtfully articulates why God must be capable not only of love and compassion, but also of violence and destruction. The demonstration of this message and its relevance for us will be the aim of this commentary.

We know nothing about Nahum the person. His name is unique in the Hebrew Bible,[5] and the accompanying description "the Elkoshite" can be understood as referring either to his father's or family's name, or to his hometown.[6] Some identify Elkosh with the village of Al-Qosh in Iraq, twenty-five miles north of present-day Mosul, across the Tigris River from Nineveh. Kurdish Jews even made pilgrimages on Shavuot to what is purportedly Nahum's Tomb. There is a saying among Kurdish Jews that "he who has not witnessed the celebration of pilgrimage to Nahum's Tomb has not seen real joy." The fate of this structure was recently newsworthy when ISIS made advances into this region.[7]

---

5. However, it appears frequently in other northwest Semitic inscriptions. See Ralph L. Smith, *Micah–Malachi*, Word Biblical Commentary (Waco, TX: Word Books, 1984), 63.
6. The *Targum Yonatan* understands Elkosh to mean his family, while Rashi understands it to refer to his hometown. Rabbi Yosef Kara also concludes that it refers to a place, though he also notes that there is an element of clever wordplay here. Elkosh can be considered a contraction of two words which express Nahum's central message: *Elokim kasheh*, God is harsh. Ibn Ezra and Radak think it could be a reference either to his family or to the place he came from.

   Some modern scholars, in explaining Nahum's familiarity with Nineveh, speculate that he was part of a group of Judahite emissaries that brought the yearly tribute from King Manasseh to his Assyrian masters. While in the capital, he would have observed Nineveh's broad roads (2:4), walls (2:5), gates (2:6), and its vast wealth (2:9). A local Christian tradition claims that Nahum was from Nineveh and that his tomb lies inside the local synagogue. See Marvin A. Sweeney, *The Twelve Prophets: Volume 2: Micah, Nahum, Habakkuk, Zephaniah, Haggai, Zechariah, Malachi*, Berit Olam: Studies in Hebrew Narrative and Poetry (Collegeville, MN: The Liturgical Press, 2000), 420.
7. Information regarding Nahum's Tomb, including the traditions that arose among the Kurdish Jewish community with regard to it, as well as its recent appearances in the news, was culled from www.myjewishlearning.com, "Nahum's Tomb: A Shavuot Like No Other"; and www.haaretz.com, "Ancient Jewish Site Near ISIS-controlled Mosul at Risk of Collapse."

Door of Nahum's Tomb at Al-Qosh

It is clear from the text that Nahum displays an intimate familiarity with both the landscape and the vegetation of Israel. Therefore, most scholars suggest that Elkosh was found in either the north of Israel (Elkosh being the old name for the first-century Galilean town Capernaum [literally, "the village of Nahum"]), or in southern Judea.

WHEN DID NAHUM PROPHESY?

Though the book does not precisely identify the historical time period in which Nahum spoke, it is clear that it was at a time when the Assyrian Empire had reached the height of its power. The book's tone makes it clear that Assyria ruled over Judah with an iron fist. Nahum describes the conquest of No-Amon (Thebes) by Ashurbanipal in 663 BCE (3:8), and prophesies about the fall of Nineveh, which was destroyed in 612 BCE. These dates, 633–612 BCE, form the range of the earliest possible date (*terminus a quo*) and the latest possible date (*terminus ad quem*) for his prophecy.[8] However, Nahum doesn't mention Babylonia, an omission which would have been inconceivable once Nabopolassar turned Babylonia into a superpower in 626 BCE.[9]

According to the tannaitic work *Seder Olam* (ch. 20), Nahum prophesied during Manasseh's rule. Manasseh assumed the throne in 696 BCE, and his reign over Judah, which ended in 641 BCE, was marked by subservience and submission to the Assyrian overlords as well as complete abandonment of Jewish tradition as it had been practiced for centuries, since the building of the Temple. Nahum prophesies about a time when the Temple will be restored to its former glory, proper sacrifices will be offered on the altar, Manasseh's lineage will be cut off, and his kingdom of idolatry erased (1:14–2:1). According to this tradition, it is possible that Nahum did not want to associate his

8. In 1923, C. J. Gadd published a tablet from Babylon which was in the possession of the British Museum. The accounts in this tablet, ABC 3 of the "Babylonian Chronicles," covered the years 616–609 BCE, the tenth to seventeenth years of Nabopolassar's rule as king of Babylon. This tablet locates the fall of Nineveh in the fourteenth year of his reign, the year 612 BCE, providing an absolute chronological peg for biblical and Assyrian history.
9. Interestingly, Josephus believed that Nineveh was destroyed 115 years after Nahum prophesied (*Antiquities* IX:11:3). However, this would place Nahum in the year 727 BCE, before the destruction and exile of the Northern Kingdom. This is problematic, as it would mean that Nahum is delivering a message that would not be relevant for over a hundred years, and that many of his comments to his Judahite audience implying past Assyrian crimes (i.e., "misfortune will not come a second time" – 1:9) would not yet be relevant, as they had not been invaded a first time by Assyria until 701 BCE. According to Maimonides, Nahum received his tradition from the prophet Joel (see introduction to *Mishneh Torah*, sect. 1).

name with Manasseh's wickedness, and therefore omitted his name from the superscription.[10]

Although these two issues would support an earlier dating, many modern scholars and rabbis prefer to date Nahum to the later end of the range mentioned above. Professor Yehuda Elitzur maintains that Nahum's prophecy about Nineveh's downfall took place either right before 612 BCE (when the city actually fell), or immediately afterward. He claims that it was Nahum's prophecy that encouraged King Josiah to side with the Babylonians in their war with the combined Assyrian and Egyptian forces. This choice is what led to Josiah's fateful and ultimately fatal decision to march out to Megiddo in 609 BCE and attempt to prevent the Egyptian forces from reaching the battle of Carchemish.[11] Elitzur's approach is adopted by Rabbi Binyamin Lau in his work on *Trei Asar*, where he speculates that Nahum's words provided the basis for the false prophets who encouraged militant responses throughout the book of Jeremiah, and ultimately led to Judah's downfall.[12]

The contemporary Bible scholar Rabbi Yoel Bin-Nun offers a different suggestion. He asserts that there is only one historical event at which Nahum could have spoken – at King Josiah's communal Passover offering in 622 BCE (see II Kings 23, II Chr. 34). Josiah had exploited the weak state of the Assyrian Empire to regain control over much of northern Israel. He wished to cement his expanded control in the same manner as his great-grandfather Hezekiah did almost a century earlier, by implementing a mass renewal of the covenant through a national Passover offering. However, argues Rabbi Bin-Nun, the people of Judah remembered what the result of Hezekiah's actions had been – the devastating invasion of 701 BCE that left Judah nearly destroyed, and soon afterward the puppet king

10. In *Seder Olam* it says that "Joel, Nahum, and Habakkuk prophesied during the days of Manasseh, but they were not identified with him because he was not righteous" (ch. 20).

11. See Yehuda Elitzur, *Nahum HaNavi: Tekufato VeSheliḥuto* (Nahum the Prophet, His Times and Mission), available online at http://www.daat.ac.il/daat/tanach/trayasar/nahum-eli-1.htm.

12. Binyamin Lau, *Eight Prophets: Bonds of Love* (Hebrew) (Rishon LeZion: Yediot Aharonot Publishing, 2016), 168–78.

Manasseh ascending the throne. With this in mind, the people thought that it was better not to provoke the Assyrians again and risk another devastating response. Nahum responded to the people's fears with a message of encouragement: "trouble will not rise twice" (1:9) and "now I will break off his yoke from you" (1:13). This message afforded the king and the people with the confidence they needed to renew and rebuild.[13]

While recognizing the textual merits of the explanation which supports a later dating, we prefer to maintain an earlier dating and follow the rabbinic explanation which has Nahum speaking during Manasseh's reign. There are several reasons for this. First, the late dating suggested by Professor Elitzur and Rabbi Lau locates Nahum at a point in time when, as a result of civil wars and the Babylonian uprising, the Assyrian kingdom had all but collapsed; all that was missing was the final deathblow. This removes not only any sense of drama from Nahum's message, but also the sense of prophecy from his words.[14] Second, as we will demonstrate in our commentary on chapter 1, there are several allusions to King Manasseh in the chapter, and reading them instead as references to the Assyrian monarch does damage to the continuity of Nahum's message.

Finally, unlike Rabbi Bin-Nun, we believe that there are earlier occasions when Nahum's message would have been equally pertinent and relevant, which can provide textual support for an earlier dating. From the time of his ascension to the throne in 697 BCE, Manasseh was a loyal vassal to Nineveh. To the account in II Kings, II Chronicles adds a surprising detail: At what is likely near the end of his reign, in the year 650 BCE, Manasseh apparently attempted to exploit the brief civil war between Ashurbanipal and his brother to rebel against Assyrian rule.[15] This rebellion was quickly

13. Rabbi Bin-Nun's explanation can be found in Lau, *Eight Prophets,* and online in Hebrew, at www.etzion.org.il, in the lecture entitled "The Days of Josiah, Part 2."
14. A contemporary example would be to say that if someone had foreseen, and in fact, guaranteed, the Soviet downfall in 1979, it would have been considered no less than a form of prophecy, whereas such a statement in 1989 would have been seen as a reasonable and unremarkable supposition.
15. Further discussion and debate regarding the circumstances of this rebellion can be found in William M. Schniedewind, "The Source Citations of Manasseh: King Manasseh in History and Homily," *Vetus Testamentum* 41, no. 4 (October 1991): 450–61, especially footnotes 3, 4, and 11.

subdued, and in 648 BCE, the Assyrians took Manasseh in chains to Babylon, where Ashurbanipal was concluding his campaign against internal insurrections. When he returned to Judah, Manasseh began to engage in a series of actions to strengthen Judah's defenses and begin the process of religiously reforming the country (see II Chr. 33:13–end).

Manasseh's rebellion raises many questions. For almost fifty years, Manasseh was a loyal vassal to Assyria. What caused him to turn against his masters, risking the prosperity and quiet that his surrender had brought to Judah? One possible explanation is that Nahum's prophecy against Assyria provoked Manasseh to rebel, as it provided him with confidence that the rebellion would succeed. If Nahum's prophecy was indeed the impetus behind Manasseh's rebellion, this would place Nahum's prophecy between 663 and 650 BCE. Alternatively, perhaps Nahum uttered his words of encouragement after Manasseh's return from captivity, as the repentant king undertook to remove idols from the Temple and rebuild Jerusalem's fortifications. This explanation would place his prophecy between 648 and 641 BCE. Either way, Nahum's words provided a glimmer of hope both to the king and to his oppressed people that a brighter future awaited them, if they repent.

STRUCTURE AND LANGUAGE

Despite his relative anonymity, scholars bestowed upon Nahum the title of "the poet laureate of the Minor Prophets."[16] In the nineteenth century, Robert Lowth exclaimed that

> none of the Minor Prophets seem to equal Nahum, in boldness, ardor, and sublimity. His prophecy too forms a regular and perfect poem ... it is truly majestic; the preparation for the destruction of Nineveh, and the description of its downfall and desolation, are expressed in the most glowing colors, and are bold and luminous in the highest degree.[17]

16. Richard Patterson, *Nahum, Habakkuk, Zephaniah*, Wycliffe Exegetical Commentary (Chicago: Moody Press, 1991), 10–11.
17. R. Lowth, *Lectures on the Sacred Poetry of the Hebrews* (London, 1839), 234.

Nahum's poetic literary arsenal is extensive. The first section is a partial acrostic. Wordplay, alliteration, assonance, and consonance appear regularly. For example, see 1:10: *sirim sevukhim ukhsovam sevuim*, "while the thorns are entangled and the drunkards are drinking"; and 2:11: *buka umevuka umevulaka*, "Empty, yea, emptied out and breached." Long poetic descriptions are constantly interrupted by short staccato commands: "And Nineveh is like a pool of water; it is since days of yore; and they flee. Halt! Halt!" (2:9). Throughout his prophecy Nahum effectively uses rhetorical questions to prove his point: "Who can stand before His fury and who can rise amid His wrath?" (1:6); "Are you better than No-Amon, which was situated among the rivers?" (3:8). Metaphors and similes appear frequently: "His wrath has reached [the earth] like fire" (1:6), "They are consumed like dry stubble, fully ripe" (1:10), "And Nineveh is like a pool of water" (2:9), "Where is the lions' den [i.e., Nineveh]?" (2:12). Additionally, readers will find many examples of irony (2:1, 8, 3:14, 15) and satire (2:12–14, 3:8–13, 14–19).

Reading Nahum properly involves identifying the book's structure. At first, this may seem to be an easy task, as the book is both relatively short and revolves around one subject, i.e., the upcoming downfall of Nineveh. Upon more careful examination, though, it becomes clear that Nahum defies easy breakdown. His poetic language rarely directly identifies the subject of his prophecy or his audience: sometimes, the subject of his words has to be inferred from context; in other places, several meanings can be maintained at once. Most scholars agree that there is a clear division in topics between the first chapter and the following two.[18] In chapter 1, Nahum first describes

18. Some scholars divide the book into two poems: the acrostic poem and the long poem (James D. Newsome Jr., *The Hebrew Prophets* [Atlanta: John Knox, 1984], 84), while others divide the book into more than two segments. David Dorsey in *The Literary Structure of the Old Testament* suggests that the entire book is meant to read as one unit, with seven symmetrical literary units centered chiastically around the end of the second chapter. His breakdown is as follows:

a. God, a terrible force of nature, avenges His enemies but is good to those who trust Him (1:2–10)
b. God will destroy Nineveh but restore Judah (1:11–2:1)

God's attributes, specifically that of vengeance, His power, and judgment of His enemies. Nahum then turns to the people of Judah and promises an end to their suffering. How this will come about is the topic of chapters 2 and 3, which describe the upcoming destruction of Nineveh with powerful and vivid imagery.[19] Within each chapter, Nahum alternates between two audiences, first speaking to, or about, the people and the city,[20] using the feminine singular form, then addressing their leadership, signified by the masculine singular form. At the conclusion of the final three sections, the activity or inactivity of a messenger is described (2:1, 14, 3:18–19). Combining these details, we divide Nahum into the following four-part structure, with the first section, A, describing God's attributes, and the next three sections alternating between messages directed at the people (B, C, D) with messages directed at the leadership (B1, C1, D1):[21]

A. 1:2–8: Divine Attributes and How God Relates to the World
Nahum begins by describing God as a God of vengeance, contrasting this attribute with God's long-lasting patience.

---

c. A vivid description of the attack upon Nineveh (2:2–11)
d. (Center) Lament over fall of Nineveh, i.e., the lions' den (2:12–14)
c′. A vivid description of the looting of Nineveh (3:1–7)
b′. Nineveh will be destroyed; it is vulnerable, like Thebes (3:8–13)
a′. Nineveh, likened to a destructive force of nature, will be destroyed (3:14–19).

However, these categories and parallels are too broadly defined and lack enough corresponding textual support to be convincing. See David Dorsey, *The Literary Structure of the Old Testament: A Commentary on Genesis–Malachi* (Ada, MI: Baker Publishing Group), 301–5.

19. As 1:1 uses multiple terms to describe the book of Nahum (including *massa* and *ḥazon*), Malbim suggests the following alternative division: chapters 1 and 2 describe the *massa* period leading to the present destruction of Nineveh, while chapter 3 presents a *ḥazon*, a vision, that depicts a future and final destruction of Nineveh. Given that Nineveh was destroyed only once, we shall not expand on this approach.
20. In chapter 1, the people he speaks to are the people of Judah and the city is the city of Jerusalem, while in chapters 2 and 3, the people he speaks to are the people of Assyria and the city is the city of Nineveh.
21. The structure presented here is similar to that identified by Joseph Blenkinsopp in *A History of Prophecy in Israel* (Louisville: Westminster John Knox Press, 1996), 122–23.

He then describes God's omniscient control over the forces of nature, and promises that the upcoming cataclysm will not affect those that trust in Him.

B. 1:9–13, 2:1: A Message of Hope to Judah

B1. 1:14: A Rebuke of Judah's King

Nahum then turns to address the Jewish people directly. He chides them briefly for their lack of faith, but then promises them that their difficulties with their Assyrian oppressors will soon come to an end. When that salvation arrives, Nahum assures the people that they will be able to resume wholehearted devotion to and worship of God. For the unnamed leader of Israel, however, there is only rebuke for establishing and continuing idolatrous practices in the Temple.

C. 2:2–2:11: Describing the Upcoming Assault on Nineveh

C1. 2:12–2:14: A First Taunt of the Assyrian king

This section describes, in a highly detailed manner, the upcoming Babylonian assault on the city of Nineveh, from the initial approach of the troops, including descriptions of colorful and dramatic battle scenes in which projectiles and missiles fly while chariots race in the streets, to the final plundering and looting of the city's treasures. Nahum then taunts the Assyrian leadership, which viewed itself as strong as lions, for being powerless to stand against the enemy.

D. 3:1–17: Describing the Devastation: Intensified and Justified

D1. 3:18–19: A Final Taunt of the Assyrian king

Nahum then revisits the devastated city, where corpses are piled so high that people fall over them in the streets. He explains how Nineveh's destruction was caused by the city's moral deficiencies and depravities. After comparing Nineveh's fate to that of No-Amon (Thebes), the Egyptian city that had been ransacked by Assyria in 663 BCE, Nahum ends with a final taunt directed at the fallen king of Nineveh, who had viewed himself as all-mighty and all-powerful.

The structure above reveals several facets of the book of Nahum that are generally overlooked. First, we see that Nahum's intended audience needed to be brought slowly to the realization that Nineveh can and would be destroyed – that God was not only capable but ready to do so. Second, the alternation between messages to the people and to the leadership exposes a disconnect between the two in their religious and political orientation. Section B makes very clear that while the Jewish people were worthy of salvation should they show trust in God, their leadership and king deserved to be destroyed. Finally, the repetition of the description of Nineveh's destruction in section D is significant. By emphasizing the sins of Assyria, Nahum ensures that no one will be able to misconstrue his message as a display of shallow nationalism and prejudice. Instead, God acts on moral principles that apply equally to all.

1:1

Superscription

> An oracle (*massa*) concerning Nineveh, the book of the vision of Nahum the Elkoshite. (1:1)

The books of Prophets begin with a superscription that identifies the prophet and his subject matter, and Nahum is no exception. These opening words stand outside the prophecy itself, and based on their form and content, it is clear that these superscriptions weren't written by the prophets themselves, but by those who collected the sacred writings, in order to provide context and continuity to the works.[1] For readers, it is important to note that these words often provide information that the prophet's original audience would not have heard. Within the first two words of the book of Nahum, the reader learns that Nineveh is the target of Nahum's prophecy, but Nahum's contemporary listeners would have discovered this only much later on in Nahum's discourse.

---

1. See O'Brien for the shifting views in scholarship regarding the relationship between the superscriptions and the contents of the prophecy (*Nahum*, 20). For a general overview of the role of the superscription and the book, see Gene M. Tucker, "Prophetic Superscriptions and the Growth of a Canon," in *Canon and Authority: Essays in Old Testament Religion and Theology* (Philadelphia: Fortress Press, 1977), 56–70.

Comparing Nahum's superscription to the opening verses of other prophetic books, we can see that while nine of the fifteen prophets are introduced with their lineage or other personal information, and the others contain at least some marker to identify the date in which they were composed, Nahum's introduction contains only very sparse and vague personal information and no time stamp at all. What we do know from the superscription is that Nahum is described by two of the terms that the Bible uses in other prophetic works to describe prophecy: *massa* and *ḥazon*. Nahum's superscription does not use the third term which appears in many of the superscriptions, *devar Hashem,* but it does include the term *sefer,* which does not appear in any of the other books. To appreciate Nahum's message, we must unlock the meaning of these terms. The following chart is a comparison of the language used in the superscriptions at the beginning of the books of the prophets:

Prophetic Superscriptions

Prophet's name	Genealogy	Other information about prophet	Date	Subject/ recipient of prophecy	Word(s) of Hashem *(devar Hashem, divrei Hashem)*	Vision (*ḥazon*)	Burden/ oracle (*massa*)
Nahum		✓		✓		✓	✓
Isaiah	✓		✓	✓		✓	
Jeremiah	✓	✓	✓	✓	✓		
Ezekiel		✓	✓				
Hosea	✓		✓		✓		
Joel	✓				✓		
Amos		✓	✓	✓	✓	✓	
Obadiah				✓		✓	
Jonah	✓				✓		
Micah		✓	✓	✓	✓	✓	

Prophet's name	Genealogy	Other information about prophet	Date	Subject/ recipient of prophecy	Word(s) of Hashem *(devar Hashem, divrei Hashem)*	Vision (*ḥazon*)	Burden/ oracle (*massa*)
Habakkuk						✓	✓
Zephaniah	✓		✓		✓		
Haggai			✓	✓	✓		
Zechariah	✓		✓		✓		
Malachi				✓	✓		✓

What is the meaning of *massa*? Most traditional commentaries understand the word to be a synonym for prophecy. It appears approximately twenty times in the Bible in reference to prophecy (in Prov. 30:1 and 31:1 it refers to wisdom), and is derived from the Hebrew root N-S-A, "to raise."[2] *Massa* is most often translated into English as either an oracle, or pronouncement, in the sense that a voice is raised up to deliver the divine message, or as a burden that a message must carry and bear. Rabbinic thought recognizes the negative connotation of the second definition: "[There are] ten designations for prophecy... and which is the severest form?... The Rabbis said: burden (*massa*), as it states (Ps. 138:5), 'As a heavy burden'" (Genesis Rabba 44:6).

The common usage of the word *massa* in the Bible is usually in relation to the destruction of one group or nation, often to the benefit of another. Looking at the appearances of the term *massa* in the prophecies of Habakkuk, Zechariah (chs. 9 and 12), and Malachi (ch. 1), we note the following pattern: After the word *massa*, God appears suddenly, acting decisively on Judah's behalf, and the description of God's

2. Other appearances of the word *massa* can be found in II Kings 9:25–26; Is. 13:1, 14:28, 15:1, 17:1, 19:1, 21:1, 11, 13, 22:1, 23:1, 30:6; Ezek. 12:10; the books of Nahum and Habakkuk; Zech. 9:1, 12:1; and Mal. 1:1. *Massa* also appears in Jer. 23:33, Lam. 2:14, and in II Chr. 24:27, but does not contain the prophecy's actual content, which does not help us ascertain its meaning. See the term "oracle" in the *Anchor Bible Dictionary*, vol. 5, ed. David Noel Freedman (New York: Doubleday, 1992), 28.

appearance is often marked by military imagery. Any doubts that arose regarding divine justice (see, for example, Hab. 1:4: "The law becomes weakened [numbed], and justice never prevails" and Mal. 2:17: "Where is the God of justice?") disappear quickly. This divine appearance is known as a theophany. It generally leads to a distinction between two groups of people: those whom God destroys and those whom God saves. In Habakkuk and Zechariah, the nations of the world stand in opposition to the Jewish people; in Malachi, the division is within the Jewish people themselves (see Mal. 3:18: "Then you will again discern between the righteous and the wicked, between he that serves God and he that serves Him not"). The use of the word *massa* at the beginning of the book of Nahum prepares the reader for this theophany, and the resulting distinction there is between those who will survive and those who will perish.

Rabbi Eliezer of Beaugency notes (commentary on 1:1) that the word *massa* is often followed by identifying the nation that receives the brunt of the prophecy, and cites as examples "the *massa* of Moab" (Is. 15:1) and "the *massa* of Damascus" (Is. 17:1). Indeed, Isaiah's diatribes against the foreign nations in chapters 13–23 are all introduced with the word *massa*. When Isaiah uttered these prophecies a century earlier than Nahum, these nations were soon to be destroyed by Assyria, if they hadn't been crushed by them already. Isaiah's underlying message was that despite these countries' efforts, attempts to defeat Assyria militarily were futile. Only with divine intervention could Assyria be defeated. Linking this book to Isaiah,[3] Nahum now delivers the remarkable message that God is indeed plotting to defeat Assyria.

---

3. Rabbi Yoel Bin-Nun has outlined a series of literary parallels between Nahum and Isaiah, and claims that Nahum was part of a coterie of Isaiah's students who sequestered themselves during the days of Manasseh. While we find some of the claims far-reaching, it is worth examining them in greater depth. Rabbi Bin-Nun's approach can be found in Hebrew at www.etzion.org.il, in the Tanakh series "*Nevi'im mul Maatzamot* – Prophets against Superpowers." The specific parallels between Isaiah and Nahum can be found in the lecture entitled "Isaiah and His Students from the Days of Manasseh until the Destruction, Part 2."

Nahum is also called a *sefer*,[4] i.e., book, as it begins with the words "book of the vision of Nahum."[5] Of all of the prophetic works, Nahum is the only one labeled a book (though others describe the process of transferring their words to writing; see Jer. 36:2, 45:1; Ezek. 2:2; and Hab. 2:2). We are sympathetic to the suggestion that Nahum originally meant his message to be read, not spoken.[6] Nahum prophesied during the reign of a king known for killing his opponents, and books were a safer form of communication. Indeed, Jeremiah chose to have his prophecy of Jerusalem's upcoming destruction delivered to his adversary King Jehoakim via scroll, rather than delivering it orally in person.

Rabbi Yoel Bin-Nun speculates that this is the proper interpretation of Isaiah 8:16: "Bind up the testimony, seal the instruction among My disciples," i.e., that Isaiah's prophecy was meant to be written down and read.[7] During Manasseh's reign, prophets who spoke against the authorities were summarily killed, forcing the prophets to teach and prophesy underground, just as thousands of years later, Jews who studied Torah in Communist Russia had to hide their activities for fear of being persecuted or perhaps sent to Siberia. Therefore, concludes Rabbi Bin-Nun, Torah became the property of a limited few, "bound up" and hidden "among the disciples." However, this interpretation is less appropriate with regard to Nahum. As noted in our introductory section on poetic devices, Nahum makes extensive usage of auditory elements, including

---

4. Rashi apparently had a different vowelization of the word *ḥazon* than our text; his *ḥazon* is vowelized with a *kamatz* and not a *ḥataf pataḥ*. As such, he reads "a book [of Nahum] of the vision," but without the construct state that attaches vision to Nahum. He interprets the vision as emanating from Jonah so many years before, about Nineveh, that in another forty days the city would be overturned. When they repented, the vision was delayed – but now, Nahum returns to Jonah's original vision of Nineveh's destruction.
5. For some scholars, the dual subscription *massa* and *ḥazon* indicates that two separate works that were attributed to Nahum were merged together, with the demarcation being between the theophany of 1:2–1:8 and the oracle against Nineveh in the rest of the book (O'Brien, *Nahum*, 33). As we are focusing on the final form of the book and not on speculation about its development, we will not belabor the issue here.
6. C. F. Keil, *The Twelve Minor Prophets*, COT (Grand Rapids: Eerdmans, 1954).
7. Heard orally from Rabbi Yoel Bin-Nun in several classes and forums.

alliteration, consonance, and wordplay, which indicates that these words were intended to be spoken and heard, not read.

Finally, Nahum is introduced as being a *ḥazon*, a vision. The root of the word *ḥazon* is Ḥ-Z-H, "see." But *ḥazon* is more than simply vision in the sense of sight. In the Bible, it refers almost exclusively to prophecy, which is generally a vision of a distant future, one that often sounds unbelievable to listeners grounded in their present-day reality. An excellent example of this is the root's first appearance in Tanakh, when God spoke to the childless and elderly Abram at the Covenant between the Pieces (Gen. 15), promising him that his progeny would be as numerous as the stars in the sky:

> The word of the Lord came unto Abram in a vision [*maḥazeh*] saying, "Fear not, Abram; I am your shield; your reward is exceedingly great.... Please look heavenward and count the stars, if you are able to count them." And He said to him, "So will be your descendants."

Similarly, Obadiah's *ḥazon* describes a glorious future to its listeners, including the final downfall of Israel's archrival Edom; while Isaiah's *ḥazon* (which we interpret to refer to his entire collection of prophecies), though it begins at the bleakest point in Jewish history until that time, concludes with twenty-seven chapters that describe a glorious redemption and salvation.

Sometimes false prophets claimed to have been the recipients of a *ḥazon*. They told their listeners to ignore the dismal present and to rest assured that if they continued faithfully in their path, a brighter future would eventually arrive. This trend became a challenge and a snare for Israel's real prophets, who were desperately trying to convince the Jewish people to learn from their deteriorating circumstances and change their ways. Jeremiah bemoaned how false prophets would use this term to claim authenticity for their message:

> So says the Lord of hosts: Pay no attention to the words of the prophets that prophesy unto you, they lead you unto vanity; they speak a vision (*ḥazon*) of their own heart, and not out of the mouth of the Lord. (Jer. 23:16)

Nahum prophesied to a downtrodden people about the upcoming fall of their oppressor, Assyria. This message must have been extremely hard to believe, and it is not hard to imagine how one could have suspected Nahum of being a false prophet. Assyria had not only been the regional superpower for over a century, having even conquered the mighty Egyptian kingdom, but also had historical roots that preceded Abraham by centuries. For a modern reader to comprehend how unbelievable Nahum's message must have sounded to his listeners, it helps to recall more recent historical events. Only several short decades ago, in the 1970s, everyone, experts and laypeople alike, believed that the Soviet empire was nearly indestructible. No one could have predicted the Soviet Union's rapid dissolution within the space of only a few years at the end of the 1980s. Nahum's listeners would have reacted with extreme disbelief upon hearing that the apparently invincible Assyrian Empire would soon crumble. The description of Nahum's prophecy as a *ḥazon* makes perfect rhetorical sense; he was predicting the demise and disappearance of an entity that had existed for over fifteen hundred years!

1:2–1:8

The God of Vengeance

Nahum begins by focusing on one specific attribute of God, that of vengeance. Divine vengeance is, in fact, the theme of Nahum's message throughout the book. Nahum will utilize his message, i.e., the upcoming deliverance of God's chosen people and the destruction of their Assyrian oppressors, to articulate why vengeance, a seemingly uncharacteristic attribute of God, plays such a vital role in understanding how God interacts with the world. Our commentary will follow Nahum as he describes God as both caring and unforgiving, as a simultaneous source of salvation and of destruction. In the conclusion to our commentary, we shall grapple with and attempt to reconcile the contradictory aspects of God in Nahum's description.

In this section, Nahum speaks, but does not directly address his listeners. Rather, he delves immediately into a description of God's attributes and omnipotence. We will call this type of speaking, where the speaker speaks out loud to listeners who hear him but does not directly address his listeners, "indirect discourse." Only in 1:9 does Nahum directly address his audience with what we will call "direct discourse"; therefore, we will treat 1:9 onward as a separate unit. Nahum's first speech can be divided into three subsections:

A. God's attributes (1:2–3)
B. God's power – His control over nature (1:4–6)
C. God's power directed against the good and the wicked (1:7–8)

Interestingly, a partial acrostic runs through these verses, beginning with the letter *alef*, and ending with the letter *kaf* (missing the letter *dalet*).[1] This may signify that these verses were once part of a larger liturgical unit, familiar to the people, which Nahum cleverly adapted for his purpose:

Verse	**Verse Transliteration**	**Hebrew Letter**	**Verse Number**
The Lord is a jealous and vengeful God	*El kano venokem Hashem*	א	2
The Lord – His way is with a tempest and with a storm	*Hashem, besufa uvise'ara*	ב	3
He rebukes the sea and dries it up	*Go'er bayam vayabeshehu*	ג	4
Mountains quaked because of Him	*Harim raashu mimenu*	ה	5

1. Some suggest that the word *umlal* (cut off) in verse 4 should read *dalal* (languish) in order to complete the partial acrostic. Partial acrostics are not uncommon in the Bible; in fact, many acrostic poems in the Bible are not complete. Duane Christensen suggests that the partial acrostic carried symbolic import: "If an entire acrostic conveys completeness, half an acrostic may well be a prophetic way of indicating incompleteness with still more to come. Assyria faces imminent judgment, but only half of what is eventually in store for her." Duane L. Christensen, "The Acrostic of Nahum Reconsidered," *Zeitschrift für die alttestamentliche Wissenschaft* 87 (1975): 25. Others suggest that this partial acrostic represents an earlier, complete, separate text which was familiar to listeners, and Nahum chose to incorporate only sections thereof. Michael H. Floyd, "The Chimerical Acrostic of Nahum 1:1–10," *Journal of Biblical Literature* 113 (1994): 421–37.

Verse	Verse Transliteration	Hebrew Letter	Verse Number
and the land raised up from before Him	*Vatissa haaretz mipanav*	ו	5
Who can stand before His fury	*Lifnei zaamo mi yaamod*	ז	6
His wrath has reached [the earth] like fire	*Ḥamato nitkha kha'esh*	ח	6
The Lord is good, a stronghold in the day of trouble	*Tov Hashem, lemaoz beyom tzara*	ט	7
and He knows them that take refuge in Him	*veyode'a ḥosei vo*	י	7
[But] with an overrunning flood He will make a full end of the place thereof	*Kala yaase mekomah*	כ	8

The foundation for Nahum's entire prophecy can be found in its opening. In a few short sentences, Nahum outlines a series of anthropopathic descriptions – i.e., descriptions of God as having human feelings and emotions – of God's attributes.

> The Lord is a jealous and vengeful God;
> The Lord is vengeful and full of wrath;
> The Lord avenges Himself upon His adversaries
> And bears grudges against His enemies.

> The Lord is slow to anger and great in power, but He will surely not acquit. (1:2–3a)

He presents God as "jealous," "vengeful," and "full of wrath," and concludes by saying that God "bears grudges" against His unnamed enemies. In verse 2, two words repeat themselves three times each – vengeful (*nokem*) and God's four-letter name (*yod-heh-vav-heh*). The rest of the book will explain how these two words are linked together.

By opening by describing God's attributes of jealousy and zeal,[2] Nahum recalls Isaiah's prophecy about the downfall that Sennacherib would experience in 701 BCE when he attempted to besiege Jerusalem (Is. 37:21–35). Isaiah predicted how the Assyrians would be forced to retreat from Judah, like cattle being dragged away, while the trapped citizens of Jerusalem would be able to leave the city and enjoy the fruits of the vineyards that surround it. Isaiah concludes, "It is the *zeal* of the Lord of hosts that will do this!" (37:32). Nahum's attribution of jealousy and zeal to God recalls Isaiah's similar attribution. The tradition of ascribing the attributes of jealousy and zeal (both possible translations of the word *kanna* or *kanno*) to God hearkens back to the Ten Commandments, and there are several other places in the Bible where God is described this way. God's capacity for jealousness and zeal appears in the prohibitions against idolatry: "You shall not make for yourself a graven image…you shall not bow down unto them, nor serve them; for I, the Lord your God, am a jealous God… (Ex. 20:3–4), and resurfaces in the command to destroy idolatry upon entering the Land of Israel: "For you shall bow down to no other god; for the Lord, whose name is Jealous, is a jealous God" (Ex. 34:14).

In the Bible, jealousy is not inherently bad. The factor that determines whether the jealousy is a reflection of an acceptable emotion, i.e., zeal, or one that is not acceptable, i.e., envy, is the nature of the relationship between the involved parties. In Proverbs, we read of the dangers of jealousy (see Prov. 14:30, 27:4), while in the case of a woman who is suspected

2. The Hebrew word for jealous, *kanno*, appears only here and in Josh. 24:19; however, the similar word (both in root form and in meaning) *kanna* occurs five times (Ex. 20:5, 34:14, Deut. 4:24, 5:9, 6:15).

of infidelity, the Bible teaches us that jealousy is sometimes warranted (see Num. 5). The expectation of loyalty and the powerful emotion of love can provoke jealousy. These strong emotions are spoken of in Song of Songs: "For love is as powerful as death, and jealousy as difficult as the grave" (8:6). Just as there is an exclusive relationship between husband and wife, there is an exclusive covenant between God and the Jewish people that binds them together irrevocably. Therefore, God's jealousy appears in the context of idolatry. When Nahum mentions jealousy, he is drawing upon a familiar biblical metaphor for God's relationship with Israel: that of husband and wife. God's jealous reaction to the people's infidelities leads to punishment (see Jer. 2:1–3:5; Ezek. 16:23, 25, 35–42), but the same divine jealousy can lead God to act on their behalf (see Is. 59:17; Ezek. 36:6–7, 38:17–23; Zeph. 3:8–17, Zech. 8:2–3). It is this powerful feeling, that of God wanting to protect his people, that leads to Nahum's primary focus in verse 2 – vengeance.

Nahum describes God as a God of vengeance three times,[3] and then adds that He bears a grudge,[4] giving readers the sense that God's anger is building to a crescendo, moving on an upward scale from jealousness to vengeance to wrath. The Hebrew word for wrath, *ḥeima*, shares the same root letters as the word for heat, and signifies a burning rage that is ready to boil over uncontrollably. The tension begins to dissipate in the verse's second half, which qualifies God's vengeance by directing it toward His foes, and limits it even further at the end: God is not yet acting, but He is waiting and holding a grudge against those who deserve retribution. The beginning of the next verse describes how the course of God's mounting anger will eventually unfold, with Nahum expressing that though God is slow to anger, ultimately the wicked will be made to pay: "The Lord is slow to anger and great in power, and will surely not acquit" (1:3).

Rashi expresses this idea in his commentary on this verse:

3. Rashi (commentary on 1:2) understands the repetition historically, stating, "Rabbi Shimon says: The three expressions of vengeance [mentioned here] correspond to the three exiles to which Sennacherib exiled Israel, as we find in *Seder Olam*."
4. The Hebrew word *noter*, which has been translated here as to "bear a grudge," means to "keep," "guard," or "maintain." It has the same meaning as the Heb. *natzar* (cf. the Old Aramaic *nitzar* with the classical Aramaic *nitar*) and also *shamar* (see Jer. 3:5, Amos 1:11).

> He is great in power, and He is capable of wreaking vengeance. The reason He did not hurry His revenge is that He is slow to anger, but ultimately, He will not acquit. (Commentary on 1:3)

Ultimately, Nahum promises, the wicked will be made to pay.

How would Nahum's audience react to Nahum's declaration of God's impending vengeance? First, it is useful to note here that at this point, no one can rest assured that they are safe from God's wrath, as Nahum has not yet identified the target of God's anger. Second, though Nahum speaks of a God who interacts with the world, it is important to understand that this must not have been what the Israelites had been experiencing. Having lived under the rule of Manasseh, the Assyrian puppet king, for decades already, it would have been natural for them to begin to wonder whether God had forgotten them. It is this skepticism on the part of Israel regarding God's presence in the world and His the concern for His people that Nahum must address. For this reason, Nahum immediately qualifies his statement that God will exact vengeance with the reminder that it will take time, and patience is necessary.

While Nahum's audience may have been mollified by the knowledge that God manages and controls His anger, they would likely have still remained with an uneasy feeling, as would modern-day readers of the book: There is a biblical commandment to "walk in the ways of the Lord" (Deut. 13:5), which is interpreted to mean that we should emulate God's attributes (Sota 14a), but the traits of God that Nahum describes here are not traits that are instinctively associated with what we usually think of as the Godlike behavior that we are instructed to emulate. Jealousy may not be inherently immoral, but it is not an emotion we are comfortable with, and acting out of anger is rarely considered appropriate. There are two biblical prohibitions which distinctly prohibit acting out of vengeance, or even holding grudges: "You shall not take revenge, you shall not hold a grudge" (Lev. 19:18). Yet, these aspects of divine behavior are the focus of Nahum's message and the source of all the devastation that will follow. How might the people reconcile these two conflicting messages?

Nahum himself may be suggesting one answer here. Having described God as a God of vengeance in verse 2, he then immediately qualifies this statement by limiting its relevance to a specific group of people: the wicked, i.e., God's adversaries and enemies. As such, vengeance is not a universal trait that God demonstrates to everyone, but one that correlates with man's behavior and iniquities. Abraham Joshua Heschel writes about this idea in *The Prophets*:

> The prophets never thought that God's anger is something that cannot be accounted for, unpredictable, irrational. It is never a spontaneous outburst, but a reaction occasioned by the conduct of man. Indeed, it is the major task of the prophet to set forth the facts that account for it, to insist that the anger of God is not a blind, explosive force, operating without reference to the behavior of man, but rather voluntary and purposeful, motivated by concern for right and wrong.... It is a secondary emotion, never the ruling passion, disclosing only a part of God's way with man.... In both its origin and duration, anger is distinguished from mercy.... "For I will not contend forever, nor will I always be angry" (Is. 57:16).[5]

However, we may not have to view God's anger as distinct from God's kindness and reduce it to secondary status, as Heschel does. Instead, it may be possible to understand God's vengeance as a natural outgrowth of His compassionate nature. Precisely because He is merciful, God may choose to act in anger. Since a merciful God cannot be indifferent to the sufferings caused and injustices perpetuated by evildoers, He must inflict retribution upon the wicked. Corruption must be punished, and justice must be restored. Heschel actually does go on to express this idea as well: "it is divine anger that gives strength to God's truth and justice" (p. 77). Nahum communicates this concept in 1:3, which emphasizes that God is "slow to anger,"[6] yet He remains powerful and "will not acquit the guilty."

5. *The Prophets: Volume 2* (New York: Harper & Row, 1962), 62–63, 77.
6. The Septuagint consistently translates the phrase *erekh appayim* as μακροθυμός, *makrothomos*, meaning "patient." I heard an alternative explanation from Dr. Jonathan Grossman, who suggests that as the Hebrew word *af* means anger, the intent of the phrase is that God's anger is lengthened – capable of reaching all the way to Nineveh from Judah.

The notion that God's anger is a natural consequence of His compassion, expressed here in Nahum, is clearly modeled after God's revelation to Moses of the divine attributes of mercy after the sin of the Golden Calf:[7]

> The Lord, the Lord, God, merciful and gracious, *slow to anger*, and abundant in goodness and truth; keeping mercy unto the thousandth generation, forgiving iniquity and transgression and sin; and *will not acquit the guilty*.... (Ex. 34:6–7)

In Exodus, God's attributes serve to emphasize His mercy and His willingness to forgive despite the gravity of the sin. Nahum both modifies this recitation and shortens it dramatically, skipping statements that describe God's mercy.[8] This serves his rhetorical purposes – first, his aim is to convince his audience that God has the capacity to punish enemies and administer justice. Second, he wants to remind his listeners that God has shown patience, which explains God's failure to act against Assyria until now, while also emphasizing that even God's patience will also run out, and justice will eventually be served. Finally, by calling to mind a source that emphasizes the fundamentally merciful nature of God in the course of proclaiming His sense of justice, Nahum is subtly signaling that even the attributes of justice and punishment of the guilty are themselves expressions of divine mercy.

Finally, the three appearances of God's four-letter name in verse 2 may balance the three appearances of God's name in the rest of the section, as shown in the chart.

---

7. For a discussion of how the listing of the divine attributes of mercy in Exodus 34 are a fundamental restatement of the divine attributes of justice listed in the Ten Commandments, see R. Menachem Leibtag's essay "Two Sins, Two Covenants," in *Torah MiEtzion: New Readings in Tanach – Shemot* (Jerusalem: Maggid Books, 2012), 463–80, available online at http://www.Tanakh.org/kitisa.htm.
8. Jonah also modifies the statement to serve his rhetorical needs, replacing the word "truth" with the phrase "forgives evil" (Jonah 4:2). However, as Jonah's primary theme is understanding how God's attributes interact with each other, and the complex relationship between mercy, forgiveness, and truth, the central phrases still remain more recognizable than in Nahum.

The Lord is a jealous and vengeful God (v. 2)	The Lord is slow to anger and great in power (v. 3)
the Lord is vengeful and full of wrath (v. 2)	the Lord – His way is with a tempest and with a storm (v. 3)
the Lord avenges Himself upon His adversaries(v. 2)	The Lord is good, a stronghold on a day of trouble for those who trust in Him (v. 7)

We see that in this parallel structure, the appearances of God's four-letter name balance and develop each other. The first appearance in the left column describes God's justice (vengeance). The first appearance in the right column signifies God's mercy. The middle appearance in the left column describes God's raging anger, and the middle appearance in the right column describes how the divine anger expresses itself through the raging storm. The final appearance in the left column describes God directing His anger at His enemies; the final appearance in the right column describes how God actively protects those who trust in Him.

Having described some of God's attributes and character traits, in the next few verses Nahum moves on to describe what God can do:

> The Lord – His way is with a tempest and with a storm; and cloud is the dust of His feet.
>
> He rebukes the sea and dries it up, and He has dried up all the rivers; Bashan and Carmel are forlorn, and the blossoms of the Lebanon are forlorn.
>
> Mountains quaked because of Him and the hills melted, and the land raised up from before Him – and the inhabited earth and all who dwell thereon.
>
> Who can stand before His fury and who can rise amid His wrath? His wrath has reached [the earth] like fire, and the rocks have been broken up by Him. (1:3–6)

These verses begin with a description of God's ability to summon storms and whirlwinds (v. 3b), which then wreak havoc with the bodies of water that surround the Land of Israel (v. 4a). As a result of God's stirring the forces of nature, the fertile lands, i.e., Bashan and Carmel, that were once part of the Northern Kingdom, dry up. Next, Nahum portrays how mountains and hills fall at God's will as they would in an earthquake, and then asks a simple rhetorical question: "Who can stand before His fury?"[9] The themes of these verses echo the words of the prophet Amos over a century earlier. The description in verse 5 of how the "hills melted" (*vehagevaot hitmogagu*) at God's appearance recalls Amos's description of Israel's eventual redemption: "and the hills of Israel will shake (*vekhol hagevaot titmogagna*) [because of the tremendous amount of grain growing on them]" (Amos 9:13). By weaving optimistic messages from earlier prophecies into his words, Nahum reassures the people that even in difficult times, redemption is not far away.

Nahum concludes by comparing divine anger to a volcano, which pours out like fire and shatters rocks. These images of God's power over nature appear elsewhere in the Bible, often in contrast to the impotent pagan gods who stand helpless before nature's fury. Nahum poetically combines images of God's power to impress upon his audience God's complete omnipotence. Implicit in his words is the idea that if nature can't stand before God, how will the wicked?

However, Nahum's portrayal of God's unlimited power serves another purpose as well. Nahum describes the utter desolation and devastation of Israel's most lush northern regions – "*Bashan* and *Carmel* are forlorn, and the blossoms of the *Lebanon* are forlorn (*umlal*)." These three areas: Bashan, which refers to the northern Transjordan plain; Lebanon, which denotes the rich northern border; and Carmel, which corresponds to the mountain range that runs into modern-day

9. The usage of rhetorical questions appears throughout Nahum (1:6, 2:12, 3:7–8) as a poetic device. David Baker discusses the use of rhetorical questions in Nahum: "Unlike a regular question, which is soliciting information, a rhetorical question assumes the answer is already known by both the asker and the asked. Instead of the statement which could have been used in its place, the rhetorical question forces the hearer to get actively involved in the discussion" (David W. Baker, *Tyndale Old Testament Commentaries: Nahum, Habakkuk and Zephaniah: An Introduction and Commentary* [Westmont: Inter-Varsity Press, 1988], 29).

Haifa, are among the most fertile areas in Israel.[10] Nahum appears to be intentionally echoing Isaiah's prophecy against the Assyrian invaders a century before: "The land is mournful and is forlorn (*aval umlela aretz*); *Lebanon* is ashamed, it withers; Sharon is like a wilderness; and *Bashan and Carmel* are clean bare" (Is. 33:9). For Isaiah, the description of devastation is meant to lead the wicked to repent and return to God, when they see the secure dwellings of the righteous (Is. 33:14–16), while Nahum chooses to use the image of devastation to remind his listeners of God's tremendous power.

Nahum's description of the Northern Kingdom of Israel as battered and beaten may serve to fulfill another rhetorical aim. Ever present in the people's memory were the repeated Assyrian invasions and incursions that had plagued Israel over the past century, ultimately leaving the area of the Northern Kingdom desolate and barren. By stating that God is equally capable of such destruction, Nahum reminds his listeners that God's power is equal to and indeed surpasses that of the Assyrians. The people of Judah had heard Rab-Shakeh, the Assyrian general, mock God's power as he stood astride the battlements during the siege of Jerusalem: "Did any of the gods of the nations ever deliver his land out of the hand of the king of Assyria?" (II Kings 18:33). Doubts must have arisen in the people's consciousness: they wondered if the devastation the Assyrians left behind pointed to some weakness in God's power, proving Rab-Shakeh's boast. During the time of the invasions in the Northern Kingdom, Isaiah had to continually remind his listeners that Assyria was only an instrument in God's hand (see Is. 10). Nahum reinforces this message decades later by alluding in 1:6 to the devastating earthquake of 760 BCE. At that time, Northern Israel fell to Assyria, but only after God flattened the former with a powerful tremor that left the surviving residents weakened and ultimately helpless to resist the

10. Some suggest that this is an example of the poetic device known as synecdoche, in which a part can represent a whole; in this case, these three geographic areas symbolize the entire earth falling before God's power. All three areas also appear in the Bible in contexts in which they poetically represent the notion that it is futile for the forces of nature to attempt to oppose God's dominion (Bashan in Ps. 68:16; Carmel in Amos 1:2; Lebanon in Ps. 29:5–6).

invasion. Nahum is arguing that just as then, it was God, not Assyria, that was responsible for Israel's downfall, so too now, it is God that will bring about the Assyrian downfall.

Having impressed this message upon his listeners, Nahum moves from the past tense to the present and future tenses:

> The Lord is good, a stronghold on a day of trouble, and is cognizant of those who trust in Him. But, with an overrunning flood He shall make a full end of her place, and darkness shall pursue His enemies. (1:7–8)

Having previously focused on the exhaustive nature of God's destructive power, and the inability of anyone or anything to stand in the face of His anger, Nahum now hones and refines his message of destruction and focuses on God's goodness and His dedication to those who are faithful to him. Rashi is keenly aware of the dramatic change in the message's tone, which reflects God's ability to perform two conflicting actions simultaneously, and quotes the *Mekhilta* (Ex. 15:3) which expresses this idea: "[God's behavior is] unlike the nature of flesh and blood [humanity], who, when he is busy with one thing, is not free to [simultaneously] do another thing."

Here, Nahum does not present God's goodness as blessing or prosperity. It is expressed, at best, as the promise of refuge when the day of reckoning arrives. By making this guarantee, Nahum is attempting to add a moral dimension to the natural disasters that plague the people: Rather than being random acts, they demonstrate that God controls the events around them, rewarding those that demonstrate their trust in Him by providing them with protection when trouble arrives. This verse marks the first time that a new category of people, "those that trust in God," are mentioned, as opposed to the "enemies" that are mentioned by name in verses 2 (*tzarav*) and 9 (*oyvav*). Subtly, Nahum has split humanity into two groups, divided by their moral choices.

Nahum buttresses the idea that during a period of divine judgment, the righteous can find sanctuary with God, as he returns to describing God's awesome power. In verse 8, he describes God's ability to "make an end" of everything through a flood, [11] a clear allusion to the Great Flood in the story of Noah (Gen. 6:9–10:32). This reference reminds us of both God's ability to punish evil and His commitment to the protection of the righteous, as God saved Noah, who is called "a righteous man" (Gen. 6:9), while drowning the wicked. Flooding also alludes to the future total and permanent destruction that will come on the day of final reckoning, as described in Jeremiah 47:2. This section of Nahum concludes with the reminder that darkness will pursue God's enemies – bringing closure to Nahum's speech, which began with his statement that God "bears a grudge against His enemies" (v. 2). The mention of darkness can be understood to indicate that unlike human armies, who cease fighting with the advent of nightfall, God does not allow night to impede Him.

The ending of verse 8 contains very difficult syntax and unidentified pronouns ("He shall make a full end, her place, and darkness shall pursue His enemies"). Who is the "her" whose place's end is approaching?[12] To what place does Nahum refer? Read with the superscription, we would assume that "her place" refers to Nineveh, and this interpretation is reflected in many translations and commentaries. However, Nahum's audience did not hear the superscription. For them, the meaning of Nahum's words were uncertain – they did not know whether God was referring to Assyria, their cruel overlord enemy – or perhaps to them. The ambiguity with regard to the identity of God's enemy in this verse continues into the next section, when Nahum finally addresses the people directly.

---

11. The devastation that Nahum speaks of is depicted as being so complete that one scholar, Gordon Johnston, suggests that Nahum's curses, so unique among the prophets, are probably derived from Neo-Assyrian treaty curses, which were considered unusually brutal. Gordon H. Johnston, "Nahum's Rhetorical Allusions to Neo-Assyrian Treaty Curses" *Bibliotheca Sacra* 158, no. 632 (October–December 2001): 415–36.
12. Perhaps reflecting the text's difficulty, instead of "her place" (*mekomah*), the Septuagint has τοὺςἐπεγειρομένους, "those who rise up." This suggests either a scribal error or a different reading, possibly *mikimeihu*. This reading makes for a more suitable parallel with "His enemies" than what appears in our text.

1:9–2:1

Comforting Judah

After his dramatic description of God's power over all creation, Nahum finally addresses his listeners directly, using the word "you":

> Why do you contemplate against the Lord? He will make a full end; trouble will not rise twice. While the thorns are entangled and the drunkards are drinking, they are consumed like dry stubble, fully ripe. (1:9–10)

He poses a simple question: "Why do you contemplate against the Lord?"[1] Until now, Nahum had presented a general, universal description of God's unlimited power. He promised sanctuary for those who trust in Him, and total destruction for those who defy Him. Now, the people hear Nahum's first direct complaint: "Why do you contemplate against the Lord?" It is unclear at first to whom the "you" in this verse refers. Is

1. In the Hebrew, the root of the word for "contemplate" (*teḥashevun*) is Ḥ-S-V, which means "to plot" when followed by the words "evil against" (*ra al*, as in verse 11). However, the preposition here is *el*, best translated as "about." When seen in context, it can be understood that Nahum is attacking the people for doubting or wondering about God's ways. Compare with: "Though I have trained and strengthened their arms, yet do they devise evil against Me" (Hos. 7:15).

Nahum talking about the Assyrian enemy? Or is he addressing another unnamed party whose behavior deserves divine rebuke? Or is Nahum speaking directly to his Jewish listeners? Or is Nahum speaking directly to his Israelite audience? Most commentaries interpret all of the negative prophecies from here until the end of the chapter (1:9–14) as being directed toward Assyria and its king. This reading is consistent with the superscription that identifies Nineveh as the subject of God's anger in Nahum's prophecy. However, the superscription was added later and was not heard by Nahum's listeners, and it is not considered part of his original message.[2] Our understanding is that the ambiguity in Nahum's words is intentional. His audience has not yet heard Nahum's fiery denouncement of Assyria. If Nahum used the words "Why do you contemplate against the Lord," his listeners would assume that he is speaking about them. Nahum hasn't yet identified the subject of his reproof and he is aware that his Israelite listeners might think that these words of rebuke are directed toward them. Nahum's usage of the word "end" (*kala*) once again is an allusion to the damage caused by Sennacherib a century before – it echoes Isaiah's portrayal of the destruction that occurred during the previous Assyrian invasion: "For the Lord God of hosts is carrying out a determined destruction (*kala*) upon the land" (Is. 10:23).

What led to the lack of faith among the people of Israel that provokes Nahum's rebuke? After decades of uninterrupted oppression, the people doubted both God's goodness and His omnipotence. If God is all-powerful, how was Israel defeated by the Assyrians? If God is just, why was a good king like Hezekiah nearly defeated while an evil king like Manasseh prospered? Prophets were murdered, idolatry reigned in the Temple, and injustice prospered, leaving Judaism nearly extinguished under Manasseh's oppressive reign. Given these circumstances, though Nahum must rebuke the people for their lack of faith in God, he must immediately encourage them as well, assuring them that despite their

2. Rashi, Radak, and *Daat Mikra* interpret the following verses (1:9–14) as directed at the Assyrians. However, many modern scholars, including *Mikra LeYisrael*, Maier, and O'Brien understand the verse to be directed toward the Jews. Our interpretation is that the listeners, for at least one brief moment, understand Nahum as directly addressing them.

recent experiences, their trust in God will not be for naught. He emphasizes that once God does act against His enemies, their destruction will complete. The Assyrians will not live to fight another round. In verse 8, Nahum told the people, *Kala yaase*, "He will make an end," in the future tense. Now, Nahum tells them, *Kala hu oseh*, "He is making an end," in the present tense, indicating that the end of the Assyrian enemy is imminent.

Nahum continues by assuring his listeners that "trouble will not arise twice" (1:9) – no foreign adversary who faces divine punishment returns to harm the Jewish people. Once Assyria is attacked, it will be defeated. The promise that "trouble will not arise twice" may also convey the message that the destruction that Assyria inflicted upon the Jewish people with the obliteration of Israel in the north in 722 BCE and the devastation of Judah in the south in 701 BCE were onetime events, never to reoccur. Verse 10 buttresses this claim. Nahum describes God's enemies as helpless, either entangled like thorns or incapacitated like drunks, unable to respond, to be consumed like dry stubble in a fire. The verse uses powerful alliteration, emphasizing the letter *samekh* – *ki ad Sirim Sevukhim, ukheSovam Sevuim* – possibly alluding to the drunken slur of one who is inebriated, as the enemy is described in the simile. Most importantly, for the first time, Nahum distinguishes between "you," his listeners (1:9), and "them," God's enemies (1:10). Finally, the people hear that they are not the target of divine vengeance:

> From you, he that devises evil against the Lord, that counsels wickedness, came forth.
>
> So said the Lord: Though they be at peace, and likewise many, even so they shall be cut down and passed over, I will no longer afflict you. And now, I will break his yoke from off you, and I will rend your bonds asunder. And the Lord shall command concerning you: No more [offspring] of your name shall be sown; from the house of your god I will cut off a graven image and a molten image; I will prepare your grave, for you have become worthless.
>
> Behold on the mountains the feet of a messenger announcing peace. O Judah, celebrate your festivals, fulfill your vows – for the wicked one shall no longer continue to pass through you; he has been completely cut off. (1:11–2:1)

The remainder of the unit is challenging, as Nahum uses many pronouns without antecedents to identify them. However, we can decipher Nahum's intentions by noting the shifting gender pronouns and singular versus plural pronouns he uses. We noted that verse 9 addressed "you" in masculine plural, a direct appeal to the Jewish people, Nahum's listeners. He follows by mocking "them" in verse 10, referring to God's still-unnamed enemies. In verse 11, Nahum charges that from "you" (feminine singular) has come forth "someone" (masculine singular) who plots evil against God. In verses 12 and 13, Nahum speaks to a feminine singular "you" – from the final verse of the section, we see that this refers to Judah (the collective term for his listeners, the Jewish people). As such, it is logical that verse 11 also refers to the Jewish people. Who then is the person referred to as *hoshev* with a masculine singular pronoun in verse 11 – "From you (feminine singular), he that devises evil (*ḥoshev* – masculine singular) against the Lord, that counsels wickedness, came forth"? Who from among the Jewish people is devising evil or counseling wickedness?

Similarly, in verse 13, which states that God will break the yoke that has oppressed Judah (the Hebrew pronoun used in the term "his yoke" is masculine singular), who is the yoke's owner? The climax is reached in verse 14. Nahum relays God's command to obliterate to an unidentified person, again masculine. Nahum concludes by finally identifying the people to whom he is speaking, when he exhorts the Jewish people to celebrate their holidays in 2:1. But who is the unknown person facing destruction? Going back and looking at the entire section as a whole may provide an answer.

Having asserted that God is capable of bringing about His enemies' downfall, and that God is ready to start carrying out the process of that downfall, Nahum now speaks directly to the Jewish people in verses 1:9–2:1. They thought ill of God, and someone who came from them plotted against Him (v. 11). Given the amount of suffering the people have borne under Assyrian oppression, these negative sentiments and plots are understandable, as the people were likely wondering: Has God forgotten us? Has He been vanquished, defeated? Nahum contends with these feelings of insecurity on the part of the people in verses 12–14. He begins by stating: "So said the Lord" – the only direct quote from God in the book. Though "they," presumably the Assyrians, are many and mighty, they will be cut down and disappear. The verbs in verse 12 that refer to the enemy appear in the past tense, leading to a sense that this will occur soon, or perhaps has occurred already. The word used for "to be cut down," *nagozzu*, is related to the Hebrew term for "to shear" (which has the Hebrew root G-Z-Z), as in shearing sheep. (In the Bible, sheep shearing almost always foreshadows the downfall of the proud, as happened to Laban in Genesis 31, Judah in Genesis 38, Nabal in I Samuel 25, and Amnon in II Samuel 13. Isaiah 5:6–7 describes how the people are humbled before God like sheep before being sheared.) God then states that although He has afflicted the Jewish people in the past, He will do so no longer. This message would have been encouraging to Nahum's listeners for two reasons. The more obvious reason is that Assyria's predicted demise signifies the end of their suffering. More importantly, Nahum reaffirms the message that any suffering that occurred in the past was not due to Assyria's strength, but came from God. This reinforces the lesson that Isaiah attempted to teach to the people decades before, when he said: *Hoy, Ashur, shevet appi*, "Woe, Assyria, [which is the] staff of My anger" (Is. 10:5). Isaiah tried to explain that Assyria's success was due to Israel's corruption of justice and abandonment of the poor, and not due to the strength of their armies, but to no avail (Is. 10:2). But now, states Nahum in verse 13, God will break the yoke (*motehu*) that Assyria holds over Judah. To symbolize the Assyrian dominance, Nahum continues with a variation of the rod metaphor used by Isaiah a century before (Is. 9:3, 10:5, 24, 30:31). Describing the breaking of the Assyrian yoke, Nahum declares the completion of Isaiah's prophecies of Assyrian domination over Judah (Is. 10) and promises their reversal (see Nahum 1:13–2:1).

Having comforted the Jewish people, Nahum then turns directly to an unnamed masculine addressee in verse 14, relating that God has three vital messages for him. First, no descendants will carry his name. This was a significant concern in the ancient world: Abraham's primary worry was that he would die childless (Gen. 15:2), and recently discovered inscriptions in Nineveh show Assyria's king Ashurbanipal praying that his son will honor and preserve his name.[3] Second, God states that idolatry, specifically graven and molten images (*pesel umassekha*), will

3. See O. Palmer Robertson, *The Books of Nahum, Habakkuk, and Zephaniah*, NICOT Commentary Series (Michigan: Wm. B. Eerdmans Publishing, 1990), commentary on 1:14.

be removed from the person's house of worship. In the final part, God declares simply that the person will die, with God preparing the grave.

But to whom is God speaking? Most commentaries assume that the king of Assyria is the mysterious masculine figure addressed. However, given the book's structure, there is another more likely candidate. Chapters 2 and 3 address the people and the city of Nineveh, but conclude with a broadside against Nineveh's leadership. If chapter 1 follows a similar pattern, first addressing the people and then their leader, then the target of Nahum's ire is none other than Manasseh, king of Judah. Until now, Nahum spoke directly to the Jewish people, scolding them for their lack of faith but promising that their sufferings would come to an end. In verse 11, he noted that someone who "devises evil against the Lord" came forth from them. Manasseh collaborated with the Assyrian oppressors, setting up idols inside the *Beit HaMikdash* itself (see II Kings 21:2–7, II Chr. 33:2–10). One of Josiah's first acts was to remove all the idolatry from Judah, and the description in Chronicles echoes Nahum's promise:

> He began to purify Judah and Jerusalem from the high places, and the asherim, and the graven images and the molten images (*hapesilim vehamassekhot*). (II Chr. 34:3)

> Out of the house of your god I will cut off a graven image and a molten image (*pesel umassekha*). (Nahum 1:14)

However, the rest of the terrible fate that Nahum predicted for Manasseh in verse 14 did not come to pass. Why not? As noted in the introduction, Manasseh suddenly, and quite inexplicably, turned on his Assyrian overlords. His rebellion led to his imprisonment, but upon his freedom and return he began the slow process of undoing the damage that he had done to the spiritual fabric of the nation. If Nahum's words were indeed directed to Manasseh, this message might have provided him with both the push and the encouragement to change his ways.[4]

---

4. If our suggestion is correct, then we are able to even further narrow the possible date for when Nahum spoke from 663 BCE (the fall of No-Amon, i.e., Thebes) to 650 BCE (the approximate historical date for Manasseh's rebellion against Assyria).

Nahum concludes his address to the Jewish people by stating that soon, announcers will proclaim the establishment of peace from the mountaintops: "Behold on the mountains the feet of a messenger announcing peace." His words echo Isaiah's promise about the future: "How beautiful upon the mountains are the feet of the messenger of good tidings that announces peace, the harbinger of good tidings that announces salvation" (Is. 52:7). Nahum uses the language of Isaiah's messianic assurances to bolster his own message with messianic overtones as well. He urges the Jewish people to celebrate the Assyrian downfall, just as Isaiah urged his listeners a century before: "Give thanks unto the Lord, proclaim His name, declare His doings among the peoples.... Sing unto the Lord; for He has done gloriously" (Is. 12:4–6). The Israelites are instructed to resume traveling to Jerusalem to celebrate Israel's traditional festivals.

Reading the Torah, we see that the pilgrimage festivals have a dual significance (Lev. 23).[5] On one hand, they mark the natural yearly agricultural cycle celebrated by all peoples (the harvest, the gathering of fruits, etc.); and concurrently, they mark the supernatural, the occasions on which God intervened in history on behalf of His people. Not surprisingly, with Assyrian influence waning away, one of Josiah's most important acts as king was a large, public celebration of Passover (II Kings 23:21–25). His act signified not only religious renewal but public defiance. The promise that the Jewish people would once again celebrate their holidays also alludes to the resumption of another central aspect of the three main biblical festivals: the public pilgrimage to Jerusalem (see Ex. 23:14–19, 34:18–26, Deut. 16:1–17). This pilgrimage, the *aliya leregel,* not only was a religious duty, but also served the vital civic function of unifying the people.[6] The Jewish people lived scattered across the breadth of the country, each person surrounded by his family and tribe. The Bible is filled with warnings against allowing tribal identities to override the people's sense of national brotherhood,

---

5. For further discussion of this point, see Rabbi Yoel Bin-Nun, "The Dual Significance of the Pilgrim Festivals," available online at https://www.etzion.org.il/en/dual-significance-pilgrim-festivals, and Rabbi Michael Hattin, "The Holiday Cycle," available online at https://www.etzion.org.il/en/holiday-cycle.
6. See Maimonides in his *Guide for the Perplexed,* III:39, who advances a similar idea when discussing the reason behind the commandment of *maaser sheni.*

as exemplified by the horrific episode at the conclusion of the book of Judges (chs. 19–21), in which the people of the town of Gibeah refuse to extend hospitality to their fellow Jews, commit brutal rape, and lead the people into a civil war. For Nahum, only when Israel would be free to travel unimpeded in its own land could unity be given a chance to develop and freedom to bloom.

In addition to the resumption of celebrating the holidays, Nahum also reminds the people to fulfill their vows and bring offerings. In the Bible, vow offerings were often made in anticipation of God acting in the future on behalf of a person or the people as a group: Jacob vowed offerings at Beit El in anticipation of his eventual safe return (Gen. 28:20–22); the people vowed to bring an offering before fighting the king of Arad (Num. 21:1–3); and the sailors on Jonah's ship vowed to bring offerings if they are saved from shipwreck (Jonah 1:6), as did Jonah himself when he was in the belly of the whale (2:10). In verse 11, Nahum began his direct address to the people mentioning one "that counsels wickedness" (*beliyaal*) who had come forth. Now, in 2:1, at the conclusion of his direct address to the people, the people are instructed to celebrate because "the wicked one" (*beliyaal*) has been completely cut off, never to tread on Judean soil again.

Finally, it is important to note that these last verses provide support for viewing Nahum as a full-fledged prophet. Contrary to the claims of critics (mentioned above) that Nahum asked nothing of his people and was therefore not a genuine prophet but merely a nationalist populist who ranted for Assyria's downfall, these verse prove that nothing could be further from the truth. Nahum made clear that the salvation that will come is not due to Judah's merits, but rather to Assyria's failing, and that once free from Assyrian oppression, the Jewish people are expected to use their newfound freedom to remove idolatry form their midst and resume their national and religious responsibilities.

2:2–2:14

The Assault on Nineveh

Having proclaimed Judah's upcoming redemption, Nahum now directs the focus of his prophecy to the Assyrians.[1] In the following two chapters, Nahum will describe the downfall of Nineveh using some of the most powerful and vivid battle imagery in the Bible. In chapter 2, Nahum describes the upcoming invasion and subsequent desolation of Nineveh, the Assyrian capital, by an enemy whom Nahum does not name. (While the Babylonians were the initiators of the sacking of Nineveh, they had many allies, all of whom had their own issues with hundreds of years of Assyrian domination, which may be why Nahum chooses to remain vague about the identity of Nineveh's destroyer.) Chapter 3 repeats these battle descriptions, as well as describing the aftermath, and also provides moral justification for the extensive devastation, which is missing from chapter 2.

1. A notable exception is the interpretation of Abarbanel, who suggests that the majority of chapter 2 is a continuation of Nahum's speech to Judah, and describes the eventual devastation of Jerusalem by Nebuchadnezzar and the Babylonians. Due to the difficulty in this approach, we will not reference it in our interpretation.

Nahum's first unit ended with Judah being told to celebrate its salvation. Now, a new audience, once again referred to in second-person feminine singular, is addressed:

> The scatterer has come up before you.[2]
>
> Man the fort! Watch the road! Strengthen your flanks! Fortify your power mightily.
>
> For the Lord restores the pride of Jacob, as the pride of Israel; for the emptiers have emptied them out, and marred their vine branches. (2:2–3)

As in chapter 1, Nahum does not immediately identify the subject of his words. He will do so later, in verse 9. Instead, with a sense of urgency, Nahum describes the sighting of the approaching enemy. As opposed to the messenger of peace who went up on the mountains to announce Judah's salvation, the enemy, a scatterer, is coming up against them. The word "scatterer" (*mefitz*) appears to suggest a play on words on the part of the prophet, relying on two Hebrew root words: *potz*, "scatter," and *nafatz*, "shatter," the noun form of this verb meaning a hammer (Prov. 25:18). The word echoes other instances where the Bible describes God leading an assault: In the Torah, see Genesis 11:8: "So the Lord scattered (*vayafetz*) them abroad from there [the Tower of Babel]"; and Numbers 10:35: "'Rise up, O Lord, and let Your enemies be scattered (*veyafutzu*)"; and in the Prophets, Habakkuk 3:6: "He stands and shakes the earth… and the everlasting mountains are dashed (*vayitpotzetzu*) in pieces"; and Zechariah 13:7: "Smite the shepherd, and the sheep shall be scattered (*utefutzeina*)." As such, the word "scatterer" can refer both to the invading army that is approaching Nineveh's walls, as well as to the guiding hand of God, who is ultimately orchestrating the entire attack.

---

2. Rashi understands that 2:2 is still addressed to the Jewish people as opposed to Assyria. He would translate the beginning of 2:2 differently. In contrast to our rendition of 2:2, "The scatterer has come up before you. Man the fort!" directed toward Nineveh, Rashi renders it "The scatterer who once came up before you (Judah) is besieged by a siege." For Rashi, this verse is a fulfillment of the principle of *midda keneged midda*, meaning measure for measure, that what someone does will ultimately come back to haunt him.

Nahum then mimics the enemy, commanding the addressee to prepare its defenses against an upcoming military assault. The sentences he uses are short and staccato, evocative of the clipped commands an army officer might bark out to his troops right before the battle commences. Nahum's call to Nineveh: "Man the fort! Watch the road!" (2:2) may have been familiar to his Judahite listeners. His call echoes Isaiah's warning to Babylon about setting up watchmen to look out for approaching invaders: "Go, set up the lookout, what he sees he will tell" (Is. 21:6) and Micah's similar warnings to Judah (see Mic. 7:4). Throughout his prophecy, Nahum draws upon his predecessor's prophecies to create a sense of authenticity and anticipation; his message is that now the ancient oracles are being realized.

Nahum then explains (v. 3) why the battle is occurring: it is because God has chosen to restore the pride and splendor of Judah and Israel. Given that Israel was exiled by Assyria, and Judah was nearly destroyed, Nahum is clearly stating that the invasion and destruction of Nineveh is the long-awaited settling of the score. Whereas previously, in prophetic literature, the phrase "the splendor of Jacob" (*geon Yaakov*) carried negative connotations and was used to refer to Israel negatively,[3] here, Nahum deliberately reverses the connotation of the phrase, using it in praise of Israel, and warning the enemy about the upcoming assault in which Israel will be raised up and the enemy will be destroyed. The Hebrew here is in the "prophetic perfect" form; Nahum speaks about future events as if they have already occurred.

Nahum continues with his poetic technique from 1:10, using nouns and verbs from the same root to create an alliterative effect (in 1:10, *sovam sevuim*; here, *vekakum bokekim*). The root B-K-K, which is used here in reference to the people of Israel, saying that in the past, they were laid to waste, normally means to empty or depopulate, a possible allusion to the Assyrian deportation of Israel in 722 BCE (II Kings 17). It may also be a subtle allusion to why God chose to reverse His earlier

3. See Amos (6:8), where Amos describes how God exclaimed, "I loathe the splendor of Jacob (*geon Yaakov*)," and Jeremiah, who uses the phrase in the context of destruction: "I will ruin the splendor of Jacob (*geon Yaakov*) and the great splendor of Jerusalem" (13:9).

decision to show Nineveh mercy at the time of Jonah, and now is proceeding with its destruction. The excessively violent manner in which the people of Nineveh treated Israel and Judah, completely ravaging them until they were *bokekim,* i.e., virtually destroyed, justifies overturning their original acquittal. In all other places in the Bible, it is God or His messengers who are referred to as *bokek* (see Is. 24:1, Jer. 51:2).

In the next verses, Nahum depicts in detail the invading army, led by God, as well as the chaos and panic on the part of the Assyrian defense inside the city of Nineveh:

> The shield of his mighty men is made red, the valiant men are in scarlet; the chariots are fire of steel in the day of his preparation, and the cypress spears are unwrapped.[4] The chariots rush madly in the streets, they jostle one against another in the broad places; the appearance of them is like torches, they run to and fro like the lightning. He admires himself of his worthiness; they stumble in their march; they make haste to the wall thereof, and the mantelet is prepared. The gates of the rivers are opened, and the palace is dissolved. (2:4–7)

As the invading forces approach Nineveh, Nahum interrupts to describe that army in very realistic terms. His emphasis on a detailed description of the army contains an important lesson for his listeners: God controls history, yet the events that will occur will take place through the natural course of events. Assyria's fall will come about by human agency (i.e., by means of the Babylonian Empire). The advancing troops are covered in crimson, on their clothing and on their armor, with torches lit and

4. The term *hare'alu,* here "unwrapped," has been translated differently by the commentators. Rashi translates it as "wrapped"; he understands the phrase as referring to the enemy generals, who are wrapped in colorful garments. Radak quotes his father, who translates it as "trembling"; he understands the phrase as referring to the Assyrian generals, who are shaking with fear. Radak himself and the *Metzudot* translate *hare'alu* as "poisoned," referring to the dipping of the spear tips into poison as part of the preparations for battle. We have followed the translation of the Mahari Kara, who explains that the metal spearheads were kept under wraps until the day of the battle.

the sun reflecting off their faces. According to Ezekiel 23:14, red was a favorite color of the Babylonian army. The usage of crimson red, the color of blood, may also have served to provoke fear among the Assyrian defenders.

In the concluding verses of the battle description (2:4–7), Nahum switches to describing the chaos and panic inside the city. Instead of proceeding in an orderly fashion, the defending chariots crowd each other while trying to navigate the narrowing streets. Assyrian soldiers run back and forth without rhyme or reason. Meanwhile, the attackers unleash a hail of flaming arrows, setting Nineveh's buildings alight. As their city succumbs to the flames, defending soldiers stumble as they madly rush to the walls, carrying mantelets (a type of small woven shield used as protection from oncoming projectiles) as they run. Nahum's short, staccato sentences reflect the hurried pace of the battle, the portrayal of which ends with the description of the flooding of the city. The flood that Nahum had predicted in chapter 1: "With an overrunning flood He [God] will make a full end of the place,"[5] is recounted here as coming to pass at the close of the battle.

---

5. There is much discussion in modern scholarship whether or not Nineveh was actually destroyed by a flood, as Nahum would suggest, or due to the assault of the Babylonians and their allied forces. According to the first century BCE Greek historian Diodorus Siculus, there was an oracle in the hands of the kings of Assyria that Nineveh would not fall "unless the river first become an enemy to the city" (Diod. II 26:9 – Diodorus's writings are available online at http://penelope.uchicago.edu/Thayer/E/Roman/Texts/Diodorus_Siculus/2A*.html#23). He continues to say that "in the third year [of the battle], a succession of heavy downpours swelled the Euphrates [Tigris], flooded part of the city, and cast down the wall to a length of 20 stades.... Thereupon the king realized that the oracle had been fulfilled, and that the river had manifestly declared war upon the city" (Diod. II 27:1–3).

   Diodorus's account of Nineveh's downfall was generally accepted until the nineteenth century, especially since the biblical account contains so many allusions to water. However, when archaeologists began to unearth the ruins of Nineveh (see earlier section, "The Historical Background"), they discovered that not only did no evidence exist for the flood account, but that it appeared that the city was actually burned. Indeed, most of Nineveh's buildings were found on top of the mound Kuyunjik, rising to thirteen meters (forty-three feet) above the plain, which would have made flooding impossible. However, many scholars suggest that as a preliminary maneuver it is likely that the attackers flooded the moats and canals that provided

As soon as the description of the battle for Nineveh ends, a description of the looting begins:

> And the queen (*hutzav*) is revealed, she is carried away, and her handmaids moan as with the voice of doves, beating upon their breasts. But Nineveh has been from of old like a pool of water; yet they flee away; 'Halt! halt!'; but none looks back. Loot the silver, loot the gold;[6] for there is no end of the store, rich with all precious vessels. She is empty, and void, and waste; and the heart melts, and the knees smite together; all loins are trembling, and the faces of them all have turned ashen. (2:8–11)

Verse 8 is considered one of the most difficult verses in the book, as it references a figure (*hutzav*) whose identity is unknown. Both Rashi and Ibn Ezra understood it to mean the queen of Assyria, describing how she is publicly humiliated as she is carried away by the invaders. Others maintain that *hutzav* refers to a statue of Ishtar, Nineveh's patron goddess. If *hutzav* is indeed the statue of Nineveh's patron goddess, we can envision the following scenario: As their city is falling, Nineveh's desperate citizens resort to a measure taken only in extreme emergency, that of removing their idol from its dwelling in its temple and displaying it publicly, hoping that the city's defenders will see it and be strengthened (similar to what Eli's sons did with the Ark of the Covenant when the Philistines attacked in I Sam. 4). This drastic measure, however, is to no avail. The statue is taken and looted like the rest of Nineveh's treasures. A cacophony arises from the city; the bitter sounds of the temple priestesses beating their breasts in mourning mix with the voices of desperate officers calling upon their retreating soldiers

---

the city's first line of defense by tampering with the flood control gates at the Khusur River. For further discussion, see Aron Pinker, "Nahum and the Greek Tradition on Nineveh's Fall," *Journal of Hebrew Studies* 6, article 8, available online at http://www.jhsonline.org/Articles/article_58.pdf.

6. According to Rashi and the *Metzudot*, it is Nahum who is directing the Babylonian army to take spoils (commentary on 2:10); while the Mahari Kara suggests that these are the words of the citizens of Nineveh themselves, pleading with the soldiers to take their riches but to spare their lives (commentary on 2:10).

to hold the line ("Halt, halt!" v. 9), without success. Nineveh, once considered impregnable as if it were surrounded by water,[7] is finished.

With Nineveh destroyed and looted, the richest city of the ancient Near East has become a desolate wasteland; and the looming question is: If Nineveh could fall, could anything be considered secure? Nahum uses a brilliant three-part alliterative with a *hapax legomenon,* words found nowhere else in the Bible, to convey the sense of desolation: *Buka umevuka umevulaka,* "emptiness, desolation, and devastation." There is also onomatopoeia here, as the Hebrew words, when vocalized, sound like the sound that water makes as it is slowly emptying out from a container. Nahum's wording echoes Isaiah's earlier prediction of Tyre's destruction: *Hinne Hashem bokek haaretz uvolkah,* "Behold, the Lord is emptying the land and devastating it" (24:1).

In describing the feelings of hopelessness and despair that will descend on Nineveh's inhabitants: *veḥalḥala bekhol motnayim, ufnei khullam kibbetzu farur,* "all loins are trembling, and the faces of them all have turned ashen" (2:11), Nahum draws upon previous ideas from both Isaiah and Joel, in which similar language was used to describe the fear of people awaiting an enemy invasion or attack. As the enemy approaches from the desert horizon, Isaiah confesses: *Al ken malu motnai ḥalḥala,* "My loins are seized with trembling" (Is. 21:3). Joel's portrayal of the Jewish people's response to the approaching enemy is even closer to Nahum's: *Mipanav yaḥilu amim, kol panim kibbetzu farur,* "People tremble (*yaḥilu*) before them; all faces turn ashen" (Joel 2:6). Through clever wordplay, some of the most terrifying prophecies ever uttered against the Jewish people are transformed into battle cries against their enemies.

In the aftermath of the battle, following the description in verse 11 of the inability of the Assyrians to protect their capital, Nahum begins to taunt Nineveh's leaders and nobility:[8]

---

7. Rashi explains the metaphor in 2:9 of Nineveh having stood like a pool of water as follows: "Since the day it was founded, it has been sitting calmly with no one disturbing it, like a pool of water that does not move from its place" (commentary on 2:9).
8. In this project we have chosen Nahum's words as mocking the Assyrians. Interestingly, Rashi understands verse 12 as a mini-lament (*kinna*) for Nineveh's former splendor (commentary on 2:12); Radak and Ibn Ezra suggest that Nahum is giving voice to the nations of the world, who are expressing their astonishment that a city like Nineveh could fall.

> Where is the lions' den? And it is pasture for young lions, where the grown lion and the old lion went, and the lion's cubs, and no one makes them afraid. The lion did tear in pieces enough for his cubs, and strangled for his lionesses, and filled his caves with prey, and his dens with prey.
>
> Behold, I am against you, says the Lord of hosts, and I will burn her chariots in the smoke, and the sword shall devour your young lions; and I will cut off your prey from the earth, and the voice of your messengers shall no more be heard. (2:12–14)

Foreign visitors to the great city of Nineveh were greeted with large reliefs carved into walls that portrayed scenes of the Assyrian kings hunting lions, as a way of demonstrating their ferocity and their bravery.[9] Now Nahum takes that image and turns it against them, asking sarcastically, "Where is the lions' den?" (2:12).[10] Additionally, not only did the Assyrians depict their king and his warriors as brave fighters capable of hunting ferocious lions, they also depicted them as being like mighty lions themselves. Nahum subtly both combines the two metaphors and reverses them. If kings hunted lions and brought their hides as trophies to Nineveh, now lions run free throughout the city, carrying their prey back to their dens. The king, whose job it was to hunt, is nowhere in sight, while lions rampage throughout the city with no one to frighten them any longer. They tear their game and bring the prey back to their caves and dens for their young to devour. The Assyrians had boasted

---

9. "The visual arts of Assyria contain depictions of the royal hunt of wild animals. The most ferocious and challenging adversary for the Assyrian king was the lion. The chase of the lion – from the chariot, on horseback, or on foot – and its ultimate dispatch with bow, spear, or dagger demonstrated the royal individual's exceptional bravery and skill" (Pauline Albenda, "Assyrian Royal Hunts: Antlered and Horned Animals from Distant Lands," *Bulletin of American Schools for Oriental Research* no. 349 [2008]).
10. The midrashic understanding of this verse is that God mourns over the loss of His people and His Temple, and therefore turns on their tormentors:

    > The Temple is called a lion.... The monarchy of David is called a lion.... Israel is called a lion.... Nebuchadnezzar is called a lion. He destroyed the Temple and took the monarchy of David and exiled Israel, and so God says, "Where is the home of the lions?" Where are My children? And then He roars for His home. (Exodus Rabba 29:9)

that they were like lions. Now these Assyrian "lions" are being hunted down, lying helpless while invaders kill her "cubs" (2:13). Assyria's propensity to engage in "lionlike" behavior has now come to an end. No longer could they despoil others, taking riches from their conquests like a lion returning with its prey in its mouth to give to its young. No longer would Assyrian messengers deliver threats, demanding tribute (see II Kings 18:17–25, 19:22, Is. 37:4, 6).

In the last verse of chapter 2, God declares "Behold, I am against you [Nineveh]" (2:14). Jeremiah and Ezekiel will employ this formulation in their denunciation of the Jewish people a generation later. Speaking against Judah's capital, Jeremiah shouts: "I am against you, Jerusalem, you who live above this valley on the rocky plateau, declares the Lord – you who say, 'Who can come against us?'" (21:13; see also 50:31, 51:25), while Ezekiel similarly states: "Therefore this is what the Lord God says: I Myself am against you, Jerusalem, and I will inflict punishment on you in the sight of the nations. Because of all your detestable idols, I will do to you what I have never done before and will never do again" (Ezek. 5:8–9; see also Ezek. 13:8–9). Like Nahum, Jeremiah and Ezekiel use the divine direct address to introduce God's words toward a guilty party, and to declare how God Himself will arrange the fitting punishment. Significantly, until now Nahum had merely alluded to God as the cause of Nineveh's downfall ("the scatterer"). In the final verse, Nahum identifies God as directly responsible for the carnage and destruction of Nineveh. This forms the bridge to chapter 3, where Nahum will reexamine Nineveh's downfall, but his words will add a moral dimension significantly absent in chapter 2.

3:1–3:19

How Could Nineveh Fall?

A new prophecy begins in 3:1 with the word *hoy*, meaning "woe."[1] This lengthy prophecy is directed at the city of Nineveh and continues throughout the majority of chapter 3, ending only in verse 18, when Nahum turns his attention to the Assyrian king. The prophecy in chapter 3 shares several structural similarities with the one in chapter 2 (2:2–14), repeating the account of the assault on the city – this time, with greater, more graphic detail – but also adds the moral justification for the devastation that befalls the Assyrians. In chapter 3, Nahum explains that it was Nineveh's own ruthless behavior toward others that caused its downfall.

The graphic depiction of Nineveh's downfall is especially evident in the first three verses of chapter 3:

> Woe to the bloody city! It is all full of deceit, robbery. There is no end to its prey.
>
> The noise of a whip and the noise of rattling wheels, of galloping horses, of clattering chariots! Horsemen charge with bright sword and glittering spear. There is a multitude of slain, a

1. This introductory formula is found in the Bible in several places, and we shall analyze it in detail in Hab. 2:6.

> great number of bodies, countless corpses – they stumble over the corpses. (3:1–3)

The word "woe" generally announces impending destruction (see Is. 3:9). It can also be used to express grief, so it could be suggested that Nahum is grieving over the Assyrians' fate, but his subsequent portrayal of the Assyrians' iniquities, which are the justification for their destruction, quickly eliminates this meaning as a possibility here.

Nahum calls Nineveh *ir damim*, literally, "the city of blood." These words can be understood to be referring to Nineveh in a direct and literal fashion: having described the battle for Nineveh and the pillaging that occurred after its defeat, Nahum could be simply describing the carnage that fills the roads. But Nineveh the "bloody city" has another connotation as well, one that justifies the extent of the devastation, which Nahum most probably also has in mind: the violent shedding of innocent blood. This meaning is apparent in many places throughout the bible, including Genesis 4:10, 11 regarding Cain; II Samuel 3:28 regarding Joab; II Samuel 16:8, where Shimei accuses David of murder; and II Kings 9:26 regarding Ahab. The prophet Micah also used the word in this sense, when he accused the wealthy people of Judah of building "Zion with blood (*damim*), and Jerusalem with iniquity" (Mic. 3:10), and Ezekiel will develop this idea even further in his indictment of Jerusalem (Ezek. 24).

Throughout the book of Nahum, the prophet takes words and phrases that had previously been used in negative prophecies against Israel and transforms them, using them instead in negative prophecies directed against Israel's enemies – here, against Assyria. Hosea used the word *kaḥash*, meaning deceit, when berating the Northern Kingdom, i.e., the Kingdom of Israel (see Hos. 7:3, 10:13, 12:1); in 3:1, Nahum uses the same word to describe Nineveh. Micah had described Jerusalem as an *ir damim*; here, Nahum uses the same phrase to refer to Nineveh.

Nahum also employs word games, using words with similar letters in the root form to convey the same meaning. When Nahum described the Assyrians as lions in 2:13, he used the word *teref* to refer to their prey. *Perek*, the word that Nahum uses here to refer to pillage, contains two of the three letters of the previous root. The connections serve to strengthen his message: the city that plundered and conquered and accumulated booty to maintain its power would now fall.

The next two verses, verses 2 and 3, contain no verbs at all until the final phrase. Instead, Nahum graphically portrays the sights and sounds of the battle's aftermath.[2] Nahum had previously described the futile attempts of the Assyrian chariots to maneuver in the streets while attempting to defend Nineveh (see 2:5). Now, any Assyrian attempts to defend their city are in the past, and the invading enemy's cavalry and charioteers ride freely in the streets, cutting down the doomed inhabitants without mercy. Piles of corpses clutter the roads, so much that the foot soldiers trip over the bodies. He uses repeated military imagery, including the words for horseman (*parash*), chariot (*merkava*), charging (*maale*), flashing/blazes (*lahav*), and voices/sounds (*kol*). Again, Nahum relies on imagery used by an earlier prophet, employing words that are echoes of the words used to describe the great battles in Joel, chapter 2. In the following excerpt from the book of Joel, the prophet describes the upcoming war against Judah:

> Before them fire devours, behind them a flame blazes (*lehava*)... nothing escapes them. They have the appearance of horses; they gallop along like cavalry (*farashim*). With a noise (*kol*) like that of chariots (*markavot*) they leap over the mountaintops, like a blaze (*lahav*) of fire consuming stubble...they charge like warriors; they climb (*yaalu*) walls like soldiers. (Joel 2:3–7)

Once again, Nahum has taken a negative prophecy that was directed toward the Jewish people and redirected it toward Israel's enemies, with Nineveh replacing Judah as the target of God's wrath. Emphasizing the extent of the deaths, Nahum uses three different words for corpses and the dead. The rarest of these, the Hebrew word *pager*, appears in only three other places in the Bible, all with terrifying connotations. David

2. In this respect, the book of Nahum may be considered an early example of the narrative technique known as impressionism, where an author portrays characters, scenes, and moods as he visualizes them at a particular moment rather than as they are in reality, often in disjointed or disconnected sequences.

uses it when he asserts that he will give the Philistine corpses to the birds in I Samuel 17:46; Isaiah uses it to describe Babylon's ultimate downfall (Is. 14:19); and in Amos's terrifying vision of the basket of summer fruits, in which he declares the finality of God's plan to wipe out Israel, he states that women will cry out that there are "so many corpses tossed everywhere! Hush" (Amos 8:3). Once again, earlier dark prophecies against Israel that were etched in the conscience of the people are transformed into visions of salvation that will lead to the downfall of their enemies.

In the next few verses, Nahum levels his most devastating accusation against Nineveh, unsparingly portraying its horrifying punishment.

> Because of the multitude of harlotries of the seductive harlot, the mistress of sorceries, who sells nations through her harlotries, and families through her sorceries.
>
> "Behold, I am against you," says the Lord of hosts; "I will lift your skirts over your face,
>
> I will show the nations your nakedness, and the kingdoms your shame.
>
> I will cast abominable filth upon you, make you vile, and make you a spectacle.
>
> It shall come to pass that all who look upon you will flee from you, and say, 'Nineveh is laid waste! Who will bemoan her?' Where shall I seek comforters for you?" (3:4–7)

Nahum accuses Nineveh of acting like a harlot and engaging in sorcery against other nations. It would now be humiliated accordingly. The harlot metaphor is a common motif in the Bible, generally signifying faithlessness and a willingness to betray sacred bonds for personal profit. For example, in Judges 16, following his visit to a prostitute in Gaza, Samson is sold to the Philistines for silver pieces by his partner Delilah; he betrayed God by visiting a prostitute and was therefore betrayed in turn by Delilah. Prophets often use the metaphor of harlotry to describe Israel's abandonment of God. In several places, the prophets describe Israel as a bride married to God (see Hos. 1–3, Jer. 2, Ezek. 16); therefore, turning to other nations for sustenance and protection becomes an act of betrayal and harlotry (e.g., Hos 1:2, 4:14). Now, this metaphor of harlotry is applied to Assyria, and specifically, Nineveh. Nineveh has been portrayed as a woman since chapter 2, and now it is called a prostitute. What did Assyria do to warrant being called a harlot? Assyrians were notorious for luring unsuspecting nations into alliances, promising protection and wealth, only to break their agreements when convenient, and enslaving them. The Kingdom of Judah had felt the brunt of Assyrian capriciousness in the past. Against Isaiah's council, King Ahaz of Judah had appealed to Assyria for help upon being attacked by his enemies, the kings of Aram and Israel, in 734 BCE (see II Kings 16:7–18, Is. 7–9). However, the respite was short-lived. When the Kingdom of Israel was destroyed a short while later, Assyria turned its gluttonous appetite toward Judah (Is. 36:16–17).

Nahum's condemnation of Assyrian sorcery in verse 4 echoes Micah's earlier denouncement of the Jewish people's involvement in witchcraft (Mic. 5:11) and reflects the Bible's condemnation of pagan worship, including the occult and perversions. Captured people would adopt the Assyrian practices, hoping to stave off enslavement, but they were ultimately exiled or sold into slavery. It is the Assyrian penchant for acts of perfidy and betrayal that lead to the severity of the shameful punishment which is to befall them, described in the next verse.

Nahum then presents God's direct response to Nineveh's iniquity, using the divine first-person, "I," seven times in three verses. The response begins with the same phrase that concluded chapter 2: "Behold, I [God] am against you." The judgment is severe, among the harshest in the Bible. In verse 5, Nahum graphically depicts Nineveh's humiliation: God will expose the city before onlookers like a captured woman is exposed before her captors, lifting her skirt so high that her nakedness is revealed.[3] The description of the future humiliation of Nineveh

3. Similar usage of this disturbing metaphor appears in Is. 47:1–3, Jer. 13:26–27, Ezek. 16:37, and Hos. 2:3–5. While scholarship notes that the personification of a city as a woman was prevalent throughout the ancient Near East, and therefore the metaphor would have been understood accordingly, explicit and horrible imagery of violence against females is a difficult metaphor for many people to accept. An excellent discussion of the issue of biblical stories and depictions of violence against women can be found in Judith E. Sanderson's "Nahum," in *The Women's Bible Commentary*

continues in the following verse, relating that dung will be thrown on Nineveh, making it even more disgusting to look upon. Those who see Nineveh in this state will have no option but to recoil, and no one will assist Nineveh or even mourn. So many nations suffered greatly at the hands of the brutal Assyrians; now, there is no one to pity Nineveh at its time of suffering.

In verses 8–11, Nahum continues to taunt the Assyrians, and in doing so, he reminds his listeners that no city is impregnable, not even Nineveh. He mockingly asks if they thought that they were somehow better or more special than No-Amon (i.e., Thebes), the once-prestigious Egyptian capital, which was destroyed and sacked by the Assyrians in 663 BCE:[4]

> Are you better than No-Amon that was situated by the river, which had the waters around her – whose rampart was the sea,

(ed. Carol A. Newsom and Sharon H. Ringe [Louisville: Westminster John Knox, 1998], 217–21), where she emphasizes that "no aspect of God's relationship with humankind can be represented... by an image that depends on a destructive view of women."

One new approach in understanding this metaphor is suggested by Daniel Smith-Christopher in his *OTL* commentary on Micah ([Louisville: Westminster John Knox, 2015], 69). In his interpretation of this metaphor as it appears in Micah, he notes that the root G-L-H can mean "to expose," and that is the meaning in Nahum 3:5 when it refers to the city of Nineveh, portrayed as a woman, but the same root can also mean "to exile." The ancient listener, aware of the Assyrian practice of stripping their captives before forcing them to march into exile, would have nodded approvingly at Nahum's choice of words – not because of any misogynic leanings, but because he would have recognized the comeuppance that had befallen the Assryians.

4. Of course, the Assyrians would answer unhesitatingly that they were better than No-Amon – after all, didn't they just defeat them in battle? No-Amon is Egyptian for "city of (the deity) Amon," and is more commonly referred to today by its Greek name, Thebes. [Though Jerome, the author of the Vulgate, the fourth-century translation of the Bible into Latin, identified it as Alexandria, this suggestion has been discredited in modern scholarship.] Thebes had been the capital of Upper (southern) Egypt and had stood at the site of modern Karnak and Luxor. Though the city straddled the Nile River, the capital section occupied the eastern side, with the river forming a barrier against access from three sides and a highly fortified wall protecting it from the fourth. Until its defeat in 663 BCE, the city was considered to be unconquerable.

> whose wall was the sea? Ethiopia and Egypt were your strength, and it was boundless; Put and Lubim were your helpers. Yet she was carried away, she went into captivity; her young children also were dashed to pieces at the head of every street; they cast lots for her honorable men, and all her great men were bound in chains. You also will be drunk; you will be hidden; you also will seek refuge from the enemy. (3:8–11)

Esarhaddon conquered the Egyptians in 671 BCE, but they revolted upon his death. In response, Ashurbanipal went to Egypt and routed them in their strongholds in the Nile Delta in 667 BCE. The survivors fled south five hundred kilometers to No-Amon, which they felt could not be beaten. However, in 663 BCE, Ashurbanipal captured No-Amon and razed it to the ground. Through the rhetorical question, Nahum establishes a clear analogy between No-Amon and Nineveh. Egypt was a mighty empire, yet it fell to the Assyrians when those countries closest to it (Put and Lubim) fought against it together with the foreign invaders.[5] Nahum is hinting that those countries that would conquer Nineveh would be its neighbors, those closest to it geographically and historically, i.e., the Babylonians and the Medes.

Nahum continues by describing the horrific end that was the fate of the people of No-Amon, and he hints that such would be the fate of Nineveh as well. As before, Nahum, in his portrayal of the destruction of Nineveh, draws from earlier prophets. This time, he draws from some of Isaiah's and Joel's darkest prophecies against Israel's enemies. Isaiah described how the children of Babylon would be "dashed in pieces (*veoleleihem yeruteshu*) before their eyes" (Is. 13:16), and Nahum similarly describes how the children of No-Amon were "dashed in pieces (*olaleiha yeruteshu*)." Joel promised that on the Day of Judgment, God

5. Concerning the Egyptian conquest, Ashurbanipal boasts how he coerced the neighboring kings to participate: "I... took the shortest road to Egypt and Nubia. During my march, 22 kings... [including] Manasseh king of Judah... brought heavy gifts to me and kissed my feet. I made these kings accompany my army over the land – as well as over the sea-route with their armed forces and their ships." James B. Pritchard, ed., *Ancient Near Eastern Texts Relating to the Old Testament*, 3rd ed. (Princeton: Princeton University Press, 1969), 294.

will contend with the nations who abused Israel and its exiles, "and cast lots (*yaddu goral*) over My people, and bartered a boy for a harlot, and sold a girl for wine" (Joel 4:3). Nahum draws on the prophecy from Joel, noting that No-Amon had faced a fate similar to that of the enemies described in Joel: as the people of No-Amon were led off in chains by their Assyrian conquerors, the onlookers would "cast lots (*yaddu goral*) for her honorable men, and all her great men were bound in chains." Having introduced his list of the continued abuses against the citizenry of No-Amon with the word *gam*, meaning "also," using the word twice in verse 10, Nahum repeats the word *gam* in verse 11, to emphasize that the unfortunate fate that had befallen No-Amon and the fate that would soon befall Nineveh are one and the same. In a drunken stupor, Nineveh is powerless to protect itself from what awaits it.

Nahum continues to taunt the Assyrians in verses 12–15:

> All your strongholds are fig trees with fruits newly ripened: when they are shaken, they fall into the mouth of the eater. Behold, your nation is [are] women in your midst! The gates of your land are wide open for your enemies; fire devoured the bars of your gates.
>
> Draw your water for the siege! Fortify your strongholds! Go into the clay and tread the mortar! Make strong the brick kiln! There the fire will devour you, the sword will cut you off; t will eat you up like a locust.

These verses describe how the Assyrians, who so strongly believed in their superiority and invincibility, will now experience their weaknesses coming to the fore. When figs are ripe, they fall easily when the tree is shaken. As seen on ancient reliefs which depict scenes from the city of Nineveh, fig trees were common in Nineveh, making this metaphor of the weaknesses of the Assyrian defenses a very personal one. The prophet continues by describing the Assyrian soldiers, whom, with the city gates wide open, are powerless to defend themselves against the upcoming assault. He compares them to women, whom in his understanding, in accordance with what would have been the common assumption at the time, are also powerless to defend themselves (see Radak). As fire consumes the city structures, Nahum returns to sarcastically barking orders at the defenders that scramble to repair the breaches in the city walls: Draw water! Make clay![6] But as is the case with regard to the commands that Nahum shouted out in 2:2, any attempt on the part of the Assyrians to actually respond to those commands and save themselves is futile. There is nothing Nineveh's defenders can do; the battle is lost.

Nahum concludes his attack on the Assyrians by comparing them to locusts:

> Make yourself many – like the locust. Make yourself many – like the swarming locusts. You have multiplied your merchants more than the stars in the sky. The locust plunders and flies away. Your commanders are like swarming locusts, and your generals like great grasshoppers, which camp in the hedges on a cold day; when the sun rises they flee away, and the place where they are is not known. (3:15–17)

At first glance, this may be interpreted as encouragement. In the Bible, the locust swarm was a feared sight (Ex. 10, Joel 1–2, Amos 7:1–3). A large horde would descend on an area and devour its plant life and crops, leaving it a bare wasteland. Similarly, the Assyrian army would invade a city, and loot and despoil it so thoroughly that nothing would remain. However, as Nahum makes clear quickly, this comparison is not a positive one. Instead he continues to mock the Assyrians, who thought themselves so strong and so invincible. Locusts, despite their tremendous numbers, can stay stationary for a long period of time in cool weather. However, once the temperature rises, they quickly leave in search of more favorable conditions. Similarly, the Assyrian army, despite their numbers, quickly fled in the heat of the battle.

The same was true for the Assyrian merchants, described ironically as numerous as "stars in the sky." Previously, the phrase "stars in

6. Commanding the Assyrian defenders to make bricks may also be an allusion to the Exodus. Israel's suffering was exemplified by their making of bricks for the Egyptians (Ex. 5), and now the Assyrians have been reduced to performing slavelike labor in a last-ditch, futile attempt to save themselves (Sweeney, *The Twelve Prophets*, 446).

the sky" was used positively to refer to the Jewish people (Gen. 15:5). When Assyria unified the ancient Near East under one rule, merchants and traders were able to prosper at levels previously unseen. Some may have felt that the web of financial ties that bound the empire together would prevent its demise.[7] However, like Assyria's military might, its financial might could not prevent its collapse, and its merchants, like its army, were no better than locusts, who fly away as soon as conditions worsen. To Nahum's Jewish listeners, the knowledge that those people who threatened their very existence for almost a century would be the ones to disappear must have brought some relief.

Nahum's usage of locusts as a simile may also be an ironic reversal of an Assyrian symbol. In the British Museum, among the exhibits from Ashurbanipal's palace that were taken from Nineveh, is a relief that depicts a royal feast commemorating his defeat of Teumman, the king of Elam. Fitting with the biblical description of peace (I Kings 5:5, Mic. 4:4), Ashurbanipal is seen reclining under vines. While servants fan him, play instruments, and bring wine, the Assyrian tyrant is content to gaze upon Teumman's head, hung from a fir tree opposite his couch. In the upper left corner of the relief is a locust sitting on top of a palm tree, while to its right, a bird swoops to catch it. This detail may have special significance, as Ashurbanipal had described the Elamites as a "dense swarm of grasshoppers." To the Assyrians, the locust may signify the last vestige of a once-dreadful enemy, now virtually eliminated.[8]

If Nahum was aware of this symbolism, he could be cleverly alluding to the reversal of fortune that has befallen the Assyrians. Instead of the Elamites, the Assyrians are the locusts, and like the Elamites before them, the Assyrians are about to be defeated. Their locustlike behavior

7. "Under Ashurbanipal, for the first time in 800 years, western Asia was dominated by a single political rule. With the vast territory of the empire under one central government, commerce could flourish throughout this area as never before" (Maier, 348). Much later in history, before World War I, a similar naïve belief permeated the thinking of many European policy makers, who thought that the commercial ties that bound European countries together were enough to prevent the outbreak of hostilities between those countries.
8. See website Associates for Biblical Research, https://biblearchaeology.org/research/divided-kingdom/2744-nahum-nineveh-and-those-nasty-assyrians.

is reflected not through their tremendous numbers and their ferocity in battle, but through their willingness to abandon their place of rest when threatened.

Like chapters 1 and 2, the final chapter ends with a shift from feminine pronouns, which signify the nation, to masculine singular pronouns, as Nahum directs one final taunt toward the king of Assyria:

> Your shepherds slumber, O king of Assyria; your nobles rest in the dust. Your people are scattered on the mountains, and there is no one to gather them. Your injury has no healing, your wound is fatal. All who hear news of you will clap their hands over you, for upon whom has not your wickedness passed continually? (3:18–19)

This is the first time that Nahum has directly identified the king of Assyria as the target of his scorn. In doing so, he creates a contrasting parallel to the endings of the previous chapters where he did not directly identify his target. In chapter 1, after speaking to Judah, Nahum speaks to an unnamed king that we have identified as Manasseh, king of Judah; in chapter 2, the description of the upcoming destruction of Nineveh is followed by God's declaration in which He speaks to the king of the lions that He is leading the war effort against him. Though it can be assumed that the king of lions is referring to the king of Assyria, Nahum prefers to leave the metaphor unexplained. Only here in chapter 3 does Nahum directly identify his target. Having already vividly described the downfall of Nineveh, Nahum now zeroes in on his final target, the Assyrian monarch, describing his downfall and punishment. He is a shepherd – but his sheep and flocks are dispersed. Nahum began his description of the assault on Nineveh with a warning that a scatterer was approaching (2:2) – and now Assyria is scattered.

The metaphor Nahum uses here of leaders as shepherds, responsible for the welfare of the people, was a common one in both the Bible and the ancient Near East. For example, David is referred to as a shepherd in II Samuel 5:2 and Ezekiel 37:24. Similarly, in the ancient Near East, the kings of Assyria and Babylonia were traditionally called "faithful shepherd" (*Mikra LeYisrael*, 60). There are many additional examples in the Bible: Moses concludes his request that God appoint a replacement for him with the plea "that the congregation of the Lord be not as sheep that have no shepherd" (Num. 27:17). Later generations remembered Moses and Aaron as faithful, successful shepherds of the Israelites, and God is also referred to as the Master Shepherd: Isaiah asks, "Where is He that brought them up out of the sea, with the shepherds of His flock?" (Is. 63:11), and the narrator of Psalms 77 praises God, saying that "You led Your people like a flock in the care of Moses and Aaron" (77:21). Other prophets also used the metaphor of leaders as shepherds, but while God is still referred to as the Master Shepherd of his flock, the human leaders of Israel are in these cases deeply problematic, failed "shepherds": Jeremiah castigates the leaders of his generation as failed shepherds, promising their replacement with more worthy ones:

> Therefore so says the Lord, the God of Israel, against the shepherds that feed My people: You have scattered My flock, and driven them away, and have not taken care of them; behold, I will visit upon you the evil of your doings, says the Lord. And I will gather the remnant of My flock out of all the countries whither I have driven them, and will bring them back to their folds; and they shall be fruitful and multiply. And I will set up shepherds over them, who shall feed them; and they shall fear no more, nor be dismayed, neither shall any be lacking, says the Lord. (Jer. 23:2–5)

Similarly, Ezekiel's screed against the corrupt leadership that led to Judah's destruction also uses this metaphor: "Woe unto the shepherds of Israel that have fed themselves! Should not the shepherds feed the sheep?" (Ezek. 34:2; see also Zech. 11:5, 13:7).

Shepherds are primarily responsible for ensuring that the herds do not wander aimlessly, entangling themselves in dangerous places. Micaiah describes how he saw "all Israel scattered upon the mountains, as sheep that have no shepherd" (I Kings 22:17), while Ezekiel lambasts Israel's leadership for not only failing to protect their people, but for abusing them instead:

> You eat the curds, clothe yourselves with the wool, and slaughter the choice animals, but you do not take care of the flock. You

> have not strengthened the weak or healed the sick or bandaged up the injured. You have not brought back the strays or searched for the lost. You have ruled them harshly and brutally. So they were scattered because there was no shepherd, and when they were scattered they became food for all the wild animals. My sheep wandered over all the mountains and on every high hill. They were scattered over the whole earth, and no one searched or looked for them. (Ezek. 34:3–7)[9]

Nahum also uses the metaphor of leaders as shepherds in verse 18, sneering at the king of Assyria, that his leadership, referred to as "shepherds," fell asleep; as a result, his people are scattered like sheep with no shepherd, who have no protection or sustenance. The king was once described by Nahum as a predator, a lion who brought strangled prey into his den to provide for his people (2:12–13) – now the lion has become the sheep, the target and prey for others.

Nahum concludes with two final remarks. First, "Your injury has no healing" – the defeat suffered by Assyria will be final, without respite or restoration. This is what Nahum alluded to in chapter 1: "trouble will not rise twice" (v. 9). Second, as a result, all those who hear of the fate of Assyria will shout, sing, and clap for joy, since at one point or another, everyone suffered under Assyrian oppression. This is reminiscent of the end of chapter 2, when the king of Assyria was told "and the voice of your messengers shall be heard no more (*lo yishama od*)." Instead of Assyrian

9. This metaphor continues into midrashic literature. Exodus Rabba 2:2 tells how a little lamb ran away while Moses was tending Jethro's flock. He chased after the lamb. When he found it drinking at a spring, Moses exclaimed, "I did not know that you ran away because you were thirsty! You must be tired." Moses then lifted the little lamb and carried it on his shoulders back to the flock. Due to this display of compassion, God declared, "Since you have mercy while leading sheep of flesh and blood, then by your life, you shall also shepherd My sheep, Israel." A similar story is told about David. The continuation of the same midrash states that he kept the big sheep penned to allow the little ones to graze first, allowing them to eat the softer vegetation. Next, he released the old sheep to graze on the medium vegetation, and finally the strongest sheep were released to graze on the toughest vegetation. Seeing this, God then declared, "Whoever knows how to take care of sheep, each one according to its strength, he is the one who shall come and shepherd My people."

edicts and decrees, "all who hear news of you (*shomei shimakha*)" will rejoice over the Assyrian downfall. These tidings, signifying freedom from tyranny and oppression, brought joy to their listeners. No one who had suffered under Nineveh's barbaric hand could mourn that it would no longer rise.

However, the reaction of glee and elation that accompanied Nineveh's destruction echoes the reaction of the nations that followed the destruction of another great city in the Bible: Jerusalem. The primary focus of the next section will be how Jeremiah utilized Nahum's poetry about the downfall of Assyria in his lamentations over the destruction of Jerusalem.

Appendix

From Nahum to Jeremiah

This commentary has regularly noted throughout when Nahum drew upon the ideas and wordings of his predecessors to formulate his ideas. By drawing on earlier, dark prophecies of punishment against Israel and redirecting them toward Assyria, Nahum's words not only were a source of comfort to Israel, but helped reinforce the idea that just as God was harsh in His punishment of Israel, He was also merciful and faithful to redeem. To express this idea, Nahum relied on earlier seers, and especially on Isaiah; specifically, Isaiah's prophecies that predict Israel's eventual salvation (compare Nahum 2:1 with Is. 52:7) and those that predict Assyria's eventual downfall (compare Nahum 1:2 with Is. 37:33, and Nahum 1:8–9 with Is. 10:22–23). But only one generation later, Israel returned to being the target of God's anger, and Jerusalem would face destruction and devastation just as Nineveh did. Did Nahum's words of comfort disappear from the people's minds? We shall look at two of the prophets who followed him, Ezekiel and Jeremiah, and see that Nahum's influence extended long after him.

We noted at the end of chapter 2 how Jeremiah and Ezekiel will employ Nahum's formulation, "Behold, I am against you!" as a formula used to introduce God's words toward a guilty party, and to declare how God himself will arrange a fitting punishment.[1] Their utilization of Nahum's prophecies is not limited to repetition of formal structural forms. Instead, they often lift Nahum's wording and thematic ideas and use them for their own rhetorical ends. In chapter 22, Ezekiel describes how God will judge the city of Jerusalem for its sins, punishing it once and for all. He begins, "Son of man! Judge, judge the city of blood!" Ezekiel has taken Nahum's description of Nineveh as "the city of blood" (3:1) and applied it to Jerusalem. Ezekiel then delivers the rebuke that he prophetically received from God in which he catalogs all of Jerusalem's sins, including murder, sexual immorality and promiscuity, social injustice, and abuse of the poor as an explanation of why the people of Jerusalem are deserving of scorn among all the nations, echoing Nahum's description of Nineveh's numerous iniquities. Then, Ezekiel relates God's metaphor in which the people are compared to metal in a crucible. Just as dross is removed from silver in a crucible, so too God will purify the people of Israel, who have become hardened by sin, by melting them with the fire of His wrath until they are purified: "As they gather silver and brass and iron and lead and tin into the midst of the furnace, to blow the fire upon it, to melt it; so will I gather you in My anger and in My wrath, and I will cast you in, and melt you... with the fire of My wrath, and you shall be melted... you shall know that I the Lord have poured out My wrath upon you" (22:20–22). Ezekiel's repeated usage of the words "wrath," "poured out," and "fire" echo Nahum's description of God's zeal and vengeance against His enemies in chapter 1.

However, it is Jeremiah who draws most heavily on Nahum's ideas and articulations. Sometimes Jeremiah uses Nahum's words without changing their context. In Jeremiah's promise of a brighter future for the Jewish people, he describes how God would "break his yoke (*eshbor ullo*)" (i.e., the yoke of Babylonian rule) and "rend your bonds asunder (*umosrotekha anatek*)" (30:8), just as Nahum had comforted Judah that God would "break his [the Assyrian] yoke (*eshbor motehu*)" and "rend your bonds asunder (*umosrotayikh anatek*)" (1:13). Sometimes Jeremiah

1. Additionally, in his brief mention of the punishment awaiting Nineveh, the prophet Zephaniah, who lived a generation after Nahum, includes several phrases that echo those of Nahum (compare Nahum 3:7, 19 with Zeph. 2:15).

uses Nahum's words to point out a positive contrast between Israel and the nations. Jeremiah promises rebellious Israel that repentance is worthwhile, since God does not "bear grudges (*etor*) forever" (3:12; see also Mic. 7:18). This language is directly reminiscent of Nahum's declaration, when speaking against Assyria, that God "bears grudges (*noter*) against His enemies" (1:2). Using Nahum's prophecy as the context, Jeremiah is subtly stating to the people of Israel that despite their transgressions, God does not consider them an enemy. In other places, Jeremiah, when prophesying against Israel and Judah, uses some of the exact same wording that Nahum had used in his imagery-filled prophecy against Nineveh. Nahum describes how God says to Nineveh that "I will lift your skirts over your face (*shulayikh al panayikh*), I will show (*vehareiti*) the nations your nakedness, and the kingdoms your shame (*kilonekh*)" (3:5). Jeremiah warns Jerusalem that a similar fate awaits it as well: "And I will also lift your skirts over your face (*shulayikh al panayikh*), and your shame shall be seen (*venira kilonekh*)" (13:26).

Nahum's influence is especially noticeable in two sections of Jeremiah's prophecies. The book of Jeremiah concludes with a series of prophecies against the nations of the world, including Egypt, the Philistines, Moab, Ammon, Edom, Damascus, Kedar, Hazor, and Babylonia (chs. 46–51).[2] In these prophecies, generally referred to as "Oracles against the Nations (OAN),"[3] Jeremiah borrows liberally from Nahum, using wording, imagery, and themes that Nahum had used to describe Assyria's downfall, but now expanding the prophecy to encompass all the nations of the world. The parallels are especially apparent in his prophecy against Babylonia (chs. 50–51). Nahum began his prophecy by declaring three times that God is a God of vengeance. Jeremiah also makes ample use of the word "vengeance" in his prophecy against Babylonia. He announces that when God chooses to act against Babylonia, "it is the time of the Lord's vengeance; He is paying her a recompense" (51:6), "for His aim is to destroy her, for the Lord's vengeance is the vengeance

2. Similar series of prophecies against the nations can be found in Is. 13–24, Ezek. 27–36, Amos 1, and Zeph. 2.
3. See John Hayes's seminal article, "The Usage of Oracles against Foreign Nations in Ancient Israel," *Journal of Biblical Literature* 87, no. 1 (March 1968): 81–92.

of His Temple" (51:11), and "therefore, so said the Lord: Behold I plead your cause, and I avenge your vengeance" (51:36). Nahum had mocked the Assyrian leadership for being drunk and asleep on their watch; similarly, Jeremiah mocks the Babylonian leadership using the language of sleep: "In their heat I will place their wine feasts, and I will make them drunk in order that they become joyful, and sleep a perpetual sleep and not awaken" (51:39; see also v. 57: "And I will make drunk her princes and her wise men, her governors and her mighty men, and they shall sleep a perpetual sleep and not awaken"). If the greatest insult that Nahum could hurl at the Assyrian army was that they had become women, it is not surprising, then, that Jeremiah described the defeated Babylonian army in the same way: "The mighty men of Babylon ceased to wage war, they dwelt in the fortresses; their might has failed, they have become like women" (51:30). A brief and by no means exhaustive list of the parallels between Nahum and Jeremiah 46–51 demonstrates how much Jeremiah drew upon Nahum's language and ideas in his own oracles:[4]

Imagery	In Nahum	In Jeremiah 46–51
References to Judah's salvation	1:12–13, 2:1, 3	46:27 50:33, 34 51:5, 10, 24, 35, 36
Threat of exile	2:8, 3:10	46:19 48:7, 11
Lion imagery	2:12–14	49:19–20 50:17, 44 51:38
Dead in the streets	3:3	50:3 51:4
The city personified as a female	3:4–7	46:19–24 47:3 48:2, 9, 18 49:4, 13 51

4. Many of these parallels are noted in O'Brien, *Nahum*, ch. 5.

Imagery	In Nahum	In Jeremiah 46–51
Others that gaze upon the city's humiliation	3:5–7	46:39 47:13 49:13, 17 50:13, 23 51:24, 37
Drunkenness as a result of warfare	3:11	48:26 51:7, 39, 57
Troops that become women	3:13	48:41 49:22, 24 50:43 51:30
Troops as locusts	3:15	46:23 51:14
Leaders as shepherds	3:18	49:7–22 50:6, 44
The incurable wound	3:19	51:8

Many of the strongest parallels, though, can be found between Nahum and the book of Lamentations, traditionally ascribed to Jeremiah (Bava Batra 14b). The parallels include the repetition of words and phrases, as well as the larger themes and motifs in each. On the simple level of repeated vocabulary, just as Nahum taunted the Assyrian king that "your injury (*shivrekha*) has no healing" (Nahum 3:19), the Lamenter asks, "For your wound (*shivrekh*) is great like the sea; can anyone heal you?" (Lam. 2:13). Nahum described how God rhetorically asks about Nineveh, "From where shall I seek comforters (*menaḥamim*) for you?" (3:7; see also 3:19); in Lamentations, Jerusalem's sorry and tragic state is intensified by the fact that "she has none to comfort (*menaḥem*) her among all her lovers" (Lam. 1:2; see also 1:9, 16, 17, 2:13). Both books attribute the destruction to God's fierce anger (*af*) in Nahum 6 and in Lamentations 1:12, 2:1, 3, 21, 22, 3:43, and 4:11, yet both are determined to reaffirm that God is good. Just as Nahum declares that "the Lord is good (*tov*) to those that trust in Him" (Nahum 1:7), Jeremiah proclaims that "the Lord is good (*tov*) unto them that wait for Him" (Lam. 3:25). Dead bodies lie piled in the streets in both Nineveh and Jerusalem

(Nahum 3:3, Lam. 2:21), and special attention is paid to the dead children of both. Nahum promised that the fate of Nineveh's children would be equal to the fate of No-Amon's children, who were "dashed in pieces at the head of the streets (*olaleiha yeruteshu berosh kol ḥutzot*)" (Nahum 3:10); Jeremiah exhorts Jerusalem to cry aloud "for the life of your young children (*olalayikh*), that faint for hunger at the head of every street (*berosh kol ḥutzot*)" (Lam. 2:19). In both, the city is gazed at in a degrading manner and mocked (Nahum 3:7, Lam. 2:15–16). Both Nineveh and Jerusalem are personified as an abject, humiliated woman whose nakedness is visible to all and whose skirts are covered in filth. God has Nahum tell Nineveh that He will "lift your skirts over your face … show the nations your nakedness, and the kingdoms your shame. I will cast abominable filth upon you" (Nahum 3:5–6). Jeremiah describes Jerusalem's sorry plight, lamenting that "all that honored her despise her, because they have seen her nakedness … her filthiness was in her skirts" (Lam. 1:8–9). While Jerusalem is not called a harlot, as Nineveh was described by Nahum (Nahum 3:4), Jerusalem's infidelities are implied by the mention of her multiple lovers (Lam. 1:3, 19).

These similarities may obscure some important differences between Nahum's portrayal of Nineveh and Jeremiah's portrayal of Jerusalem. While Nahum briefly mentions Nineveh's sins, they are not the focal point of his message. Instead, he focuses on the upcoming punishment and destruction of Nineveh. In Lamentations, Jeremiah lists Jerusalem's sins at the beginning of the lament, as an attempt to justify the scale of the punishment ("Jerusalem has grievously sinned, therefore she is become as one unclean"; Lam. 1:8), but Jeremiah will actually go on to devote far greater attention and empathy to Jerusalem's suffering and her hopes for eventual redemption. Indeed, the verses show that even when Jerusalem admits to wrongdoing, she attempts to downplay her sins and instead hope that God's wrath and punishment will be directed elsewhere, toward more severe transgressors: "The Lord is righteous; for I have rebelled against His word" Jerusalem admits, but continues, "Hear, I pray you, all you peoples, and behold my pain …. Let all their wickedness come before You; and do unto them, as You have abused me for all my transgressions" (1:18, 22). Another most significant difference is that while Nineveh received no sympathy from Nahum, Jeremiah still refers to Jerusalem, sinful as she may be, as a daughter (1:6, 2:1, 2, 5, 8, 13).

Finally, Jeremiah poetically allows Jerusalem to plead its own case before the listeners, while Nineveh is never given a voice. This is because Nahum does not focus on Nineveh's sufferings to engender sympathy among his listeners, but to convince them of God's justice with regard to His severe punishment of Nineveh. Nahum's allusions to Nineveh's wickedness serve to justify the punishment that it has received. Unlike Jerusalem, Nineveh will not be rebuilt.

Even with the many differences, there are important moral lessons that could be learned by the people of Jerusalem from the echoes of Nahum's prophecy against Assyria in the words of Jeremiah's laments for Jerusalem. One can imagine the cheers of joy that would have arisen from Nahum's audience when he first uttered his prophecy of punishment and destruction against Assyria. It is easily understandable that the oppressed nation would rejoice upon finally hearing the tidings that they had waited centuries for – the tyrant would fall at last. Indeed, not to rejoice at the sign of salvation would seem to be a moral failing, reflecting ingratitude. However, there is a fine line between celebrating one's own redemption and finding pleasure in the suffering of others. Obadiah criticizes the nation of Edom for this. They are worthy of punishment because they "looked on the day of your brother on the day of his disaster... rejoiced about the children of Judah on the day of their destruction... spoken proudly on the day of their distress" (1:12). The shouts of joy and celebration with which Nahum's audience most probably reacted, however, may have obscured Nahum's essential message, i.e., that God is a God of justice, and anyone's sin will eventually be punished. A mere one generation later, Jeremiah berated the people of Judah for their failings. The many parallels between the book of Jeremiah and the earlier book of Nahum would have caused Jeremiah's audience to be more acutely sensitive to the irony of the fact that the very words and phrases with regard to which the people rejoiced only years earlier, now have become their laments and cries.

Additionally, Jeremiah's usage of Nahum has the effect of redeeming Nahum from a simplistic and mistaken reading that may have been prevalent among his listeners and is definitely prevalent today. Read alone, Nahum could have been understood as the vision of a chauvinistic and nationalist cheering of the deserving destruction of a hated enemy. We've noted several times that Nahum would draw upon some of the darkest prophecies against Israel in the prophetic reservoir and transform them into oracles against the hated Assyrians. The people at the time of Jeremiah might have mistakenly understood Nahum to be expressing that God is acting out of favoritism, i.e., God loves the Jewish people more than He does the Assyrians, so once the latter are punished, they will be also be destroyed and exiled, but that wouldn't necessarily be the case with God's chosen people. But once Jeremiah recycles Nahum's apparently triumphant exaltations at the devastation of Nineveh into laments to describe Jerusalem's downfall, any nationalistic elation that Jeremiah's audience may have felt quickly dissipates, and the truth becomes clear: God does not capriciously punish one nation over another because of prejudice. Instead, each country will stand or fall based on its own moral merits. What God loves is goodness; what God hates is evil. Good deeds bring reward and evil is followed by punishment, irrespective of one's birth or nationality. The one consolation for Israel is that God allows Israel to learn from its mistakes, and therefore, unlike Nineveh, Israel will be given the chance to repent and eventually return to its land.

Conclusion

Nahum's Message Today

There are several major themes in the book of Nahum that we have identified and explored in our study. First, we have demonstrated that the book is much more than a simple prediction about Nineveh's impending downfall and demise. Rather, the account of the impending destruction serves the greater purpose of being a vehicle for Nahum to address several major theological issues and provide his perspective. In chapter 1, Nahum began by describing the nature of God: His attributes, and how He interacts with the world. He began by saying that God is righteous and just (1:2–3). Therefore, though God is patient and slow to anger, iniquity cannot be ignored, and the time to judge the guilty will arrive. Divine anger, wrath, and vengeance also demonstrate God's justice. Those who oppress Israel will not be allowed to do so forever; they will eventually face their recompense. Nahum continued with a description of God's total mastery over nature, using allusions to earlier historical events, eventually stating his main point here, i.e., that just as God demonstrated control over nature in the past (see 1:4–8), so too God has total control over history, and now He would intervene on behalf of the Jewish people (see 1:9 until the end of the chapter), which is what justice demanded.

A second major theme in the book of Nahum is the idea that God controls the historical forces that run the world. Having demonstrated that God's sovereignty over nature is unquestioned, Nahum proceeds to show that God is sovereign over history as well. Nahum expresses this message by describing a very human battle between Nineveh and its invaders, and its aftermath. The identity of the invaders is not revealed, and this creates ambiguity for Nahum's audience and readers of Nahum as to whether the "scatterer" who led the forces against Nineveh was human or divine. Only at the end of the second chapter is the ambiguity resolved, when Nahum states that it is God who declares "I am against you!" In this manner, Nahum expresses that while it was the Babylonians, Scythians, and Medes who fought against Assyria, they were no more than puppets in God's hand. A reader of Nahum can see that he is reformulating a classic biblical lesson, which was taught by many other prophets in their bible to their respective audiences. The lesson was best formulated by Isaiah almost a century before Nahum spoke. Regarding the rise of the Assyrians, Isaiah declared in God's name that they are "the staff of My anger" (Is. 10:5). This is the traditional prophetic approach to understanding history, and the one that Nahum wished to teach as well: when we step back from the commotion and chaos of human politics and interactions, we can discern God's guiding hand, and we should know that in the end, evil will be punished and good rewarded. One of the writers of Psalms exclaims that this is God's greatness: dramatic events occur, yet "Your footsteps remain hidden."

And yet, discomfort remains. Nahum does not merely predict Nineveh's doom; he revels in it. Throughout the book, his tone is satirical, mocking, and seemingly indifferent to the fate of Nineveh's population as they face the same cruel fate they inflicted on so many others.

Several ideas have been proposed to help modern readers navigate these issues and understand why God would have allowed such a cruel punishment and how Nahum could have appeared so heartless. One approach suggests that Nahum, like other prophets, is not expressing his own personal viewpoint but is conveying a higher, more heavenly truth. Israel's shame is also a desecration of the divine name (see Ezek. 36:19–23); therefore, the humiliating removal of a people who had degraded and exiled Israel was appropriate. Gleason Archer remarks:

> Identifying himself completely with God's cause, [Nahum] could only regard God's enemies as his own, and implore God to uphold His own honor and justify His own righteousness by inflicting a crushing destruction upon those who either in theory or in practice denied His sovereignty and His law.[1]

A second approach, prevalent in current scholarship, is to provide the historical context of Nahum's words. As noted in the section discussing the history of the Assyrian Empire, it is difficult to fault Nahum for demonizing them as brutal and vicious, as these were attributes that the Assyrians proudly boasted about, with each king trying to outdo his predecessor as the cruelest and most ruthless leader to ever have sat on Nineveh's throne. Therefore, Bible scholar Peter Craigie writes sympathetically about Nahum that "in order to understand its force and power, one must first attempt to enter Nahum's world ... Assyria claims a place of preeminence among evil nations ... it embarked upon a path of imperial expansion which knew no limitations of human decency and kindness."[2] Several modern scholars share this sympathetic view, and portray Nahum as the biblical prototype for resistance literature against tyranny.[3]

These approaches, however, simply shift the frame of the question. If Nahum is representing God's perspective or reflecting Nineveh's values, the glaring discomfort with the extreme nature of Nineveh's punishment as well as with Nahum's aggressive and unsympathetic tone and words still remains. Therefore, this commentary wishes to propose a third approach, one which assumes that Nahum must be more than the prophet who was offended, either for his people's sake or on his God's behalf. To portray him as such is to reduce him to a nationalist or theological cheerleader, whereas this commentary wishes to advance the belief that Nahum's theology is actually much deeper. Looking through the Bible, one can see that the dominant pattern in stories of large-scale wrongdoings and subsequent punishment is as

---

1. Quoted in Patterson, 21.
2. Quoted in O'Brien, *Nahum*, 112.
3. Ibid.

such: God will right wrongs and perform justice, but with few exceptions (Sodom and Gomorrah, the Great Flood, the plagues in Egypt), God exercises His sovereignty through the lens and limitations of the natural world. In the case of Nineveh, this is the case, and as such, it is in line with human nature both that Nineveh's destroyers were violent and oppressive, and that their rapine behavior toward the city would in turn lead to their own eventual downfall. This pattern is common in biblical history and theology. Evil can serve a purpose within the divine plan; wicked nations can be instruments of God's punishment. Isaiah describes how the king of Assyria was considered God's instrument of punishment against Judah: "The Lord will cause to come upon you and your people and your ancestral house such days as never have come since Ephraim turned away from Judah – that selfsame king of Assyria" (Is. 7:17). Though Assyria credited its feats to its own abilities, stating that "By the might of my hand have I wrought it, by my skill, for I am clever" (10:13), Isaiah understood that Assyria was merely God's instrument: "Does an ax boast over him who hews with it, or [does] a saw magnify itself above him who wields it? As though the rod raised him who lifts it, as though the staff lifted the man!" (10:15). And yet, Isaiah, as well as another prophet, Amos (see Amos 3:11, 6:4), do not question why God chooses to use such a cruel nation to carry out His judgment.[4] Once God chooses to work through people, to whom He ascribes a large measure of free will, the instruments He uses are necessarily flawed. God's goodness and the fallibility of humans do not contradict each other.[5]

---

4. On the other hand, it is fascinating to note that only a couple of decades after Nahum, Habakkuk will question and decry God's use of the wicked Babylonians to punish Judah: "Why do you look on the treacherous, and are silent when the wicked swallow those more righteous than they?" (Hab. 1:13). This idea will be discussed further in the section on Habakkuk.
5. This understanding is best articulated in Rabbi Eliezer Berkovits's *Faith after the Holocaust* (Jerusalem: Maggid Books, 2019). Rabbi Berkovits argues that concealment is not only one of God's essential qualities, it is a necessity for humanity to function – and that human freedom is the whole purpose of Creation:

    The hiding God is present; though man is unaware of Him, He is present in His hiddenness. Therefore, God can only hide in this world. But if this world were altogether and radically profane, there would be no place in it for Him to hide. He can only hide in history. Since history is man's responsibility, one would,

Examples from contemporary history demonstrate the difficulty, if not impossibility, of locating moral perfection in even the most worthy causes. The Allies that fought against Nazi Germany in World War II undoubtedly committed terrible atrocities in war, yet to suggest that it would have been better for them not to fight at all because of these abuses borders on callousness, if not immorality. In Nahum we see that God made the decision that Assyria's sins and transgressions spanning over fifteen centuries of brutality necessitated its total destruction, even though that decision included the possibility that it would be carried out by a very flawed people.[6] Nahum knows that God will work in ways that he cannot understand, and he does not question God regarding Nineveh's horrific downfall. Instead, Nahum focuses on proclaiming God's righteousness and justice at a time when his despondent listeners refuse to believe that salvation from Assyria is even possible. When Nahum lived and prophesied, the answer to the Israelites' questioning whether God could or would punish the wicked was uncertain. As Elizabeth Achtemeier wrote, "[The book of Nahum] is not primarily a book about human beings, not about human vengeance and hatred and military conquest, but a book about God. And it has been our failure to let Nahum be a book about God that has distorted the value of this prophecy...."[7] Therefore, Nahum had to rejoice at Nineveh's downfall – not because of the suffering it entailed but because only through it could God prove

in fact, expect Him to hide, to be silent, while man goes about his God-given task. Responsibility requires freedom, but God's convincing presence would undermine the freedom of human decision. God hides in human responsibility and human freedom.... God can be neither good nor bad. In terms of His own nature, He is incapable of evil. He is the only one who *is* goodness. But since, because of His very essence, He can do no evil, He can do no good either.... Goodness for Him is neither an ideal nor a value; it is existence, it is absolutely realized being. Justice, love, peace, mercy are ideals for man only. They are values that may be realized by man alone. God is perfection. Yet because of this very perfection, He is lacking – as it were – one type of value; the one which is the result of striving for value.... Man alone can strive and struggle for the good; God is Good. Man alone can create value; God is Value. (pp. 63, 108)

6. Habakkuk, in turn, will indeed struggle to understand this aspect of God's ways.
7. Quoted in Julia O'Brien, *Challenging Prophetic Metaphor* (Louisville: Westminster Press, 2008), 115.

His faithfulness to Israel and His justice to the world. We conclude with Heschel, who articulates this idea beautifully in his book *The Prophets*:

> The ultimate meaning in history lies in the continuity of God's concern. His wrath is not regarded as an emotional outburst, as an irrational fit, but rather as part of His continued care. Because the prophets could not remain calm in the face of crimes committed by men and disaster falling on men, they had to remember and remind others: God's heart is not made of stone.[8]

8. Heschel, *The Prophets: Volume 2*, 193.

Habakkuk

Introduction

When the talmudic Sage R. Nahman bar Yitzḥak wished to bring a supporting biblical verse for his opinion about which biblical verse best shows that Judaism could be reduced to one principle, he turned to the eighth book of *Trei Asar*, Habakkuk.[1] Declaring that "the righteous will live by his faith," Habakkuk's statement provided Judaism's response to that ever-present question: Why do good people suffer and wicked people flourish? The relevance of Habakkuk's message and his spiritual struggles are timeless. Hints of the book's early popularity are evident in *Pesher Habakkuk*,[2] a commentary on Habakkuk dated to the latter half of the first century BCE, discovered among the Dead Sea Scrolls. The commentary is written in the *pesher* style, i.e., verses from the text[3] followed by the author's attempts to apply the material to the events of his time. In the modern era, Rav Aharon Lichtenstein *zt"l* would regularly praise Habakkuk for its importance and relevance.[4]

1. Makkot 24a.
2. The commentary was labeled 1QpHab, which stands for Cave 1, Qumran, *pesher*, Habakkuk.
3. The *Pesher* commentary that was found is on the first two chapters of the book only.
4. Heard in an unpublished lecture on the importance of learning Tanakh, delivered at Yeshivat Har Etzion, February 6, 2003.

Pesher Habakkuk from the Dead Sea Scrolls

Nahum indirectly addressed the question of why the righteous suffer and the wicked flourish. By describing the approaching downfall and destruction of the Assyrian Empire, Nahum expressed confidence in the ultimate triumph of good over evil. Habakkuk is much more skeptical. He sees that one evil's demise is merely replaced by an even greater evil. Seasons turn, injustice continues to reign, and God apparently remains silent. Habakkuk does not accept facile answers; rather, he turns directly to argue with God. The reader is invited to follow the dialogue between Habakkuk and God: Habakkuk's questions and spiritual yearnings followed by God's responses, and finally Habakkuk's dawning comprehension and acceptance of the divine message.[5]

Who was Habakkuk? The first verse identifies Habakkuk only as a prophet and provides no additional information. Since there is very little information about the identity of Habakkuk in the book of Habakkuk,

5. The different approaches of Nahum and Habakkuk can be seen in the structures of their books. Nahum begins with a theophany, in which he confidently describes God's attributes and His involvement in the world, and this serves as his basis when he goes on to chronicle the course of the downfall of the Assyrian Empire. Habakkuk takes the opposite approach. He first decries the apparently arbitrary nature of historical events, and only through his conversation with God is he slowly able to come to a point where he can confidently sing a psalm of praise to God in which he recognizes and even praises God's involvement in historical events.

commentaries and historians examined the meanings of his name and looked elsewhere in the Bible as well as in variant manuscripts of the book to try to gather more information about this prophet. The Hebrew root of his name, H-B-K, means to embrace. Possibly based on this, one early rabbinic tradition suggests that Habakkuk was the son of the Shunammite woman whom the prophet Elisha revived, as Elisha promised her that "about this time next year you will embrace a son" (II Kings 4:16).[6] Given the vast chronological gap between the time of that event and the time of Habakkuk's prophecy, this midrash is best understood thematically and not as a literal identification.

The Latin commentary Jerome interpreted his name differently. In the same vein as the first interpretation, Jerome draws on the physical nature of the meaning of the root H-B-K, i.e., embrace, but uses the word in the sense of a physical struggle and suggests that Habakkuk means "wrestler," explaining that his name is an appropriate one for him "because he wrestled with God" (*quia certamen ingreditur cum Deo*; prologue to Hab.). A third suggestion with regard to the question of Habakkuk's identity focuses not on the meaning of his name, but on one of his attributes, proposing that Habakkuk is Isaiah's student, the "watchman" mentioned in Isaiah 21:6, as Habakkuk describes himself as a "watchman" waiting for the divine response (2:1). This connection is literary and almost certainly not a historical identification, as there is a chronological gap of almost a century between the two figures.[7]

The Septuagint identifies Habakkuk as the person who fed Daniel in the lion's den[8] but this is highly unlikely, as it would place Habakkuk

6. Zohar, introduction 7b, quoted by Shimon Bakon in "Habakkuk: From Perplexity to Faith," *Jewish Quarterly* 39, no. 1 (January 2011): 25–30.
7. However, there are a series of parallels between Isaiah's prophecies and Habakkuk's, which may suggest that Habakkuk can be considered as a successor to Isaiah's prophetic tradition. We shall examine the most prominent of these parallels in the beginning of our discussion of chapter 2.
8. The Greek version of the book of Daniel contains three lengthy additions that are rejected by Judaism but accepted by various Christian denominations as part of the canon: The Prayer of Azaria and the Song of the Three Children (attached to Dan. 3), the story of Susanna (ch. 13 in the LXX text of Daniel), and the account of Bel and the Dragon (ch. 14 in the LXX text of Daniel). In the account of Bel and the Dragon, Daniel outwits the priests of the Babylonian idol Bel and defeats a dragon worshipped by the populace. As a punishment for his insolence, he is thrown into a lion's den for

as having lived a century after the dating of his prophecy.[9] Many scholars suggest that Habakkuk was a Levite who served in the Temple, as he is identified as one both in the superscription to the Septuagint version of the book of Habakkuk as well as in variant manuscripts of the book found in the Dead Sea Scrolls. Habakkuk's prayer in the book's concluding chapter is reminiscent of the style of Psalms and lends credence to this suggestion, as some psalms are believed to have been composed by Levites, who were traditionally responsible for the musical proceedings in the Temple.[10]

Habakkuk does not date when his prophecy occurs. Based on the text, we can ascertain that the prophecy was uttered at a time when the Babylonians, also known as the Chaldeans, were replacing (or about to replace) the Assyrians as the world's superpower (1:5–11), which would place the prophecy after 630 BCE. If the wickedness that caused corruption and social injustice was caused by the rule of the king of Judah, then the period when Josiah reigned must be ruled out, as he was a righteous king. Therefore, the most likely date for Habakkuk's prophecy is Jehoiakim's reign. Jeremiah specifically censures Jehoiakim for abusing his power (see Jer. 22), and specifically threatens him with a Babylonian invasion (see Jer. 25). Scholars point to other possible dates, including the reign of Manasseh or Josiah's younger years, before he undertook to reform the country politically and spiritually. These were not only years of moral debauchery and social injustice, but also ones that saw the first signs of the weakening and dissolution of the Neo-Assyrian Empire.

---

seven days but is miraculously saved and even fed by an angel, who brings Habakkuk from Judah bearing stew and bread for Daniel to eat.

9. For discussions of the additions to the book of Daniel in the Septuagint, see A. C. Myers, *The Eerdmans Bible Dictionary* (Grand Rapids: Eerdmans, 1987), 448–49, and Bruce M. Metzger, ed., *The Oxford Annotated Apocrypha*, expanded ed. (New York: Oxford, 1977), 209–18.

10. Ralph L. Smith in *Micah–Malachi, WBC* (Waco: Word Press, 1984), 93, explains this logic: "One manuscript of Bel and the Dragon says that Habakkuk was the son of Jesus of the tribe of Levi. This later tradition that Habakkuk was of the tribe of Levi, along with the fact that he is one of only three men in the OT to be called a prophet in the superscription of his book, and the fact that he is presented as a prophet in the musical chapter (3:1) of his book, suggests that he may have been a Levite and a professional or temple prophet."

By this time, visions of future Babylonian domination would not have been so far removed from reality that Habakkuk's listeners would have scoffed in disbelief.[11]

Rabbinic tradition places Habakkuk several decades earlier, during the reign of Manasseh (*Seder Olam*, ch. 20). This is a very plausible assumption, as two prophets who spoke during the reign of Manasseh's successor Josiah, Jeremiah and Zephaniah, quote from Habakkuk (cf. Hab. 1:8 with Jer. 4:13, 5:6; Hab. 2:10 with Jer. 51:58; Hab. 2:12 with Jer. 22:13–17; and Hab. 2:20 with Zeph. 1:7). Apparently, they were familiar with Habakkuk's prophecies already and adapted them to fit their messages and audiences. If Habakkuk did indeed speak these prophecies during the reign of Manasseh, it was likely uttered when King Ashurbanipal of Assyria was engaging in campaigns to subdue the rebellious Babylonian provinces between 652 and 648 BCE, the same time when King Manasseh was imprisoned in Babylonia by the Assyrians for his alleged disloyalty.

While Nahum remains the prophet-poet par excellence, Habakkuk doesn't lack for imagery or poetic devices. However, Habakkuk presents his prophecy differently. He invites the listener to eavesdrop on his conversation with God as he wrestles with issues of divine justice, an approach which leads to his prophetic style being much closer to prose-like narrative. But there are also poetic elements to his writing: His prophecy utilizes proverbs (see 1:9, 2:6), allegory (see 2:15–16), simile and metaphors (see 1:8, 9, 11, 14–17, 2:5, 7, 8, 15, 16, 3:4, 8–10, 11, 14, 19), rhetorical questions (see 1:12, 2:13, 18, 3:8), alliteration and assonance (see 1:6, 10, 2:6, 7, 15, 18, 3:2), as well as many forms of parallelisms (1:2, 2:4, 2:12, 3:17–18).[12]

---

11. There is a trend among some recent scholars to emend the word *Kasdim* (Chaldeans) to *Kittîm* (Cypriots). With this, they argue that Habakkuk is referring in 1:6 to the Macedonians under Alexander the Great, and therefore date the book to this much later period. This drastic emendation is both unnecessary and unconvincing; indeed; scholars since the time of Albright have noted that the Hebrew in Habakkuk contains many aspects of the older Biblical Hebrew. See W. F. Albright, "The Psalm of Habakkuk," in *Studies in Old Testament Prophecy Dedicated to T. H. Robinson*, ed. H. H. Rowley (Edinburgh: T. and T. Clark, 1950), 10.
12. For a fuller discussion of Habakkuk's capabilities as a poet, see Robert D. Haak, "'Poetry' in Habakkuk 1:1–2:4," *Journal of the American Oriental Society* 108, no. 3 (July–September, 1988): 437–44.

The structure of Habakkuk's prophecy is easy to ascertain, and it reflects the book's fundamental theme. Each of the three chapters indicates a different encounter between Habakkuk and God. Each dialogue opens with the prophet's lament (and implied petition), and follows with God's response to Habakkuk's plea. Habakkuk then responds to God's answer – differently in each chapter. While in the first chapter, God's detailed response spurs only more questions from Habakkuk, in the second chapter, Habakkuk is able to internalize God's short response so thoroughly that the bulk of the rest of the chapter has Habakkuk moving on to describe the travails that will befall various sinners and transgressors. Both sections begin with a question (1:2, 1:12), and each of the answers begins with an imperative (1:5, 2:2). The third chapter is obviously distinct from the first two chapters. Instead of dialogue, questions, and answers, there is prayer and praise. Habakkuk recalls God's interventions throughout history on behalf of His people, beginning with taking them out of Egypt, leading them through the wilderness, and bringing them to the Promised Land (3:3–15). This praise forms a fitting conclusion to what came before.

1. Two Dialogues between Habakkuk And God
   - A. 1:2–4: Habakkuk Laments Social Injustice
   - A1. 1:5–11: God's Answer about Judah's Upcoming Punishment through Babylonia
     Habakkuk begins by protesting God's apparent inaction in the face of rampant injustice and violence: because God ignores what is occurring, the wicked thrive at the expense of the righteous. God responds by announcing the surprising strengthening of the Babylonians, describes their newfound strength, and how the subsequent invasion will rectify matters by exacting punishment.
   - B. 1:12–17: Habakkuk's Second Question about Babylonia and Injustice
   - B1. Ch. 2: God's answer about Babylonia
     1. 2:1–3: Introduction to the Answer
     2. 2:4–5: The Lord's Indictment of Babylon

Habakkuk protests that God's use of the Babylonians is an even greater injustice than the evil that they are coming to punish. He continues by describing the overwhelming domination that the Babylonians will enjoy, and announces that he will wait for God to respond. God answers by announcing a future judgment on the Babylonians for their own unrighteous acts. Until that happens, God urges patience and trust.

3. 2:6–20: God Sentences Evildoers (Babylon)

This latter portion takes up the remainder of the chapter. It consists of a series of taunts against various groups of evildoers, including the arrogant of spirit, those who build their houses and cities with injustice, and those who abuse their neighbors. Consistently, Habakkuk reminds the listeners that he is speaking about the Babylonians. These taunts are presented in the form of a series of woes, each containing characteristic features of woe oracles, including invectives, criticism, and threats.

2. Habakkuk's Prayer

C. 3:1: Introduction to the Hymn

D. 3:2–15: Vision of God in History

E. 3:16–19a: Habakkuk Reacts to the Vision

F. 3:19b: Concluding Musical Notation

The third chapter of Habakkuk is a prayer of thanks that has the form of a psalm. He describes God's greatness as it was manifested from the earliest times in Jewish history, at times such as the Exodus from Egypt, the giving of the Torah, and the protection Israel received in the wilderness. At the conclusion of the prayer, Habakkuk describes how reflecting on these occurrences helps him strengthen his faith.

1:1

Superscription

The oracle that Habakkuk the prophet did see. (1:1)

As in Nahum, Habakkuk's introductory verse gives us no information about the prophet's family lineage, background, or time of the prophecy; if we are to identify these, we will have to deduce them from the context. What the superscription tells us is the nature of Habakkuk's message. It is a *massa* – which means "oracle" but can also mean "burden." As noted in the introduction to Nahum, the word *massa* connotes a demarcation between two groups of people, those whom God destroys and those whom God saves. This division can be between the Jewish people and the nations of the world, or within the Jewish people themselves. Often, a foreign nation is identified, the one that is the target of the prophecy and that will receive the brunt of the predicted calamities. Here, however, the use of the word *massa* sets up a misleading expectation for the reader. We expect to hear about good and evil, and how God will save the righteous and punish the wicked. As Habakkuk quickly discovers, God has other plans.[1]

1. Some wish to suggest that the Hebrew root Ḥ-Z-H refers to another version of prophecy, known as a *ḥazon* (literally, "vision"). While some suggest that this means

But where does Habakkuk's actual prophecy begin? Does it begin immediately with verse 2, when Habakkuk complains to God about the apparent triumph of injustice and corruption? Ibn Ezra maintains that the first several verses are not prophecy, suggesting that in these verses Habakkuk is simply delivering the complaints of the people to God about the treatment that they've suffered. According to this explanation, his prophecy only begins with God's response in verse 5. But we will read the book differently, and propose that the prophecy does indeed begin with verse 2, as we see religious value and validity both in Habakkuk's complaints as well as in God's response. Only read together as part and parcel of a unified message does the book convey its full theological impact.

---

that the ultimate prophecy will not occur until the distant future, which is consistent with the ultimate message of this book, this isn't true for other appearances of the word (see Is. 1:1).

1:2–1:11

The First Dialogue between Habakkuk and God

Habakkuk plunges immediately into his central complaint: the apparent triumph of evil in the world, and the resulting effect that it has on the good and righteous. His direct and unforgiving questioning of God's ways is the premise for the entire book.

> How long shall I cry, God, and You will not listen? I cry out unto You of violence, and You will not save. Why do You show me iniquity and look upon immorality; and plunder and violence are before me; and the one who bears quarrel and strife endures. Therefore Torah has become impotent, and justice does not go out forever, for wicked surround the righteous; therefore, justice emerges perverted. (1:2–4)

His complaint, which goes on for these three verses, begins with two questions – for how long, and why. As noted above, some do not view these three verses as being part of the actual prophecy; but we shall adopt the approach that they are.

In verse 4, the culmination of his complaint, Habakkuk decries the success of the "wicked," but to whom is he actually referring? The answer to this question will not only help us understand his complaint, but also provides a valuable clue as to the dating of his prophecy. Three possibilities present themselves. One suggestion is that they are the Jewish kings of this period, whose corrupt rule over the people led to untold suffering and resignation. As such, dating Habakkuk's prophecy to either Manasseh's reign (696–641 BCE) or to Jehoiakim's reign (608–597 BCE) makes sense, but it would not make sense to date the prophecy to the reign of Josiah (639–608 BCE), who is described as one of Judah's great kings (II Kings 23:25). The divine response that the Babylonians are serving as the instrument of God in order to deliver divine punishment (vv. 5–11) means that God is using outsiders to punish his people on account of their evil rulers. If so, Habakkuk is echoing Isaiah's message to Judah a century before, that the Assyrian invaders of that time were in fact *shevet appi* – the rod of God's wrath. (Is. 10:5).

The second approach suggests that the "wicked" mentioned at the beginning of the prophecy are foreigners, and refers to Judah's Assyrian overloads. For centuries, their empire seemed invincible, but it would disappear at the hands of the Babylonians within decades, a shockingly speedy time frame by the standards of ancient history. This approach would also date the prophecy to Manasseh's reign, as we know that the next significant king, Josiah,[1] began the process of removing Assyrian sovereignty from both Judean and Israeli territories (II Kings 23:15–20), so by that point, Habakkuk would not be referring to the Assyrian overlords as the main enemy.

The third and final approach also posits that the "wicked" are foreigners. However, it proposes that Habakkuk is complaining not about any existing injustice, but rather about the injustice in the vision of the future that he has to deliver. As such, the entire book deals with one question only: Why will the wicked Babylonians succeed? Rashi[2] is the

1. The king Amon, Josiah's father, reigned between Manasseh and Josiah for a very short time.
2. Rashi (commentary on 1:2) says: He [Habakkuk] foresaw with *ruaḥ hakodesh* that in the future Nebuchadnezzar would rule the world and [in doing so] cause trouble for Israel, as the matter is stated in his prophecy (1:6): "For behold, I raise up the Chaldeans, etc." He was complaining about this.

first one to suggest this understanding, and it is based primarily on the beginning of verse 3, "Why do You show me iniquity," positing that the word "show" is referring to the visions of the future, when Babylonia would oppress Judah. Further support for this explanation can be found in verse 13, where Habakkuk contrasts the successes of the wicked Babylonians with the impending doom of the (relatively) righteous people of Judah. The first two approaches, which claim that Habakkuk is complaining about existing injustices, understand the word "show" in verse 3 to be referring to Habakkuk's reaction to seeing to the violence that surrounds him. Our commentary follows a talmudic understanding of 1:13, which will be explained in full later, which claims that the evildoers mentioned in Habakkuk's complaint in 1:2–4 and the Babylonians mentioned later in 1:13 are not referring to the same group of people.

Habakkuk has three complaints, each building upon the last. First, God has not answered him, despite the fact that Habakkuk has been crying for help: "How long (*ad ana*) shall I cry (*shivati*) and You will not listen." The word *shivati* denotes a cry for help that expects a response (see Job 19:2, 24:12, Ps. 18:6, 119:147, Is. 58:9, Jonah 2:2, Lam 3:8). Literarily, Habakkuk alludes to this expectation of response by cleverly employing consonance (the repetition of consonants or of a consonant pattern) to frame verse 2: *shivati* (I cry out) and *toshia* (You will save). Habakkuk's expectation of a response from God is emphasized by his opening question: How long (*ad ana*)? In the Bible, the words "how long" (*ad ana*) appear in several places where God, or God's prophet, laments the Jewish people's failure to listen to and trust in God (see Ex. 16:28, Num. 14:11, and Josh. 18:3). Habakkuk turns the question around, dramatically turning the tables to God, and asks, Why aren't You behaving in a manner consistent with Your promises that good will be rewarded?

But the reason for Habakkuk's anger is not limited to the apparent never-ending successes of the wicked. He is disturbed by something far greater. Beyond asking how long the wicked will prevail, Habakkuk asks a second, more important question: Why? Decrying the situation around him, he employs four separate words to describe the corruption: iniquity (*aven*), oppression (*amal*), destruction (*shod*), and violence (*ḥamas*). The word "violence" (*ḥamas*) is used frequently in Habakkuk – six times in the course of one short book: 1:2, 3, 9, 2:8, and twice in 2:17, and means more than just physical brutality. *Ḥamas* describes the abuse of the weak by the powerful, who act without fear or restraint. Jeremiah uses this word when bemoaning the rampant violence in his time (Jer. 6:7, 20:8), and the sentiment is echoed by Ezekiel (Ezek. 45:9), while Zephaniah uses the word to describe how the corruption of the religious leadership in his day caused violence to the Torah itself (Zeph. 3:4). More ominously, the word *ḥamas* is reminiscent of its first appearance in Tanakh, in Genesis 6:11: *Vatimalei haaretz ḥamas,* "And the earth was filled with violence." There it is used to describe the state of the earth right before God destroyed it with the Flood. From this original appearance in Genesis, we learn that when *ḥamas* is left unchecked, and theft and murder go unpunished, God moves quickly to punish the entire nation, not just the guilty. The Torah warns against the failure to stem wickedness and bloodshed, saying that the land itself will simply not tolerate it: "So you shall not pollute the land in which you are; for blood pollutes the land and no expiation can be made for the land for the blood that is shed on it, except by the blood of him who shed it. And you shall not defile the land in which you live, in the midst of which I dwell; for I the Lord am dwelling in the midst of the sons of Israel" (Num. 35:33–34). Later in the Bible, the prophets who lived at the time leading up to the destruction of the Northern Kingdom decry the *ḥamas* they see around them (see Jer. 6:7, Ezek. 7:23, and 8:17). Yet now, Habakkuk laments, in the face of rampant *ḥamas* God is silent. Why?

Habakkuk concludes his laments by focusing on the consequences of God's failure to respond (the words *al ken,* used twice in verse 4, mean "therefore" or "because of this." The accusation is a powerful one: he claims that God's nonintervention is itself a form of injustice. As evil gains strength, the Torah becomes impotent, justice does not prevail, and the wicked surround the righteous. Also, as wickedness prospers, people's understanding of justice is perverted (see *Metzudat David,* commentary on 1:4). Habakkuk describes the Torah as impotent using the Hebrew word *fug,* which generally means "grow numb." The same word is used to describe Jacob's stunned reaction to the news that his son Joseph still lived (Gen. 45:26), and to describe the feeling of the psalmist's hands stretched out to God in untiring supplication (Ps. 77:3, Lam. 2:18, 3:49). Using it here together with the word Torah, Habakkuk is saying that God's word is seen as ineffective, unable to counter the corruption that surrounds it. The effect that God's passivity has on justice (*mishpat*) is no less severe – Habakkuk mentions it twice in the verse. At first, justice cannot proceed; when it finally does, it is a crooked and twisted shadow of itself. The state of justice is a key consideration in Habakkuk's prophecy, and together with righteousness it becomes the literary hook to the next section when God will respond to Habakkuk's challenge (vv. 5–11).

In verses 5–11, God replies to Habakkuk's complaint, saying that not only will He do something, but that the process of punishing the evildoers is actually already very much underway:

> Look among the nations, and behold, and wonder marvelously; for, behold, a work shall be wrought in your days, which you will not believe though it be told you. For, lo, I raise up the Chaldeans, that bitter and impetuous nation, that march through the breadth of the earth, to possess dwelling-places that are not theirs. They are terrible and dreadful; their law and their majesty proceed from themselves. Their horses also are swifter than leopards, and are fiercer than the wolves of the desert; and their horsemen spread themselves; yea, their horsemen come from far, they fly as a vulture that hastens to devour. They come all of them for violence; their faces are set eagerly as the east wind; and they gather captives as the sand. And they scoff at kings, and princes are a laughingstock to them; they deride every stronghold, for they heap up earth, and take it. Then their spirit does pass over and transgress, and they become guilty: even they who impute their might unto their god.

God does not speak to his prophet directly; instead, He directs His message at His people, speaking in the second-person plural. God warns the people that they will be astonished, for He is sending the Chaldeans, i.e., the Babylonians, to chastise Judah (vv. 5–6), and spends five verses describing the ferociousness of the Babylonian army (vv. 7–11): They are not just militarily powerful, but also greedy, wicked, and recognize no god but themselves. Special attention is given to their horses, the measure of military might at that time. Just as God used Assyria a century before to punish the wicked, God is saying that He will now use an even crueler nation to punish the wrongdoers.[3] When the Chaldeans invade, no differentiation will be made between the good and the bad; instead, all will suffer the wrath of their swords. God's answer is unsatisfying. Habakkuk complained about the violence that surrounded him – and God's response is to bring even more violence.

The first verse of God's answer stresses an element of surprise, i.e., that the Kingdom of Judah will be in some way surprised, or astonished. What is the surprise? According to the simple understanding of the verse, the surprise is that the Babylonians, so long trodden upon by the Assyrians, would not only liberate themselves from Assyrian rule, but overthrow and replace their masters. The rabbinic dating of Habakkuk to the time period of Manasseh's reign supports this interpretation. However, the real surprise is probably not the announcement that the Babylonians will achieve both their freedom and, ultimately, world dominion, but rather the fact that it is the Babylonians who were chosen by God to serve as His instrument of justice.

Though God does not directly respond to the theological questions in Habakkuk's challenge, God throws Habakkuk's own words back at him throughout His response. Was Judah guilty of committing violence (vv. 2, 3)? Then Judah too shall in turn suffer violence at the hands of a violent nation (v. 9). Habakkuk asked why justice (*mishpat*) could not proceed (*yetze*) (v. 4); God describes how the Babylonian army's "law (*mishpat*) and their majesty proceed (*yetze*) from themselves" (v. 7). Habakkuk questioned: "Why do You show me (*tareini*, root R-A-H) iniquity and look upon (*tabbit*, root H-B-T) immorality?" (v. 3). Accordingly, God's response begins with the words "Look (*re'u*) among the

3. So said Amos to the corrupt Northern Kingdom: "For, behold I will raise up against you a nation, O House of Israel, says the Lord God of hosts, and they shall oppress you from the approach to Hamath until the brook of the Arabah" (6:14). See similar usages in I Kings 11:14, 23 with regard to the adversaries that God raises up against Solomon, and in Is. 5:26, 9:10, and 10:5, when Isaiah announces that the Assyrians are to be "raised up" to punish the wicked of Judah.

nations, and behold (*vehabbitu*)" (v. 5). The repetition is more than a simple literary hook that connects the first question-and-answer pair. It demonstrates that though at first glance God's answer to Habakkuk appears to sidestep the prophet's questions entirely, and in fact, even strengthen them, in truth, God has heard His prophet.

Important to God's answer is the nature of the metaphors used to describe the Babylonian invaders. Habakkuk is trying to understand how God functions in human society, and what the effects of evil reign are on order and justice. As seen above, God responds to Habakkuk by describing the Babylonian army. But who are they? The rapidly advancing forces are likened to swift leopards and fearsome wolves, to vultures that swoop down upon their helpless prey, and to the windstorm that shifts vast stores of sand as it sweeps through the dunes, leaving havoc behind. The shift to animal imagery, reminiscent of an animal kingdom where the law of the jungle applies and survival of the fittest rules, and then to imagery describing the capricious nature of the desert winds, only heightens the chasm between Habakkuk's search for order and the seemingly arbitrary nature of God's response. God has answered, but the dialogue has just begun.

1:12–2:4

The Second Dialogue between Habakkuk and God

> Are You not from everlasting, O Lord my God, my Holy One? We shall not die. O Lord, You have ordained them for judgment, and You, O Rock, have established them for correction. You that are of eyes too pure to behold evil, and that cannot look on immorality, how can You watch treachery and be silent, as the wicked swallow up those more righteous than he? And makes men as the fish of the sea, as the creeping things, that have no ruler over them? They take up all of them with the angle, they catch them in their net, and gather them in their drag; therefore they rejoice and exult. Therefore they sacrifice unto their net, and offer unto their drag; because by them their portion is fat, and their food plenteous. Shall they therefore empty their net, and not spare to slay the nations continually? (1:12–17)

God's answer to how He would bring judgment against the wicked only intensifies Habakkuk's question. Habakkuk cannot reconcile himself to God's usage of the Chaldeans, a people more corrupt than Judah itself was, to punish His people. The prophet begins the second dialogue, as he did the first dialogue, with a rhetorical question. He makes six statements that in isolation would be considered standard declarations of faith, but here they are uttered only to be called into question:[1]

1. Are You not from everlasting, O Lord my God,
2. My Holy One? We shall not die.[2]
3. O Lord, You have ordained them [the Babylonians] for judgment,
4. and You, O Rock, have established them for correction.
5. You that are of eyes too pure to behold evil,
6. and that cannot look on immorality,

Only once Habakkuk has established these basic affirmations does he complain, calling all of them into question:

---

1. The middle two statements, that God set up the Babylonians to be His instrument of justice (specifically, to punish the Assyrians), are consistent with earlier teachings, as we have seen from Is. 10:5.
2. According to tradition, this text is one of the eighteen *Tikkunei Soferim* (though there are approximately thirty instances of *Tikkunei Soferim* in rabbinic literature), places where the scribes (traditionally understood to be the *Anshei Knesset HaGedola*) emended, fixed, or corrected the text, on the grounds that the original text was either unbecoming or possibly blasphemous. There is support for such emendation in the Talmud: "R. Ḥiyya bar Abba said in the name of R. Yoḥanan: 'It is better that one letter be removed from the Torah than that the divine name be publicly profaned'" (Yevamot 79a). Though some commentaries (Ibn Ezra, Rashba, and others) suggest that *Tikkunei Soferim* are not actual changes in the text, but rather places where the original author acted like one who corrects a text to protect God's honor, most are of the opinion that in fact the texts were actually emended. In our case, the original text was considered to be "You [God] cannot die," and the problem is that the mere suggestion that God could even be considered a mortal being capable of dying is too objectionable. Further reading on the subject of *Tikkunei Soferim* can be found in M. Zipor, *Tradition and Transmission: Studies in Ancient Biblical Translation and Interpretation* [Hebrew] (Tel Aviv: 2001), 79–165 (with an excellent summary available online at http://www.biu.ac.il/JH/Parasha/eng/behaalot/tzip.html); W. Emery Barnes, "Ancient Corrections in the Text of the Old Testament (*Tikkun Sopherim*)," *Journal of Theological Studies* 1 (1900): 387–414, also available online at http://www.archive.org/stream/journaltheologio2unkngoog#page/n404/mode/2up; and Avrohom Lieberman's "Tikkunei Soferim, an Analysis of a Masoretic Phenomenon," in *Hakirah: The Flatbush Journal of Jewish Law and Thought* 5, 227–36, also available online at http://hakirah.org/Vol%205%20Lieberman.pdf.

> How can You watch treachery and be silent, as the wicked swallow up those more righteous than he? (1:13)

Habakkuk first attacks God on theological grounds. In his first complaint (vv. 2–4), Habakkuk complained about the effect of injustice on his own people, but now God is using an even worse people to end the previous injustice. How does justice have any meaning if evil is replaced by an even greater evil? Rabbinic thought places Habakkuk's questions in Moses's mouth:

> R. Yoḥanan further said in the name of R. Yosei: Three things did Moses ask of the Holy One, blessed be He, and they were granted to him. He asked that the Divine Presence should rest upon Israel, and it was granted to him.... He asked that the Divine Presence should not rest upon the idolaters, and it was granted to him.... He asked that He should show him the ways of the Holy One, blessed be He, and it was granted to him.... Moses said before Him: Lord of the Universe, why is it that some righteous men prosper and others are in adversity, some wicked men prosper and others are in adversity?.... [You must] therefore [say that] the Lord said thus to Moses: A righteous man who prospers is a perfectly righteous man; the righteous man who is in adversity is not a perfectly righteous man. The wicked man who prospers is not a perfectly wicked man; the wicked man who is in adversity is a perfectly wicked man. Now this [saying of R. Yoḥanan] is in opposition to the saying of R. Meir. For R. Meir said: Only two [requests] were granted to him, and one was not granted to him. For it is said: And I will be gracious to whom I will be gracious, although he may not deserve it, and I will show mercy on whom I will show mercy, although he may not deserve it. (Berakhot 7a)

R. Yoḥanan and R. Meir argue about whether Moses received an answer to the eternal questions of theodicy. What is interesting is that the Talmud, when discussing a different statement of R. Yoḥanan in the name of R. Shimon bar Yoḥai with regard to the question of whether one is or is not allowed to provoke the wicked, to which the Talmud brings support texts for both options, derives one of its answers from a clever textual reading of Habakkuk's question, and that answer is also helpful in answering the theological question from the earlier passage of who prospers versus who suffers adversity:

> [R. Yoḥanan's] opinion, which says that it is a mitzva to confront the wicked, is referring to a perfectly righteous man, while this opinion, which says that one may not confront the wicked, is referring to a man who is not perfectly righteous. For R. Huna said: What is the meaning of the verse "Why do You watch treachery and be silent, as the wicked swallow up those more righteous than he" (Hab. 1:13)? Can then the wicked swallow up the righteous? Is it not written: "The Lord will not leave him in his hand" (Ps. 37:33)? And is it not written further: "There shall no mischief befall the righteous" (Prov. 12:21)? [You must] therefore [say]: He swallows up the one who is only "more righteous than he," but he cannot swallow up the perfectly righteous man. (*Berakhot* 7b)

R. Huna teaches that one can learn from the fact that Habakkuk said "as the wicked swallow up those more righteous *than he*" and not simply "as the wicked swallow up the righteous man," that the extra words imply that the second person is righteous only in comparison to the first person but is not actually a perfectly righteous person.[3] According to this understanding, when a person or nation is completely righteous, they can be assured of protection from evil. But once both parties are not fully righteous, or rather, partially evil, and the only difference is a

3. Parenthetically, this reading rejects the understanding that the subject of Habakkuk's original complaint was in fact the vision of the upcoming Babylonian invasion, which explicitly states that the Babylonians are more evil in comparison to another party, either the Assyrian oppressors or the people of Judah themselves. This idea is similar to the approach of Abarbanel mentioned at the beginning of the book of Habakkuk, who, in consistency with his interpretation in Zephaniah, chapter 2, writes that the Jews of the time were not righteous, and that the original complaint refers to the current evil in society that Habakkuk sees:

> Habakkuk's issue and complaint here wasn't regarding the upcoming destruction of Judah and Jerusalem, for he knew that they deserved it due to their sins.... However, he complained of Nebuchadnezzar's success in conquering all of the kingdoms, for because of his evil he was unworthy of such success and power.

matter of degree, then God will allow the more wicked to prevail over the lesser wicked. Though R. Huna accepts this theodicy, Habakkuk is not satisfied with it and his burning questions remain.

Once the question of theodicy is posed – i.e., how can God's goodness and omnipotence be defended in light of the existing evil – on the fundamental level, Habakkuk attacks God on the practical level, by bringing parallels to the two parts of God's first response to him. God revealed that He would send the Babylonians to dispense punishment to Judah, and then spent several verses (vv. 7–11) describing the might and ferocity of the Babylonian army. In verse 13, Habakkuk reacts to the first part of God's answer, indicating his displeasure with God's choice of the Chaldeans to punish evil and the injustice that such a response entails. Then, in verses 14–17, he reacts to the second half of God's answer, i.e., the description of the ferocity of the Babylonian army. Habakkuk expresses the natural reaction that one would have to God's answer: He comes to the conclusion that since greater evil will triumph over other lesser evils by means of brute strength, man will never live in justice and harmony. If so, people are no different from, or any better than, the fish of the sea, who are "creeping things that have no ruler," that swim in the ocean in quiet desperation until they are ultimately trapped in the fisherman's net.[4] The net makes no distinction between right and wrong or good and evil; all those who are trapped will die.[5] Habakkuk concludes by comparing the Babylonians to fishermen, who symbolically worship their nets, the source of their bounty.

4. Malbim interprets the second half of v. 14, "creeping things that have no ruler," as a new metaphor, referring to insects and not fish. He posits that this is an intensification of the previous metaphor – unlike fish, whose watery dwelling place offers some protection from outside predators, land-based insects are completely exposed and unprotected. This commentary maintains that both references are to fish, as the verses continue by describing how they are hunted without respite, and insects are not generally hunted (for usage of the Hebrew root word R-M-S with fish, see Gen. 1:21).

5. Malbim notes that three separate Hebrew words are used to describe the Babylonians' nets in vv. 15–16: *ḥerem, ḥakha,* and *mikhmeret.* He suggests that these terms parallel the three types of conquests the Babylonians carried out: *ḥakha* refers to conquests of large countries (Job 40:25 uses the word *ḥakha* in the context of capturing large fish), *ḥerem* refers to the conquest of medium-sized countries (the *ḥerem* net catches the average-sized fish), and finally the *mikhmoret* refers to the conquest of large areas of land (a *mikhmoret* is spread over the water).

And since no one will stop them, they will fish without end, until all the people are caught.

Habakkuk emphasizes his dissatisfaction with God's answer to his first complaint by repeating key words from his first complaint here. Habakkuk asked why before ("Why do You show me iniquity"; v. 3), and now he asks why again ("Why do You watch treachery and be silent, as the wicked swallow up those more righteous than he?"; v. 13). The first discussion of the effects of God's actions are introduced using the repetition of the word "therefore" (*al ken*) – "Therefore Torah has become impotent... therefore, justice emerges perverted" (v. 4). Similarly, in the conclusion to Habakkuk's second complaint when discussing the ramifications of God's first answer, the word "therefore" (*al ken*) is repeated three times – "therefore they rejoice and exult... Therefore, they sacrifice unto their net.... Shall they therefore empty their net, and not spare to slay the nations continually? (vv. 15–17). Additionally, the words for justice and judgment (*mishpat*; vv. 4, 12), righteous and wicked (*tzaddik* and *rasha*; vv. 4, 13), oppression (*amal*; vv. 3, 13), and look and behold (from the roots R-A-H and H-B-T; vv. 3, 13) connect Habakkuk's second complaint with the first. The literary effect of this repetition is that Habakkuk is stating that the questions he raised at the beginning of the book have not yet been answered.

At this point, the reader would expect another answer from God to Habakkuk's new complaints, but instead, Habakkuk states that he will wait:

> On my watch I will stand, and I will set myself upon a fortress, and I will look out to see what He will speak to me and what I will reply (*ashiv*) when I am rebuked[6] (alternatively, "I will withdraw my rebuke"). (2:1)

His wait is ultimately rewarded by another response from God:

---

6. The expected parallelism with the first section would have Habakkuk saying "and what He (God) will respond (*yashiv*) to my rebuke," employing the verb *yashiv* rather than *ashiv*. *Daat Mikra* suggests this interpretation, and this is indeed the reading of the Syriac translation, a fifth-century translation from Greek to a Syriac version of Aramaic, attributed to Rabbula, a bishop of Edessa, and commonly referred to as the *Peshitta* (see Sweeney, vol. 2., 470n32).

> And the Lord answered me and said: Write the vision and explain it upon the tablets, so that one may read it swiftly. For there shall be another vision for the appointed time; and He shall speak of the end, and it shall not fail; though it tarry, wait for it, for it shall surely come; it shall not delay. Behold, it is puffed up; his soul is not upright within him, but the righteous shall live by his faith. (2:2–4)

Habakkuk's second chapter appears to begin a new section. As noted, a reader would expect another answer – how will God respond to Habakkuk's new charges, i.e., his second complaint at the end of chapter 1? Instead, we have Habakkuk declaring emphatically that he will wait. He does so in sentences marked by first-person pronouns (v. 1: "On my watch, I will stand, and I will set myself… and I will look out… speak to me, and what I will reply when I am rebuked…. And the Lord answered me"). The use of first person signifies a break from the style of his earlier questioning in 1:12–17, in which second- and third-person pronouns predominated. But these sentences are still linked to the previous section in both their content and language. In his second complaint he lamented: "And You, O Rock, have established them for correction/rebuke (*lehokhiaḥ*)" (1:12), while here in 2:1 Habakkuk speaks of "what I will reply when I am rebuked (*tokhaḥti*)," where *lehokhiaḥ* and *tokhaḥti* are from the same root.

Habakkuk begins with an announcement, declaring that he will assume the role of a watchman. In the Bible, the watchman served two roles: to look for approaching messengers (see II Sam. 18:24–28, Is. 21:6–8, 52:7–10) or to warn of approaching dangers (see I Sam. 14:16–17, II Kings 9:17–20, Ezek. 33:2–6). By using this metaphor, Habakkuk is hinting that he is searching for communication from God. This is different from the role that other prophets played when serving as watchmen: while other prophets, such as Jeremiah, Ezekiel, and Hosea, assumed the role of watchman in order to convey divine instructions downward to the people (Jer. 6:17, Ezek. 3:16–21, 33:7–9, Hos. 9:8), Habakkuk waits for an answer to the challenges that he hurled upward to God. Additionally, the metaphor of the prophet as watchman also contains a hint about Habakkuk's realization with regard to the nature of the answer that he will receive. Unlike the regular city guard, who is content to see what is in front of his eyes, the watchman looks further into the horizon.

Similarly, Habakkuk realizes that the events described in God's answer will not occur soon, but only much later, in the not-so-near future.

Habakkuk describes the specific physical posture that he will assume while waiting for God's response. Such a description is rare among the prophets. What is its purpose? Abarbanel suggests that verse 1 is descriptive, and refers to the preparations that a prophet would go through in order to receive prophecy. But the specific verbs used ("stand," "set myself") appear to convey a deeper message, emphasizing the depth of Habakkuk's resolve and determination to wait until God responds to his challenge of "Why are You silent in the face of injustice." Sensing an almost impudent tone in Habakkuk's words, Rashi provides more background for this rare emphasis on the prophet's posture (commentary on 2:1):

> Habakkuk dug a round hole and stood within it, declaring, "I will not budge from here until I hear what He will say to me regarding this, my question – why does He look and see the prosperity of a wicked man [without responding]?"

The source of Rashi's explanation is the rabbinic account of Ḥoni the Circle Maker:

> Once it happened that the greater part of the month of Adar had gone and yet no rain had fallen. The people sent a message to Ḥoni the Circle Maker, "Pray that rain may fall." He prayed and no rain fell. He thereupon drew a circle and stood within it in the same way as the prophet Habakkuk had done, as it is said, "On my watch I will stand, and I will set myself upon a fortress." He exclaimed [before God], Master of the Universe, Your children have turned to me because [they believe] me to be a member of Your house. I swear by Your great name that I will not move from here until You have mercy upon Your children! (Taanit 23a)

According to the Talmud and later, Rashi, the similarity between Habakkuk and Ḥoni the Circle Maker is not limited to the impudent and demanding manner in which they approached God,[7] but extends to the very physical posture they assumed in prayer.

Habakkuk waits patiently but is prepared to receive God's response at any moment. The words *ashiv al tokhaḥti* in verse 1 can be translated in two ways, either "I will respond to the rebuke given to me," meaning that Habakkuk has already prepared a retort to the rebuke he expects to receive as a result of his impudent challenge to God, or "I will withdraw my rebuke," referencing Habakkuk's rebuke to God, meaning that Habakkuk is declaring that if he receives a proper answer, he will withdraw his complaint. Who is the one rebuking Habakkuk? One suggestion is that it is God who will be reprimanding him, as a result of Habakkuk's challenge. Another approach suggests that Habakkuk will be censured by his listeners. A person who wrestles publicly with difficult theological issues is likely to be hushed by those around him, who might say to him: "You can't say that out loud!" Rashi supports this view: "For they reprove me to my face [saying] one should [not] criticize the divine standard of justice" (commentary on 2:1, see also Ibn Ezra ad loc.). Radak and Abarbanel suggest that the rebuke was of a different nature: The ones reproving Habakkuk were not self-righteous individuals who were shocked that he could challenge God in such a way, but rather disgruntled listeners who had agreed with Habakkuk's complaints against God in the previous chapter and had come to the conclusion that worshipping God is not worthwhile. Now, they are rebuking Habakkuk, asking him what he as the prophet will do about it. According to this explanation, Habakkuk is saying that he understands that it is up to him to figure out how to respond to them.

Habakkuk does not have to wait long; God responds to Habakkuk in verse 2. His reply is very different from the answer He gave Habakkuk in chapter 1. There, God bypassed the prophet to speak to the people, speaking

---

7. The Talmud concludes its account with an implicit acknowledgment that Ḥoni's behavior was unconventional, if not impudent:

> Shimon b. Shataḥ sent him word, saying: "If you were not Ḥoni, I would order that you be excommunicated. But what shall I do with you, since though you are impudent toward God, He forgives you and indulges you like a spoiled child who is petulant toward his father, and is nevertheless forgiven and indulged? To you the verse may be applied, 'Let your father and your mother rejoice, and let she that has born thee be glad'" (Prov. 23:25).

in the second-person plural. Now, God speaks to the prophet directly in the second-person singular. Previously, there was no introduction that separated God's response from Habakkuk's question. Now the verse states explicitly, "The Lord answered me and said." Habakkuk's wait was not in vain.

God begins by directing the prophet to write down the vision that will come, and explain it clearly, so that it will spread among the entire nation. God is addressing Habakkuk directly here, but the message is not for Habakkuk alone. Habakkuk has been giving voice to the people's spiritual struggles; now they are to receive their answer in a vision. However, after verse 2 states that the vision should be written down so that its message can be read and disseminated swiftly among the people, verse 3 not only suggests that there will be a delay, but that it is likely that this vision is to be replaced by a different vision (this reading is based on understanding the Hebrew *od ḥazon lamoed* as referring to a different vision).[8] The commentators addressed this apparent redundancy – what are the two visions and why are they needed? Rashi suggests that the two visions are in fact one and the same, and the word *od,* which indicates a redundancy, alludes to the two prophets who will deliver the vision, first Habakkuk and then Jeremiah (commentary on 2:3). He then quotes the *Targum Yonatan,* who interprets this differently. The *Targum Yonatan* reads the word *ketov,* a word in the command form, meaning "write," as *katuv,* the past participle of the word, meaning "written." According to the explanation of the *Targum Yonatan,* the redundant language refers actually to an earlier incident: God is telling Habakkuk that the answer to his question had already been written in the Torah long ago, that is, that the punishments the Jewish people were to endure were a direct result of their failure to keep the laws of *Shemitta* while they dwelled in their land.

God's response can be summarized as saying: there will be an answer, but it will be delayed. What exactly will be delayed? The text is ambiguous. Is it the appearance of the second vision that will be delayed,

8. *Od ḥazon lamoed* can also be translated as "the vision is yet to come," with the reference being to the same vision (see Is. 56:8 for an example of *od* as meaning "yet"), and it is plausible that this is how the Septuagint translates this verse, but this commentary has chosen to adopt the understanding of the vast majority of traditional commentaries (see above *Metzudot,* ad. loc, and others).

or will the vision itself appear without delay, but its implementation and realization will be delayed? The Talmud suggests an answer which is quoted and expanded upon in the commentary of Abarbanel. This explanation suggests that the two visions signify two different redemptions. The first vision is the promise that after seventy years of Babylonian exile, the people will be redeemed and return to Israel. The second vision refers to the ultimate redemption, i.e., the messianic era, and it is this vision whose fulfillment is delayed. In a discussion about the issue of calculating the exact time for the coming of the Messiah, the Talmud writes:

> What is the meaning of the verse "*Veyafe'aḥ* (and He shall speak) of the end, and it shall not fail" (Hab. 2:3)? R. Shmuel bar Naḥmani quoted R. Yonatan, "May the bones of people who calculate the time of the coming of the Messiah disintegrate [*tipaḥ*]." [Because of these people], the people say, "Since the time has come and he has not come, he is not coming." Rather, wait for him – "Though he tarry, wait for him" (Hab. 2:4). (Sanhedrin 97b)

To provide support for this interpretation, Abarbanel argues that the usage of the word "end" (*ketz*) in verse 3 never applies to an intermediary pause, but denotes only a final end. He suggests that it is for this reason that the first vision about Babylonia, which was of a fixed duration, was written down and not hidden from the public, but that the second vision was kept hidden.

The climax of this vision, and in fact, of the entire book, is verse 4: "Behold, it is puffed up; his soul is not upright within him, but the righteous shall live by his faith." God contrasts the proud and haughty, who appear to be enjoying momentary material success, with the righteous, who survive through faith. The meaning of the first half of the verse in Hebrew is uncertain, and commentaries have struggled to decipher its meaning. Rashi understands it as referring to the vice of being insatiable, which he claims is the main vice of the wicked:

> "It is puffed up" [is to be understood as meaning that] the soul of the wicked man is always feverous and longing of desire, desiring to swallow and never satisfied. *Uppela* (which has the root A-P-L) is an

> expression of defiance, as in (Num. 14:44) "And they acted defiantly" (*vayaapilu*, which has the root A-P-L) .... "His soul is not upright within him" [means that] his spirit is not satisfied within him, and he never says, "What I have already acquired is enough." Therefore, retribution shall come upon him. (Rashi, commentary on 2:4)

Radak has a different opinion regarding the question of what the main vice of the wicked is, maintaining that it is pride and arrogance. Both understandings of the word *uppela*, whether insolent and defiant (Rashi) or prideful and arrogant (Radak), can find support in the descriptions of the wicked person's behavior in the following section. Abarbanel has a third explanation, depicting the wicked as one who fumbles in darkness. He understands the word *uppela* in the verse not to mean puffed up, but rather as deriving from the word *afel*, which means darkness. Unlike the righteous, who walk in the light of certainty, the wicked one fumbles in the darkness and lives in a state of uncertainty, never sure what step to take next.

The identity of the wicked person, or group of people, to which the first half of verse 4 refers is also unclear. The commentaries are divided on this issue. Rashi, Radak, and Ibn Ezra all assume that it refers to the Babylonians. Rabbi Eliezer of Beaugency, Abarbanel, and Malbim disagree, maintaining that Habakkuk is referring to the arrogant Jews among the people of Judah. While the identity and chief negative trait of the evil person or people is unclear, Habakkuk states clearly that the defining feature of the righteous person is *emuna*, the meaning of which we will attempt to define and understand in the coming paragraphs. The Talmud declares that this verse represents the central pillar of Judaism:

> Rabbi Simlai expounded: Six hundred thirteen commandments were revealed to Moses: 364 negative commandments, corresponding to the days in the solar year, and 248 positive commandments, corresponding to the parts of the body. When David came, he summed up the 613 commandments in eleven principles .... When Isaiah came, he summed up the 613 commandments in six principles, for Isaiah said, "(1) He that walks in righteousness and (2) speaks peaceably; (3) he that despises profit from fraudulent dealings, (4) that waves away a bribe instead of grasping it, (5) that stops his ears

> from hearing of infamy, and (6) shuts his eyes from looking upon evil: Such a one shall dwell in lofty security" (Is. 33:15–16).... When Micah came, he summed up the 613 commandments in three principles, for he said, "It has been told to you, O man, what is good, and what the Lord does require of you: (1) only to do justly and (2) to love mercy and (3) to walk modestly with your God" (Mic. 6:8).... Isaiah reconsidered and summed up the 613 commandments in two principles when he said, "Thus says the Lord: (1) keep justice and (2) do righteousness" (Is. 56:1). (Makkot 23b–24a)

When Habakkuk came, he summed up the 613 commandments in one principle, for he said, "The righteous shall live by his faith (*emuna*)" (Hab. 2:4).[9]

What does *emuna* mean? The simple translation is "faith," and this meaning can be inferred from the introduction to God's promise to Abraham in Genesis 15:6: And he believed (*he'emin*) in the Lord, and He accounted it to him as righteousness (see also Neh. 9:8). But if one examines the usage of this word in other places in the Bible, it becomes clear that the word *emuna* means more than faith in the sense of simple belief. For example, in the account of the Exodus from Egypt, during the battle with the Amalekites in which Aaron and Hur assist Moses in holding his hands up, outstretched in prayer, the word *emuna* is used to mean steady: "Now Moses's hands were heavy; so they took a stone and placed it under him, and he sat on it. Aaron and Hur supported his hands, one from this [side], and one from that [side]; and his hands were steady (*emuna*) until sunset" (Ex. 17:12). The idea of *emuna* indicating steadiness is also reflected in the word's usage in many locations in Psalms, where it reflects God's attribute of reliability and constancy (see Ps. 88:12, 89:2, 3, 6, 9).

Additionally, to what does the possessive suffix *o* in the word *emunato* in verse 4 refer? Does the suffix *o*, which can mean either "his" or "its," mean "his faith," and the verse is saying that the righteous one

---

9. This verse became one of the dividing points between Jewish and Christian thought. In the talmudic quote, the question asked is what principles underlie the commandments. But none of the speakers would have suggested that these ideas come to replace the commandments. Conversely, Paul quotes this verse three times in the New Testament (Rom. 1:17, Gal. 3:11, Heb. 10:38), and interprets it to mean that salvation can be achieved through faith alone, unencumbered by commandments.

will live by his reliability and steadfast nature, i.e., his sense of clarity and certainty in life will allow him to succeed? Or does it mean "its faith," with the "its" referring to the vision, i.e., "the righteous one will live by the reliability of the vision," referring to the belief that God's vision will ultimately bring a resolution to the challenges that Habakkuk posed?

While the verses in Habakkuk do not clarify whether or not there is a promised answer, we may be able to gain some perspective on the issue by comparing this section with a different, parallel prophecy, one which served as an inspiration for Habakkuk, in Isaiah chapter 21:

Isaiah 21:1–9	**Habakkuk 1:1, 2:1–3**
1: The burden (*massa*) of the wilderness of the sea. As whirlwinds in the south sweeping on, it comes from the wilderness, from a dreadful land. 2: A grievous vision (*ḥazut*) is declared unto me.... 6: For thus has the Lord said unto me: Go, set up (*haamed*; root A-M-D) a watchman[14] (*metzappeh*; root TZ-P-H), let him declare what he sees (*yireh*; root R-A-H)!... 8: And he cried as a lion: "Upon the watchtower (*mitzpe*; root TZ-P-H), O Lord, I stand continually in the daytime, and I am set in my watch (*mishmarti*) all the nights." 9: And behold (*vehinneh*), there came a troop of men, horsemen by pairs. *And He [the Lord] answered and said:* "Fallen, fallen is Babylon; and all the graven images of her gods are broken unto the ground."	1:1 The burden (*massa*) that Habakkuk the prophet did see.... 2:1 I will stand (*e'emoda*; root A-M-D) upon my watch (*mishmarti*), and set me upon the tower, and will look out (*etzapeh*; root TZ-P-H) to see (*lirot*; root R-A-H) what He will speak by me, and what I shall answer when I am reproved. 2 *And the Lord answered me, and said:* "Write the vision (*ḥazon*), and make it plain upon tables, that a man may read it swiftly. 3 For the vision (*ḥazon*) is yet for the appointed time, and it declares of the end, and does not lie; though it tarry, wait for it; because it will surely come, it will not delay." 4 Behold (*hinneh*)...

10. A similar portrayal of the prophet as a watchman on the tower can be found in God's charge to Ezekiel (33:2): "Son of man, I have appointed you a watchman (*tzofeh*, which has the root TZ-P-H.), unto the House of Israel; and when you shall hear a word at My mouth, you shall give them warning from Me."

The numerous structural parallels between the two prophecies, including similar metaphors as well as the introductory word "behold" (*hinneh*),[11] suggest that Habakkuk is intentionally echoing Isaiah's famous prophecy regarding the downfall of the Babylonians, which ends with "Fallen, fallen is Babylon; and all the graven images of her gods are broken unto the ground" (Is. 21:9), in order to reassure and give hope to his listeners: Though Habakkuk could not promise the immediate downfall of the Babylonians, who would oppress his people – indeed, Jeremiah predicts that Judah will be ruled by Babylon for seventy years[12] – the allusions to Isaiah's vision of Babylonia's destruction would have been recognized by his listeners, and might have comforted them.

In summary, Habakkuk has once again complained to God, and this time he receives an answer addressed to him. The vision he receives does not directly and openly answer the questions he asks in his complaint at this point, and Habakkuk will not respond to God's response until the end of chapter 3. But the vision does provide guidance to Habakkuk about how he and the people should live their lives at a time when the Divine Presence appears absent: through *emuna*. Another important aspect to note in this section is that this is the first time that God has spoken directly to Habakkuk. Though the answer is lacking, the knowledge that God listened and responded is in itself meaningful.[13]

11. Adele Berlin suggests that every appearance of the word "behold" (*hinneh*) in the Bible implies a shift in the perspective of the speaker (*Poetics and Interpretation of Biblical Narrative*, 62). In the context of prophecy, the word "behold" (*hinneh*) suggests that the prophet is the recipient of sudden information that "comes from afar" (i.e., the distant future).
12. Jer. 25:11.
13. I was privileged to hear a similar thought from Rabbi Dr. Norman Lamm with regard to the end of the book of Job. After raising such tremendous and important questions of theodicy, and valiantly demolishing the shallow and simplistic theological certainties of his well-meaning friends, Job seems to cower at God's appearance and surrender meekly, without even a whimper. Why does the man who so boldly challenged creation capitulate so quickly? Rabbi Lamm suggests that whatever Job may not have gained in intellectual certainty, what he did gain from the dialogue with God was the certainty that God exists and listens to the cries of humanity. Just being in God's presence for the first time was enough for him for now. This line of thought is in disagreement with scholars who see both Habakkuk and Job as cowering and humbled due to God's display of power and might (see, for example O' Brien, *Nahum*, 80).

2:5–2:20

Visions of Woe for the Wicked

Following his dramatic exchange with God, Habakkuk begins to demonstrate to his listeners that ultimately, evil will never prosper. He does so in a series of five statements that taunt the wicked's attempts to be successful, and each statement begins with the word "woe."

> And furthermore, surely he whom wine betrays, a haughty man whose dwelling shall not remain, who widened his desire like the netherworld, and he is like death and shall never be sated, and he gathered all the nations to himself and collected to himself all peoples.
>
> Shall not all these take up a parable against him and [take up] ridicules and riddles against him? And he shall say, "Woe to him who increases what is not his! How long? And who loads himself with many pledges!" Will not those who bite you arise suddenly, and those who startle you awaken? And you shall become plunder for them. Since you have plundered many nations, all remaining peoples shall cast you away, because of the

> blood of man and the violence done to the land, the city, and all its inhabitants.
>
> Woe to him who gains evil gains for his house to place his nest on high, to be saved from the hand of an evil one. You have advised shame for your house, to cut off many peoples, and you have sinned against your life. For a stone shall cry from the wall, and a chip shall answer it from a beam.
>
> Woe to him who builds a city with blood and establishes a city with injustice. Behold, is it not from the Lord of hosts? And peoples shall toil until they are sated with fire, and nations shall weary themselves only for vanity. For the earth shall be filled with the knowledge of the glory of the Lord, as the water covers the seabed.
>
> Woe to him who gives his friend to drink, who adds your venom and also makes him drunk in order to gaze upon their nakedness. You have become sated more from disgrace than from honor. You, too, drink and become clogged up. The cup of the right hand of the Lord shall be turned upon you, and disgrace upon your glory. For the violence of Lebanon shall cover you, and the plunder of cattle shall break them, because of the blood of man and the violence of the land, a city, and all its inhabitants. What did a graven image avail that its maker has graven it? A molten image and a teacher of lies, that the maker of his work trusted in it to make mute idols?
>
> Woe to him who says to the wood, "Awaken!" To the mute stone, "Arise!" Shall it teach? Behold, it is overlaid with gold and silver, and no spirit is within it.
>
> But the Lord is in His Holy Temple. Silence the whole earth before Him. (2:5–20)

Demonstrating the futility of evildoing, verses 5–20 provide the beginning of God's response to Habakkuk. As God is referred to in the third person throughout this section (vv. 13, 14, 16, 20) we understand that Habakkuk is the speaker in theses verses. This is his first attempt to convey the meaning of the visions he has received, and he does so in the five "woe" (Hebrew: *hoy*) prophecies that he will utter. These prophecies begin in verse 6, with each one detailing the upcoming fate of and punishment that awaits evildoers.[1] Though the opening verse of this section, verse 5, doesn't begin with the word "woe," its explanation of how wine misleads the haughty is a topic which is clearly in line with the subject matter of the "woe" prophecies. Instead, verse 5 begins with the word *ve'af*, meaning "and furthermore," a connector word which links this verse and the coming verses with the previous visions, transforming the subsequent "woe" prophecies into elaborations of those previous visions.[2] These verses contain one central, unifying theme – the reversal of fortune that inevitably befalls the wicked. By engaging in wicked acts, the oppressor plants the seeds of his own destruction. Though God stated that the ultimate answer to Habakkuk's questions will become clear only in the future, the beginning of an answer to Habakkuk's questions of theodicy begins to crystallize in these verses: The apparent prosperity of the wicked is temporary and fleeting. It is precisely those actions that bring them success that will ultimately bring their downfall as well. The oppressor consumes wine heartily, but wine will eventually deceive him. The nations that he conquered and looted will later take part in deriding him.

Habakkuk's five "woe" prophecies appear to speak about individuals,[3] but throughout the section, he avoids identifying his tar-

---

1. The word "woe" is considered to be an interjection, usually a lament. It occurs fifty times in the Prophets. While it appears six times in reference to mourning for the deceased (see I Kings 13:30), it usually introduces a direct threat or warning regarding upcoming divine punishment.
2. Throughout Tanakh there are several instances where the Hebrew phrase *af ki* is used, meaning "how much more so." For example: "How much more so (*af ki*), if the people had eaten today of the spoils of their enemies, which they found, would there not now have been a greater slaughter..." (I Sam. 14:30); "But will God indeed dwell on the earth? Behold, the heaven and the heaven of heavens cannot contain You; how much more so (*af ki*) this temple that I have erected" (I Kings 8:27). See also Prov. 11:31, 15:31, 17:7.
3. Rashi interprets the "woe" passages as referring to the Babylonian kings. For example, on verse 2:5, Rashi writes, "[The wine and dwelling in the verse are Belshazzar's] dwelling and his residence shall not remain in existence, for he [Belshazzar] was arrogant. He said, under the influence of the wine, to bring the vessels of the Temple; and he drank with them. That action shall cause him to be slain, and the seed of Nebuchadnezzar to be destroyed, for an arrogant man is a scorner; he shall not have a dwelling. Neither he nor his dwelling shall remain in existence."

gets directly. This tactic allows his message to be universal. The ambiguity makes the prophecies difficult to decipher, and are thus introduced as a parable (*mashal*), as a mocking poem of ridicule (*melitza*), and as riddles (*ḥidot*).[4] However, the prophecy's context makes it clear that Habakkuk is cleverly utilizing personification to refer to the nation of Babylon and its eventual downfall.

The conquered nations, referred to as the nations that Babylonia "gathered to himself" in verse 5, become the speakers in the "woe" parables, introduced in verse 6 as "all these": "Shall not all these take up a parable against him and [take up] ridicules and riddles concerning him?" (2:6). By having the conquered nations become the speakers, Habakkuk is empowering them, converting them from helpless victims to judge and jury over the Babylonians. These downtrodden nations reappear in verse 8: "Since you have plundered many nations"; verse 10: "You have advised shame for your house, to cut off many peoples"; and verse 13: "And peoples shall toil until they are sated with fire, and nations shall weary themselves only for vanity." Verse 17 concludes with special mention of the violence committed against one particular nation: "For the violence of Lebanon shall cover you, and the plunder of cattle shall break them." Though many commentaries attempt to link these prophecies with specific historical events or personalities, generally ones from the Babylonian dynasty,[5] Habakkuk chooses to maintain the anonymity

4. The three terms *mashal, melitza,* and *ḥidot* appear together at the beginning of Proverbs (1:6). On its own, the word *mashal* can mean "song" (see Num. 21:27–30, I Kings 5:12), "proverb" (see I Sam. 10:12, Ezek. 12:22), or "parable" (Ezek. 17:2, 21:5). It can also connote prophecy, as in Balaam's visions (see Num. 23:7, 18, 24:3, 15, 20, 21, 23). In Is. 14:4 (also a prophecy against Babylon) and in Mic. 2:4, the word carries a negative connotation, used as a taunt to its subject. The word *melitza* is derived from the Hebrew word for scorn or ridicule (*lamed, yod, tzadi*). *Ḥidot* throughout Tanakh are passages that require interpretation (see Judges 14:12–19). The *Metzudot* here suggests that the difference between *melitza* and *ḥida* is whether the message is given in clear or esoteric language. Malbim suggests that the *melitza* is the interpretation of the other forms.
5. For example, Rashi identifies "the righteous one" of verse 4 as "Jeconiah the king, whom this wicked man will lead to exile – his righteousness shall stand for him, and on the day this one [Nebuchadnezzar] is cast out of his grave, Evil-Merodach shall raise Jehoiachin's head and place his throne above the thrones of the kings," and the

of both the speaker and the target. By making the literary choice to keep the identity of the target of God's wrath anonymous, Habakkuk creates a template of the wicked that remains relevant to this day.

The five "woe" prophecies that are directed at the Babylonians each reflect a fundamental flaw in their national character:

- "Woe to him who increases what is not his…" (v. 6): usury and greed.
- "Woe to him who gets evil gain for his house that he may set his nest on high" (v. 9): pride.
- "Woe to him who builds a town with bloodshed" (v. 12): murder and injustice.
- "Woe to you who make your neighbors drink, who mix in your venom even to make them drunk so as to look on their nakedness!" (v. 15): immorality/cruelty.
- "Woe to him who says to a piece of wood, 'Awake!'" (v. 19): idolatry.

Each of these prophecies can be considered self-contained, and all discuss the reversal of fortune that will overtake the oppressor. But if one considers the five prophecies as a unit, there is a noticeable progression in the way that God appears. In the first two prophecies, God is not found. The punishment of the wicked comes either from the oppressed who rise up after an upper limit of suffering has been reached, or as a result of the very nature of the injustice, which causes the oppressor's injustice to collapse upon itself. But in the three following prophecies, God plays a more prominent role. Through the expanded mention of God in these prophecies Habakkuk hopes that the people will begin to

---

drunken one in verse 5 as "Belshazzar…the one whose wine shall betray him, for he drank as much wine as a thousand" (Dan. 5:1). (Radak identifies the drunken one as Nebuchadnezzar, but without providing textual support) Rashi suggests that the wicked one of verse 15 who gives his neighbor to drink is "the wicked Nebuchadnezzar, who would give the kings wine to drink, in order to intoxicate them and practice sodomy upon them, as we state in Shabbat 149b…or Belshazzar, who gave the princes to drink with the vessels of the Temple, because of which they were smitten with *tzaraat* and intoxicated by the wrath of the Holy One, blessed be He."

understand that it is God that is responsible for Babylonia's loss of wealth and might and eventual downfall, just as they had come to understand that Babylonia's successes had come from God.

The first "woe" prophecy describes how the oppressor, who profited from charging excessive interest rates, eventually finds himself becoming the victim of an even more exacting creditor. Verse 8 moves from the individual level to the national dimension. Babylonia rapaciously plundered the nations that it conquered, and also took populations hostage to ensure the loyalty of the remaining people of the conquered nations; but the goods they acquired would ultimately be looted by the Persian conquerors, and so on. This prophecy ends with the statement that the punishment comes as a result of the damage inflicted on both man and the land: "All remaining nations shall cast you away because of the blood of man and [because of] the violence done to the land, the city, and all its inhabitants." This phrase will reappear at the end of the fourth prophecy in verse 17, bookending the first four sections that describe crimes committed by people against other people.

The second "woe" prophecy describes how the oppressor profited from his greed. Habakkuk imagines him utilizing his ill-gotten gains as he builds the foundation of his house.[6] He places his dwelling in a high place, believing that this will make him immune from retribution. The idea of one mistakenly believing that a high place will provide an escape echoes both the story of the Tower of Babel as well as Obadiah's taunt of Edom: "Though you make your nest as high as the eagle, and though you set it among the stars, I will bring you down from there, says the Lord" (Ob. 1:4). In powerful poetic language, Habakkuk describes how the very bricks and beams of his house will cry aloud to condemn him.

The third "woe" prophecy depicts the expanding reach of the wicked, detailing how he first profits unjustly, then builds himself a palace with the ill-gotten gains. After that, he founds a city – but in a manner that oppresses its inhabitants, whether physically or financially.

6. Rashi and Radak understand this imagery literally, explaining that it refers to the great palaces built by Nebuchadnezzar. Ibn Ezra expands the understanding of the word "house" to encompass all of Babylonia. The *Metzudot* translates "his house" as referring to his descendant, i.e., the dynasty that Nebuchadnezzar tried to establish.

The prophecy ends by describing how the evil one's efforts to preserve his ill-gotten gains will eventually come to naught. Jeremiah will draw on Habakkuk's words in this prophecy in the conclusion of his prophecy about Babylon:

Habakkuk 2:13	**Jeremiah 51:58**
Behold, is it not from the *Lord of hosts*? And *peoples shall labor* until they are sated *with fire*, and nations shall *weary* themselves only *for much futility*.	So said the *Lord of hosts*: The broad walls of Babylon shall be overthrown and her lofty gates shall be burnt *with fire*, and *peoples shall labor for much futility*, and kingdoms in much fire, and they shall be *weary*.

Habakkuk's focus on the city as a source of iniquity is not new. A century earlier, Micah attacked the corrupt rulers of Judah whose greed turned Jerusalem into a metropolis of injustice:

Habakkuk 2:12	**Micah 3:10**
Woe to him who *builds* a city *with blood* and establishes a city *with injustice*.	Each one *builds* Zion *with blood* and Jerusalem *with injustice*.

Significantly, it is in this third "woe" prophecy that the reader for the first time discovers who is behind the reversal of fortune for the wicked, as Habakkuk identifies God as the cause of the downfall of the oppressor. The verse that begins: "Behold, is it not from the Lord of hosts" is the central verse of all five "woe" prophecies. Though people may toil strenuously in order to conquer others and enrich themselves, ultimately their efforts will be in vain if God so wills it. When people will come to understand that God is the ultimate arbiter of people's successes and failures, His glory will be as openly apparent in the world as water in the sea. Because of the apparent reference to a more final redemptive time, some commentaries (Radak, Abarbanel) suggest that Habakkuk has ceased prophesizing about the specific downfall of the Babylonians here and is now prophesizing about the End of Days (paralleling the interpretation of the two visions above in 2:2 and 2:3). Indeed, Habakkuk's imagery draws upon the conclusion of Isaiah's vision of the messianic redemption: "For the land shall be full of knowledge of the Lord as water covers the seabed (Is. 11:9).

The fourth "woe" prophecy describes how wicked people abuse their weaker neighbors by intoxicating them and then taking advantage of them.[7] Earlier in this chapter (2:7), it was the oppressed who rise up and avenge themselves against their oppressors. Now, Habakkuk declares that it is God Himself who will cause the oppressor to drink. The image of God proffering the glass of wine for one to drink as a representation of upcoming punishment and destruction appears elsewhere in the Prophets. Isaiah described the destruction of Jerusalem as the result of being forced to drink God's wine of anger: "Awake, awake, stand up, O Jerusalem, that has drunk at the hand of the Lord the cup of His fury; you have drunken the beaker, even the cup of staggering, and drained it" (Is. 51:17). Similarly, Jeremiah announced the destruction of the nations that opposed Babylonian rule as follows:

> Then took I the cup of the Lord's hand, and made all the nations to drink, unto whom the Lord had sent me.... And all the kings of the north, both near and far, one after the other, and all the kingdoms of the earth that are upon the face of the earth; and the king of Sheshach shall drink after them. And you shall say to them: So said the Lord God of Israel: Drink, become drunk, and vomit, fall and you shall not rise, because of the sword that I am sending among you. (Jer. 25:17–27)

Verse 18 marks a shift in subject, switching from addressing interpersonal transgressions to describing the spiritual sin of idolatry. Idolatry is the subject of the fifth and final "woe" prophecy (the fifth prophecy begins in

---

7. Rashi continues to interpret these verses as referring to the Babylonian kings: "This is the wicked Nebuchadnezzar, who would give the kings wine to drink, in order to intoxicate them, and practice sodomy upon them (see Shabbat 149b). Another explanation: In *Seder Olam*, it [this verse] is expounded regarding Belshazzar, who gave the princes to drink with the vessels of the Temple, because of which they were smitten with *tzaraat* and intoxicated by the wrath of the Holy One, blessed be He. On that night he [Belshazzar] was slain" (commentary on v. 15).

verse 18, even though the word "woe" doesn't actually appear until verse 19). Like other prophets (see, for example, Is. 2:11), Habakkuk understands the practice of idolatry as being the desire to worship "one's own handiwork" (Is. 2:11). In these verses, he demonstrates the ultimate futility of idol worship, making the point that despite the efforts of idol worshippers to demonstrate to themselves and others that their idols afford those who worship them material and spiritual gain, in reality idols do no such thing, and the enterprise is fundamentally foolish. Additionally, there is an essential paradox in idol worship to which Habakkuk alludes: The idol that was fashioned by human hands cannot assist or guide its "maker," since by definition anyone who creates is always greater than his creation. Habakkuk mocks the idolater, who must speak for his idols like a ventriloquist speaks on behalf of his wooden dummy, pretending that they are alive. In contrast to these idols, Habakkuk concludes, "But the Lord is in His Holy Temple. Silence the whole earth before Him." Unlike the mute idols, for whom man has to speak in a futile attempt to animate them, man has to approach God in silence. Only then, out of a sense of silent humility, can God's voice be heard.

3:1–3:2

Superscription and Petition of Habakkuk's Prayer

> A prayer of Habakkuk the prophet concerning the *shigyonot*. O Lord, I heard a report of You; I feared, O Lord, Your work. In the midst of the years, revive it; in the midst of the years, let it be known. In anger You shall remember to be merciful. (3:1–2)

Chapter 3 begins an entirely new section of Habakkuk's prophecy. Instead of the questioning and dialogue that comprised the first two chapters, Habakkuk breaks into prayer. That chapter 3 comprises a new section is evidenced by its new superscription, "A prayer of Habakkuk the prophet concerning the *shigyonot*." This is the only time in the Bible that the words "prophet" and "prayer" appear together. At first glance, this chapter appears to be an independent entity, unrelated to the previous two chapters. [1] We

1. Some argue that the absence of chapter 3 in the Habakkuk *pesher* among the Dead Sea Scrolls (and a similar phenomenon in the Barberini Greek parallel to the Septuagint) reinforces the claim that this chapter is an independent entity. The discovery of scrolls of the book of Habakkuk that contain all three chapters in both the Muraba'at Caves near the Dead Sea and in the Greek Nahal Hever scrolls, also found in the wilderness of the Judean Desert, functionally neutralizes this view. More likely, the

will demonstrate how upon closer examination, it is clear that it is actually closely linked to the rest of the book in terms of both its themes and its vocabulary, and that it represents the culmination and completion of God's answer to Habakkuk's questions. The chapter begins and ends with Habakkuk speaking in the first person – the first time a prayer, the second time an expression of trust, with a dramatic description of how God has intervened in the past to save the Jewish people comprising the bulk of the middle of the chapter.

There are a number of stylistic and linguistic elements which connect this chapter with the book of Psalms, and Radak in his commentary here was the first to point this out. The construction of the first sentence, "A prayer of Habakkuk the prophet concerning the *shigyonot,*" matches the construction of the opening sentences of many chapters in Psalms, and a form of the word *shigyonot* itself appears in only one other place in the Bible, as *shigayon,* in Psalms 7:1. Additionally, the last two words of chapter 3, apparently a musical direction, which can be translated as "to the Conductor (*lamenatze'aḥ*) [to play] with my melodies (*binginotai*)" appear frequently in Psalms (the words "to the Conductor" appear fifty-five times in Psalms). Another link is the word *sela;*[2] this word appears three times in this chapter (vv. 3, 9, 19), and the only other book of the Bible in which this word appears is Psalms. Finally, the word "prayer" used in the superscription here also appears frequently as a superscription in Psalms (see Ps. 17, 86, 90, 102, 142, as well as 72:20). Radak advances the idea that this prayer was written as a poetic song, like those in Psalms, and expresses the prophet's praise to God for His protection throughout history while the Jewish people undergo the tribulations of exile. We will discuss these elements of

---

writers of the Habakkuk *pesher* in Qumran ignored the third chapter because it did not serve their exegetical purpose.

Interestingly, Ibn Ezra also interprets chapter 3 as separate from the first two chapters, referring to Habakkuk's prayer before an upcoming drought. This is not the approach of the majority of commentaries, however, and we will not reference it in our work.

2. The Talmud in Eiruvin (54a) interprets the word *selah* to mean "forever," a view supported by both *Targum Yonatan* and *Metzudat Tziyon* (commentary on 3:3). Ibn Ezra suggests that the word could mean "true" or "certain," or that it was a musical notation (a view also held by Radak).

connection between Habakkuk and Psalms in our interpretation of this prayer.

As mentioned above, the word *shigyonot* appears in one other place in the Bible: In Psalms, chapter 7, it appears in the singular form: *shigayon*. There, Rashi offers four interpretations of the meaning of the word *shigayon*. His first suggestion, quoting the philologist Menaḥem ben Saruq, is that it is a type of musical instrument, and that is most likely its meaning in Habakkuk, though that is not how Rashi interprets the word in Habakkuk.

Rashi in Habakkuk interprets the word *shigyonot* in accordance with his understanding in his last three interpretations in Psalms, i.e., the understanding that the word means an error or lapse in judgment:[3]

> Habakkuk is begging for mercy for himself because he had spoken rebelliously [against God]: (1:4) "Therefore Torah is slackened," and (1:14) "You have made man like the fish of the sea." [and thereby he had] criticized the divine attribute of justice. (Rashi, commentary on Hab. 3:1)

3. His other three interpretations of the word *shigayon* in Psalms 7:1 are based on understanding the word as meaning "error" or "lapse in judgment," which in this context would be referring to several incidents in David's life in which he might have acted wrongly. In his various interpretations, Rashi details these events, which, according to rabbinic thought, were events in which David later regretted his actions, and therefore in this chapter of Psalms, he might have been repenting for or praying about those regrettable incidents. Rashi refers to each of these incidents as a *shigayon*. Moed Katan 16b describes how David sang a song to celebrate Saul's downfall, but that he later regretted his behavior. According to this view, David is apologizing for this incident in Psalms, chapter 7. Sanhedrin 95a attributes indirect responsibility to David for the massacre of the priests at the city of Nob, and Rashi suggests that David is praying here that he won't be punished for that incident. David's stay there led Saul to assume that the inhabitants were rebelling against his rule. According to the midrash, David chose to fight Goliath's brother Ishbi as penance, but later regretted his choice, believing that Israel would not survive without him. Finally, Rashi suggests that David uttered this psalm after cutting off the corner of Saul's robe, an act for which, according to rabbinic thought, he was punished in I Kings, chapter 1.

In Psalms, the word prayer (*tefilla*) appears as the superscription to chapters that petition God to answer a prayer that was offered out of a feeling of helplessness. This is the case in Psalm 102:[4]

> A prayer for a poor man when he enwraps himself and pours out his speech before the Lord. O Lord, hearken to my prayer, and may my cry come to You. Do not hide Your countenance from me; on the day of my distress extend Your ear to me; on the day I call, answer me quickly. (vv. 1–3)

Habakkuk's prayer is another example of this phenomenon. Habakkuk's complaints to God earlier in the book demonstrate his feelings of helplessness. Despite these earlier feelings, Habakkuk begins his prayer here with a personal petition, acknowledging that he has heard of God's reputation for saving His people in the past, and asks Him to please do so again. Habakkuk then declares that he stands in awe of God's work. The Hebrew word for "Your work" that Habakkuk uses is *paalekha*, the root of which is P-A-L. God used a word from the same root in His answer to Habakkuk at the beginning of the book: "For a work shall be performed (*fo'al poel*) in your days that you will not believe" (1:5). Habakkuk's usage of the term *paalekha* here echoes God's usage of *fo'al poel* in chapter 1, and indicates that Habakkuk has internalized and accepted God's answer there.

Habakkuk's petition contains two requests. First, a time limit: "In the midst of the years, revive it; in the midst of the years, let it be known." Habakkuk requests: Please do not delay the defeat of evil; let the redemption take place in our lifetime, or at least, let it be known clearly that punishment will surely come. Second, and more important, Habakkuk pleads: "In anger, You shall remember to have mercy."[5] Even when punishing the Jewish people, please do not abandon us entirely.

4. Other examples include Ps. 17:1, 86:1, 90:1, and 142:1.
5. On a homiletical level, Radak suggests that the *gematria* of *raḥem*, 248, is the same as that of Abraham (spelled *alef, bet, resh, heh, mem*). He explains that Habakkuk is pleading with God, saying, "When You are angry, remember Your covenant with Abraham."

Even when the attribute of justice reigns, allow the attribute of mercy to remain. Habakkuk alludes here to the tension that exists between the need to punish the wicked and the inevitable effects that the destruction has upon the righteous. This tension will become one of the focal points of Zephaniah's prophecies, as he attempts to provide a way for the good people to escape the upcoming cataclysm.

3:3–3:19

Habakkuk's Prayer: Content and Reaction

Having prefaced his prayer with petitions, Habakkuk now begins to recall God's greatness as manifested in history:

> God came from Teman; yea, the Holy One from Mount Paran, with everlasting might. His glory covered the heavens and His splendor filled the earth. And there was a brightness like the light; they had rays from His hand, and there was His strength hidden. A pestilence went before Him, and sparks went out at His feet. He stood and meted out to the earth; He saw and caused nations to wander. And the everlasting mountains were shattered; the everlasting hills were humbled. The ways of the world are His. Because of iniquity I saw the tents of Cushan; the curtains of the land of Midian quaked. (3:3–7)

This section, which continues until the end of 3:15, is the largest of the chapter, and is considered a theophany, i.e., an appearance of God. The section can be divided into two subsections: the dramatic approach of God from the south (vv. 3–7) and the description of God's wrath during a battle with cosmic evil (vv. 8–15). The chapter concludes with the prophet's grateful response (vv. 16–19). Bookending the prayer is the word "hear:" In verse 2, Habakkuk stated that he had "heard" a report of God's actions (which the prayer clarifies to mean God's previous interventions in history on behalf of the Jewish people). In verse 16, Habakkuk says that he "heard" and his insides quivered, as God is soon to act again.

Habakkuk begins by paraphrasing the beginning of Moses's final speech to his people: "The Lord came from Sinai and shone forth from Seir to them; He appeared from Mount Paran and came with some of the holy myriads; from His right hand was a fiery law for them" (Deut. 33:2). Before he died, Moses reminded the people never to forget the Exodus from Egypt and their trek to Sinai, where they would receive the Torah.[1] For Habakkuk, these two events, i.e., the Exodus from Egypt and the giving of the Torah at Sinai, become the foundation of his prayer and his praise.[2] His prayer also alludes to Deborah's song of praise after she defeated Sisera: "Lord, when You went forth out of Seir, when You marched out of the field of Edom, the earth trembled, the heavens also dripped; also the clouds dripped water. The mountains melted at the presence of the Lord, this (was at) Sinai, because of the presence of the Lord, the God of Israel" (Judges 5:4–5). By alluding to Deborah's song, Habakkuk is reminding the people that just as God intervened to defeat the people who oppressed Israel then, so too will God reappear to overthrow those who oppress Judah now. Referring to God as "the Holy One" also invites the reader to contrast Habakkuk's words here with his words to God at the beginning of his second challenge: "Are You not from everlasting, O Lord my God, my Holy One?" (1:12). There,

---

1. According to Rashi, Habakkuk is also alluding to an ancient rabbinic tradition that when God came to give the Torah, He also went to Esau and Ishmael to offer it to them, and they did not accept it. Habakkuk includes this reference in order to reawaken God's original affection for the Jewish people, and to remind his listeners why they were originally worthy of God's affection – when others rejected God's word, Israel accepted it.
2. The *Metzudot* adds another dimension to this praise. He interprets the references to Edom and Ishmael as alluding to the miracles that God performed for the Jewish people on their way to the Land of Israel (see Deut. 2:31, 3:3).

he was challenging God; now he sees God as a source of glory that fills the world with light.[3]

Verse 5 describes how God uses pestilence (*dever*) and fiery bolts (*reshef*) to defeat His enemies. *Dever* was one of the Ten Plagues that brought down the Egyptians and freed the Israelites from slavery (Ex. 9:3); *reshef* appears in Psalms 78:48 to describe the thunderbolts that God sent against the Egyptian flocks.[4] The next two verses describe how God's appearance, His "standing" upon this world, causes mountains to crumble, hills to bow, and the earth to tremble. Just as this section began with the mention of countries found to the south of Israel in the desert (Teman and Paran), it ends (v. 7) with the terror that has overtaken the countries of the south (Cushan and Midian). Verse 6 ends with a simple phrase, "The ways of the world are His," expressing the idea that God's ways are eternal, by which Habakkuk implies that God can once again intervene in history.

While the next verses (8–15) continue with the theophanic description that emphasizes God's might and alludes to historical events from Israel's past,[5] they shift from a detached third-person description of God's approach and actions to directly addressing God:

---

3. Rashi expands the historical associations found in Habakkuk's prayer far beyond the explicit list that we have developed, including in his list the entire spectrum of history, spanning from primeval events such as the Flood, the Tower of Babel, and Creation itself (as hinted to by the reference to "the light," with the definite article "the" preceding "light" alluding to the great light of Creation), to later events in history, including the victories won by Joshua, Saul, David, and Hezekiah against Israel's enemies.
4. As understood there by the *Targum*, Ibn Ezra, and Radak. Rashi brings a midrash that identifies the *reshafim* as large birds that stole the Egyptian's animals from them as they attempted to run, with their slaughtered animals over their shoulders, to escape the hail plague, though he too notes that according to its simple meaning *reshafim* means bolts of fire. Here in Habakkuk 3:5, Rashi understands the opening verses as poetically describing the giving of the Torah at Sinai, and interprets the *reshafim* as referring to the fiery angels that accompanied God.
5. Abarbanel suggests that this subsection (vv. 8–15) contains historical allusions to instances in which the Jewish people sinned but their repenting was followed by God immediately waging wars on their enemies. According to Malbim, this subsection begins in v. 7, and refers to the miracles that will occur during the time of the final messianic redemption, beginning with the return of the ten lost tribes from Cush.

> Was the Lord angry with the rivers? Is His wrath against the rivers, or His fury against the sea? Only that You rode on Your steeds with Your chariots of salvation. Your bow revealed itself; the oaths to the tribes were a perpetual statement; You split the earth into rivers. Mountains saw You and quaked. A stream of water passed. The deep gave forth its voice. The heaven raised up its thanks. The sun and the moon stood in their dwellings; to the light of Your arrows they go, to the brightness of the lightning of Your spear. With fury You tread the earth; with wrath You trample nations. You went forth to rescue Your people, to rescue Your anointed. You have crushed the head of the house of the wicked, uncovering it from the foundation to the neck, forever. You pierced the heads of his villages with his own war clubs. They storm to scatter me. Their joy was when they could devour a poor one in secret. You trampled in the sea with Your steeds, a heap of many waters. (3:8–15)

As God's involvement in history becomes more real to Habakkuk, he becomes more personally involved. Are You angry with the sea or the waters? asks Habakkuk rhetorically. The references to God's horses and chariots of deliverance appear to be allusions to the Splitting of the Sea and the splitting of the Jordan River. The mention of God's horses and chariots is a clever, ironic twist. It was the Egyptian cavalry and their charioteers that posed a mortal threat to the Jewish people at the time of the Exodus; now, in the retelling of the story, it is God's horses and chariots that are poetically portrayed as having overcome the Egyptian horses and chariots. Verse 9 then shifts to simple and short statements that Habakkuk makes about God, who, having unsheathed His bow and His rods, is described as preparing His weaponry. The next few verses (10–12) describe how the natural world is thrown out of its natural order as God wages war on His enemies: mountains rock, water turns upstream (or split), and the depths of the earth roar, while the sun and moon stand still. The idea of reversal of fortune, so prominent in the "woe" prophecies of chapter 2, reappears in the second half of verse 13 and in verse 14, most poignantly apparent in the phrase "You pierced the heads of his villages with his own war clubs." The description of God's battle against the nations concludes in verse 15 by returning to the imagery of horses that trample and the foaming of waters, allusions to the Splitting of the Sea that appeared in verse 8. While it is not clear from the verses who is the beneficiary of God's actions,[6] the central message of these verses is unmistakable: Just as God intervened in the past to redeem Israel from its enemies, Habakkuk has no doubt that He will do so again in the future.

In summary, Habakkuk envisions the appearance of God, full of splendor, might, and glory, and describes the resulting battle with the world, which will cause the earth to tremble, the water to split, and the heavenly bodies to stand still. Verse 12 makes clear that God has gone to war because of His indignation with regard to the evil and injustice in the world, and verse 13 clarifies the corresponding principle, that this was all done for the benefit of the Jewish people. These two verses recall Habakkuk's two petitions to God, i.e., the petition that He should act in his days, represented by going to war, and that when He does go to war, He should temper His anger with mercy. The allusions to God's historical interventions in history that permeate the prayer, including references to the Ten Plagues against Egypt, the splitting of both the Sea of Reeds and the Jordan River, the stopping of the sun and moon in the skies over Israel as Joshua fought, and the flooding of the Kidron Valley to assist Deborah and Barak in their fight against Sisera, all serve to remind the listeners that God has acted on Israel's behalf in the past and will do so again in the future.

Habakkuk concludes by expressing the effect that this final vision has upon him personally:[7]

---

6. For example, in v. 10, Rashi and the *Metzudot* understand the shaking of the mountains and the flowing of waters as an allusion to the entry of the Jewish people into the Land of Israel in Josh. 3–4, while Radak suggests that the mountains are a metaphor for the Canaanite kings who heard of God's miracles while Israel was in the desert. In verse 13, Rashi suggests that the "anointed one" that God saves refers to Kings Saul and David, while the *Metzudot* suggests that it refers to Hezekiah, who was saved from the Assyrians (*Daat Mikra* notes that every king of Judah is considered an "anointed one"). Radak interprets "Your anointed" as referring to the Jewish people in the times of the Messiah and the war of Gog and Magog.
7. Rashi adopts the approach of the *Targum Yonatan*, who understands that Habakkuk is expressing how the Babylonians will react to the news of their upcoming destruction, and the later joy of vv. 18–19 describes Israel's reaction. Given the intensely personal nature of Habakkuk's prophecy, we have chosen to interpret that Habakkuk is depicting his personal reaction to his deeper understanding of God's plan for history.

> I heard, and my inward parts trembled; my lips quivered at the sound. Decay entered my bones, and I quaked in my place, that [the time] I would rest is destined for a day of trouble, to bring up a people that will troop back. For a fig tree shall not blossom; neither is there produce on the vines. The labor of the olive tree shall fail, and the grain field shall not produce food. The flock shall be cut off from the fold, and there shall be no cattle in the stalls. Yet, I will rejoice in the Lord; I will jubilate in the God of my salvation. God the Lord is my strength. He made my feet [as swift] as the hind's, and He guides me on my high places. To the Conductor [to play] with my melodies! (3:16–19)

While the vision initially caused the prophet to physically tremble and shake, he is now capable of relaxing and remaining calm when the enemy invades. While he eloquently describes the devastation that warfare will inflict on the Land of Israel – the demise of Israel's natural bounty, including the fig trees, olive trees, and vineyards and the disappearance of flocks and herds – he is still able to respond with confidence and tranquility: "Yet, I will rejoice in the Lord; I will jubilate in the God of my salvation." Like the deer that confidently leaps over dangerous crags in the mountains, Habakkuk states that with God's help, he will be able to persevere and continue forward.

Rabbi Shalom Carmy describes the process in which a religious person can move from frustration and suffering to acceptance and joy as follows:

> The human being who yearns to stand before God thus is possessed of an unwavering integrity of commitment and an unflinching honesty that can absorb hard truths about the world and oneself. Such an individual longs to make his own the joyous affirmation with which the Psalmist concludes his meditation on the mystery of evil: "As for me, the nearness of God, that is my good" (Ps. 73:28).[8]

8. Hayyim Angel, *Peshat Isn't So Simple: Essays on Developing a Religious Methodology to Bible Study* (Jersey City: Ktav Publishing, 2014), 295, quoting Rabbi Shalom Carmy, "Tell Them I've Had a Good Enough Life," in *Jewish Perspectives on the Experience of Suffering* (Northvale, NJ: Jason Aronson, 1999), 148.

In conclusion, we note that Habakkuk's prayer in chapter 3, which describes his growing sense of faith and trust in God's ways, parallels his original dialogue with and challenges to God in chapter 1. He lamented over the prevailing wickedness in 1:2–4; he prays for deliverance in 3:2. He reported God's description of the impending march against and attack on the Babylonian hordes in 1:5–11, but finds a parallel antithesis in his description of how God intervened in history in 3:3–15, portraying Him as the Divine Warrior, much more powerful than any human force. Finally, his lament of injustice in 1:12–17 is balanced by his unconditional expression of trust in God's ways in 3:16–19. Repeated or similar language connects the two chapters as well, inviting parallels:

Habakkuk 1	Habakkuk 3
O Lord! How long will I cry and You will not *hear*! (1:2)	O Lord, I *heard* a report of You. (3:2) I *heard*, and my inward parts trembled; my lips quivered at the sound. (3:16)
I cry out to You of violence, and You will not *save*! (1:2)	You went forth to *save* Your people… (3:13) Yet, I will rejoice in the Lord; I will jubilate in the God of my *salvation*. (3:18)
Therefore Torah is slackened, and justice does not go out forever, for a *wicked* man surrounds the righteous… (1:4) Why should You gaze upon traitors, be silent when a *wicked* man swallows up one more righteous than he? (1:13)	You have crushed the head of the house of the *wicked*. (3:13)
See among the nations, and look, and wonder with amazement, for He is *performing a deed* (*fo'al poel*) in your days. (1:5)	O Lord, I heard a report of You; I feared, O Lord, *Your deed* (*paalkha*). (3:2)

By concluding with wording that is reminiscent of the wording with which he began the book, Habakkuk shows that he has both literally and figuratively come full circle in his journey to understand God's ways.

Conclusion

Faith That Questions

Habakkuk's audacity is not unprecedented in the Bible. Some biblical figures, including Moses, David, Job, and Jeremiah, attempted to make sense of the world and the events occurring around them by trying to decipher God's ways, as is clear both from the text itself and from midrashic traditions.[1] Others, moved by a tremendous sense of empathy and inability to stand by idly in the face of injustice, felt empowered to stand before God and actively challenge Him, holding Him accountable for what occurs in history. Abraham firmly believed that the Lord is a God of justice, and it is precisely this faith that led him to challenge God directly when God announced that He would destroy wicked Sodom: "Is it just to destroy indiscriminately the righteous and the wicked.... Shall not the Judge of all the earth not do justice?" (Gen. 18:23, 25). When the murmurings among the Jewish people in the desert erupted into Korah's rebellion, God threatened to exterminate the entire congregation, but Moses stood in His way: "Will one man sin, and You will be angry with the entire congregation?" (Num. 16:22). The

1. The issue of God's justice and theodicy are addressed in Psalms 92, Jeremiah 22, and the entire book of Job. See also the talmudic discussion of Moses's questioning to understand God's justice in Berakhot 7a.

angel wished to appoint Gideon as a judge, in order to lead his people away from oppression, but Gideon demurred: "Please my Lord, if the Lord be with us, why then has all this befallen us? And where are all His wonders that our forefathers told us of, saying, 'Did not the Lord bring us up from Egypt?' But now the Lord has forsaken us, and He has delivered us into the hand of Midian" (Judges 6:13). Gideon does not accept the simple theological equation that the people have sinned and therefore deserve punishment; rather, he challenges God, saying: If You are the God of history, who intervened on Israel's behalf in the past, why are You silent now? Significantly, God's response to Gideon is "Go, with this your strength, and save Israel from the hand of Midian" (6:14). Radak asks what strength is God referring to, and answers that the strength that allowed Gideon to challenge God on behalf of the people is precisely the strength that will give Gideon the ability to redeem them.

Habakkuk does both: he attempts to decipher God's ways through laments and reflection, but also reaches the understanding that he must actively challenge God. He wonders about God's ability to remain seemingly silent while suffering and pain continue to rage unabated, and laments this situation: "How long, O Lord, shall I cry out and You not listen? Shall I shout to You 'violence' and You not save?" (1:2). But instead of screaming pointlessly to the heavens, Habakkuk engages in dialogue in which he actively challenges God's decisions. In 1:4, he asks God why He has seemingly turned a blind eye to injustice: "Torah is numbed…judgment emerges deformed." Does He not see that His seeming indifference to injustice causes God's own aspirations to be perverted? These laments and challenges reveal Habakkuk's essential character: he wants goodness to succeed. He hates evil and sin passionately, and he understands how when left unchecked, they lead to a fundamental breakdown of society. And he understands that now, the proper religious response is not to passively accept everything that occurs, but to question and even challenge God. And because Habakkuk shows that he shares God's visions and hopes for the future, God ultimately answers his questions, not just once but twice, with an increasing level of closeness and intimacy each time.

Just as Habakkuk was willing to question, he was also willing to listen and to learn. After he had prayed, questioned, and challenged, he was ready to stand with confidence "upon the watchtower," watching and waiting for the divine response and meaning. By going through the process of questioning and challenging followed by waiting and then listening, he was able to come to the understanding that though his questions weren't answered immediately, it did not mean that answers do not exist. Sometimes, passive patience is enough – other times, a person must work actively to develop a sense of faith. Habakkuk demonstrates how faith can be built. Pay attention, he says – watch how evil ultimately crumples under its own weight. The building built on a foundation of sin will collapse. Habakkuk's process of prayer, active challenge, waiting, and listening was completed by a final component, that of learning from history. The God that he had accused of indifference was the same God that he knew had performed tremendous miracles for the children of Israel. God did not abandon His people before, and Habakkuk understood that ultimately, God would save them this time as well. Though redemption may tarry, it would arrive.

Zephaniah

Introduction

The prophet's job of reprimanding the Jewish people for their failings and warning them of the resulting tribulations was never a popular one. To be a prophet at a time when the people finally enjoyed a respite from oppression and persecution, and to have to tell them that their peace and quiet was only a temporary illusion, would make a prophet's job even more unpleasant. Zephaniah prophesied at a time when Judah finally began to assert its independence from Assyria and enjoyed a period of prosperity and peace under King Josiah's reign. Like Isaiah's iconic lone watchman on the watchtower perceiving the growing Babylonian storm clouds forming in the distance (Is. 21), Zephaniah foresaw and understood the devastating nature of the upcoming catastrophe that would befall the people. While his people enjoyed quiet, Zephaniah spoke of the upcoming "day of the Lord," in terms more terrible and terrifying than any prophet before him.

We do not know much about Zephaniah the person besides his ancestry. His name could mean "the Lord hides" (or "has hidden"), "the Lord's watchman," or "the Lord's treasured."[1] If his great-great-grandfather Hezekiah was indeed the great King Hezekiah of Judah (726–697 BCE;

1. In the Bible, four separate people carry the name Zephaniah: the prophet of our book, the priest asked to rebuke Jeremiah in Jer. 29, a member of the Kohath family in

see II Kings 18–20), then Zephaniah came from royal stock, which gives added meaning to his criticisms of the behaviors of princes and nobility (see, for example, 1:8: "And it shall be on the day of the Lord's slaughter, that I will visit upon the princes, and upon the king's sons…"). He was the first prophet in Judah to be able to prophesize openly since Isaiah and Micah during the reign of Hezekiah almost a century earlier. Zephaniah boldly delivered his message in front of Josiah. Much of his prophecy refers to Jerusalem specifically; he even names its gates, which indicates his familiarity with the capital, as would befit a king's descendant (see 1:10–11). Additionally, Zephaniah draws heavily upon preceding prophetic works, so much so that one modern scholar goes so far as to assert that "the message of Zephaniah [is] basically an echo, a reformulation of earlier prophetic material," and asks, "[What] originality does Zephaniah evince?"[2] As we will note in our commentary, Zephaniah is indeed heavily reliant on earlier material, but his prophecy is not merely a repetition or compendium of other books. Rather, he draws from older texts in highly original ways, adapting previous familiar voices in a unique manner and creating an independent book that clearly expresses his own unique message. Rabbinic tradition suggests that his audience was the educated nobility of Judah: "Jeremiah prophesied in the markets, Zephaniah in the synagogues, and Huldah with the women." (*Pesikta Rabbati* 26). This claim is evidenced in the book by his repeated references to the princes, prophets, and priests (see 1:8–9; 3:3–4).

As a poet, Zephaniah does not use as many poetic devices as Nahum did, but instead uses a terse, staccato style to convey his ideas.[3] He often repeats the same words over and over, a device which serves to link ideas together and frame sections. His central message is that the people have to prepare for the upcoming cataclysm which he calls *yom*

I Chr. 6, and the priest in Zechariah's vision in Zech. 6. The name appears ten times in the Bible, twice spelled with a *vav* at the end of the word.

2. Greg A. King, "The Message of Zephaniah: An Urgent Echo," *Andrews University Seminary Studies* 32, no. 2 (Autumn 1996): 212; see nn4, 5. He quotes Martin Buber, who called Zephaniah "a 'compendium' of prophetic teaching."

3. "Zephaniah's style is chiefly characterized by a unity and harmony of composition plus energy of style. Rapid and effective alternations of threats and promises also characterize his style." Larry Lee Walker, "Zephaniah," in *Daniel–Malachi*, vol. 7 of *The Expositor's Bible Commentary*, 540.

Hashem, “the day of the Lord.” To emphasize his point, he repeats this phrase and emphasizes the word “day” throughout his prophecy, especially in the following central verses of the first chapter:

> The Lord’s great Day of Judgment is almost here; it is very rapidly approaching!
> There will be a bitter sound on the Lord’s Day of Judgment;
> at that time warriors will cry out in battle.
> That day will be:
> a day of God’s anger,
> a day of distress and hardship,
> a day of devastation and ruin,
> a day of darkness and gloom,
> a day of clouds and dark skies. (1:14–15)

Additionally, Zephaniah has a tendency to engage in clever wordplay. For example, in his prophecy against the Philistine coastal cities, he plays twice on their names and eventual fates:

> For Gaza shall be deserted (*Azza azuva*)
> and Ashkelon shall become a wasteland.
> Ashdod, at noon they shall drive her out,
> and Ekron shall be uprooted (*Ekron te’aker*). (2:4)

Zephaniah also utilizes traditional poetic devices like metaphor and simile, literary/historical allusions, personification, alliteration, repetition, and refrain. In general, though, he forsakes poetic devices, preferring to overwhelm his listeners with the import and gravity of his message:[4]

---

4. J. M. P. Smith writes, “Zephaniah can hardly be considered great as a poet.... He had an imperative message to deliver and proceeded in the most direct and forceful way to discharge his responsibility. What he lacked in grace and charm, he in some measure atoned for by the vigour and clarity of his speech. He realized the approaching terror so keenly that he was able to present it vividly and convincingly to his hearers. No prophet has made the picture of the day of the Lord more real” (*A Critical and Exegetical Commentary on Micah, Zephaniah and Nahum*, p. 176, available online at https://archive.org/details/criticalexegetic24smituoft/page/n6).

The book states that Zephaniah prophesied during the reign of King Josiah (639–608 BCE; see 1:1). Josiah was only eight years old when he ascended to the throne after his father's assassination. He started his program of religious reforms in the twelfth year of his rule, four years after he began his own process of personal spiritual awakening (see II Chr. 34:3). Before then, we can safely speculate that the kingdom was run by royal officials who had served under his wicked father and grandfather. Judah began to look different, however, once Josiah began his program of actively ridding Judah of idolatry. Assyria was a no longer a factor, and Josiah was also able to annex former areas of the Northern Kingdom under his rule. The discovery of the book of the Torah in the Temple, in 621 BCE (see II Kings 22: 3–13), combined with the prophetess Huldah's reiteration that a divine decree of anger still hung over Judah (see II Kings 22:14–20), provided additional impetus for Josiah to bring the people to repentance, and gave even more urgency and intensity to his efforts to eradicate idolatry from the country.

Josiah began his program of religious reforms in 627 BCE. Did Zephaniah prophesy before or afterward? He makes no explicit reference to Josiah or the reforms. He often quotes from the book of Deuteronomy, which Rashi suggests was the book that Hilkiah discovered while repairing the Temple in 622 BCE (commentary on II Chr. 34:14). Quoting from Deuteronomy would serve to enhance the authority of the prophet as well as Josiah, who used this important discovery to consolidate a series of religious and political reforms. The moral and spiritual conditions that Zephaniah lamented could easily describe two time periods. One likely period would have been the earlier portion of Josiah's reign, when the monarch was still a child and Manasseh's wicked influence still permeated the kingdom. However, he could also have prophesied after Josiah's attempts to reform the people. Despite the king's best efforts, and the drama of discovering a hidden Torah scroll in the Temple, perhaps the people still persisted in their apostasy and immorality.

Others suggest that despite the mention of Josiah in the superscription, Zephaniah prophesied during the reign of Jehoiakim. At that time, it was becoming clear that the Kingdom of Judah was tottering on its last legs. Zephaniah made constant references to the fact that only a remnant of the nation would survive the upcoming cataclysm, and that they would have to return to Israel to take possession of the land again (2:3, 2:7). This implies that the kingdom was facing a viable threat of annihilation and exile, something not true in the early days of Josiah, when the Assyrian Empire was still standing and the Babylonians had not yet consolidated their control over Mesopotamia.[5]

Most lean toward an earlier dating, for several reasons. Even in Josiah's time, the threat of exile remained a distinct possibility, as per the threat of the anonymous prophets during Manasseh's reign (see II Kings 21:10–15). The religious practices that Zephaniah describes, especially the Canaanite syncretistic rites, were characteristic of Manasseh's rule (1:4–5, 9).[6] This is also true of his criticism of the socioeconomic ills and the extensive inequality that plagued Judah. The country had an upper class that would parade itself in international fashion (see 1:8), supported by international trade and business enterprises (see 1:10–11) while exploiting the labor of the lower classes (see 1:12–13, 18). These traits reflected a society more internationally involved, not the Judah under Josiah's rule, which tended toward isolationist policies. Rabbi Yoel Bin-Nun has argued that not only do the prophecies in chapter 1

5. We shall suggest the possibility that the book contains several different prophecies, spanning the different time periods mentioned above.
6. The references to Baal do not prove decisively that Zephaniah prophesied before Josiah's reforms. While Josiah managed to erase public idolatry, rabbinic thought speaks of an undercurrent that Josiah's reforms did not manage to fundamentally change the people's ways:

   > R. Yehuda said that Rav said … [that] Josiah said [to himself]: "Since he [Pharaoh Neco] puts his trust in his idols, I will prevail over him"…. On what did Josiah rely? On the divine promise contained in the words, "And no sword shall pass through your land" (Lev. 26:6). What sword? Is it the warring sword? It is already stated [in the same verse], "And I will give peace in the land" – it must then refer to the peaceful sword. Josiah, however, did not know that his generation found but little favor [in the eyes of God]. (Taanit 22b)

   This idea is expanded in the midrash:

   > Josiah did not know that his entire generation worshipped idols. What did the scoffers of his generation do? They would put half of the idol on one door, and half on the other door. [Josiah] would send two wise men to purge their homes from idols. They would enter, but find nothing. As they left, [the scoffers] would have them close the door, so that, on the inside, the idols would be reattached. (Lamentations Rabba 1:18)

provide the blueprint for Josiah's religious reforms, the prophecies against the nations in chapter 2 serve as the blueprint for Josiah's political program of the expansion of Judah's borders (see II Kings 23:1–25, II Chr. 34:32–35:19). Accordingly, Zephaniah's prophecy may have been the catalyst for Josiah's great reformation, providing Judah with its last great moments of independence and glory. Finally, an early dating is supported by Jeremiah's rebuke of Jehoiakim's corruption, in which the prophet praises Josiah for his efforts to build the country's corrupt social fabric, something that Zephaniah later decried in his prophecy:

> [Jehoiakim] says, "I will build myself a wide house with spacious upper chambers," and he cuts out windows for himself, and it is ceiled with cedar and painted with vermilion. Shall you reign, for you compete with the cedar? Your father [Josiah] – did he not eat and drink and perform justice and righteousness? Then it was well with him. He judged the cause of the poor and needy; then it was good. Is not that the knowledge of Me? says the Lord. (Jer. 22:14–16)

Based on Malbim's commentary, we suggest a multifaceted approach to dating Zephaniah's prophecies. This approach suggests that chapter 1 and the first three verses of chapter 2 are his earlier prophecies, and were likely uttered at the beginning of Josiah's reign (639–627 BCE). Not only was the religious situation that Zephaniah spoke out against similar to the state of the people in those years, but despite the decree that hung over the nation due to Manasseh's wickedness, reform was still possible, as evidenced by Josiah's actions. When Josiah matured, he undertook a series of religious and political reforms, which led to an expansion of Judah's borders, similar to those prophesied about in chapter 2. Sadly, the people failed to take advantage of this opportunity, which ended up being their final chance to change their ways. Assyria fell, Josiah died in battle, and the country lost its independence, first to Egypt and then to Babylonia. As the decree was sealed, Zephaniah altered his message accordingly. He understood that Josiah's noble efforts were in vain. The result of this understanding is his prophecy in chapter 3, which can therefore be dated to a later period, according to this approach.

The theme that dominates Zephaniah's prophecy is the description of the upcoming "day of the Lord" – an idea so prominent that

Zephaniah references this day almost two dozen times in this short book. Previous prophets had already spoken about the "day of the Lord" as a day when the nations would be punished and Israel delivered (see, for example, Amos 8:1–3, Hos. 1:4, Is. 4:4, and Mic. 5:10–11). However, Zephaniah expanded this idea far beyond his predecessors.[7] Zephaniah emphasizes that not only is this day a terrifying day, a day of judgment, but also that it is quickly approaching (1:7). He does not speak in generalities, but rather targets both the corrupt leadership (Zeph. 1:8, 3:2, similar to Is. 3:1–3; see also Ezek. 34), as well as the people, who can be described as complacent at best ("I will punish the people, those who are thickening upon their lees, those who are saying in their hearts, 'The Lord will not do good, nor will He do evil'" [Zeph. 1:12]).[8] He expresses that it is a combination of both social injustice and idolatry that will cause the upcoming upheaval (1:4–6, 9, 3:1–3), which will encompass both Judah and its neighbors, even expanding to the entire world. Survival and deliverance are not guaranteed, even for the righteous. However, the survivors among Israel and the righteous among the nations will joyously return to Jerusalem, eventually. Zephaniah emphasizes that people cannot force God's hand; they are to wait quietly (1:7) and patiently (3:8), do acts of kindness and righteousness (2:3), and hope that God's wrath will pass over them. Zephaniah's audience is not exclusively Jewish; he alternates between prophecies that are directed toward Israel and those that are directed toward the entire world.[9]

---

7. Walter Kaiser expresses this idea in his book: "Obadiah, Joel, Amos, and Isaiah had all spoken of this day, but Zephaniah alone emphasized more strenuously than them all the universality of its judgment while also surprisingly predicting the conversion of the nations as one of its fruits" (Walter C. Kaiser Jr., *Toward an Old Testament Theology*, 223).
8. Similar to Amos's declaration that people "who are at ease ... who feel secure" (Amos 6:1) are slated for punishment.
9. Explaining Zephaniah's alternation between prophecies directed at the Jewish people and the universal prophecies, Malbim suggests distinguishing between two types of prophecies of redemption in the prophetic literature. Prophecies that were expected to occur within the prophets' lifetime were generally directed at the particular situation of Israel and Judah. However, there was an additional layer of prophetic meaning, more universal in scope, which spoke of peace and prosperity for all mankind (commentary on Zeph. 3:1).

Ascertaining the structure of the book is difficult. As Adele Berlin notes, despite its small size, there is no consensus on how to divide the book, nor are there any internal markers to indicate how to divide it.[10] Based on the repetition of prophecies which alternate between those directed at the nations and those directed specifically at Israel, we suggest the following outline for the book:

I. The Announcement of the Upcoming "Day of the Lord" (1:1–2:3)
   i. Judgment of the whole world (1:2–3)
   ii. Judgment of Judah and Jerusalem (1:4–16)
      a. for idolatry (1:4–6)
      b. for social injustice (1:8–13)
      c. "The day of the Lord" (1:7, 14–16)
   iii. Judgment of the whole world (1:17–18)
   iv. God exhorts the people to pursue justice and humility (2:1–3)

II. The Resulting Punishment of Judah and Jerusalem(2:4–3:8)
   i. The upcoming destruction of the nations (2:4–15)
      a. Judgment of the Philistines (2:4–7)
      b. Judgment of Ammon and Moab (2:8–11)
      c. Judgment of Cush (2:12)
      d. Judgment of Nineveh (2:13–15)
   ii. The upcoming destruction of Judah and Jerusalem (3:1–5)
   iii. The destruction of the nations (3:6–7)
   iv. Zephaniah calls upon the righteous (3:8)

III. The Redemption of Judah and Jerusalem and the Nations (3:9–end)
   i. Purification of the nations (3:9)
   ii. Purification and return of Israel/Celebration in Jerusalem (3:10–19)
   iii. Israel and the nations celebrate in Jerusalem (3:20)

10. "The book of Zephaniah is a short book, and, aside from the superscription that introduces it, there are no editorial insertions to suggest how it is to be subdivided.... Modern translations and commentaries differ considerably in their subdivision into sections.... The lack of agreement in dividing so small a body of text is truly amazing" (Berlin, *Zephaniah: A New Translation*).

The table below clearly demonstrates the parallels between the various sections:

Section	I. The Day of the Lord (1:1–2:3)	II. The Resulting Punishment (2:4–3:8)	III. The Redemption (3:9–end)
Introduction: universal focus	(1:2–3) The upcoming destruction of the world	(2:4–2:15) Specific predictions about the upcoming destruction of Judah's neighbors	(3:9–10) The remaining nations are redeemed
Main remarks: directed toward Judah and Jerusalem	(1:4–16) The upcoming destruction of Judah and Jerusalem for the sins of (a) idolatry and (b) social injustice	(3:1–5) Repetition of the sins of the leadership, which include (a) idolatry and (b) social injustice	(3:11–18) Redemption of the Jewish people and their return to the Land of Israel, on a day that will be designated for rejoicing.
Summary: universal focus with emphasis on Judah	(1:17–18) Wealth cannot prevent universal destruction	(3:6–7) The example of the destroyed nations as a warning to Judah	(3:19–20) The Jewish people become a source of God's pride and glory among the nations
Instruction: directed toward the righteous	(2:1–3) The directive to gather together, behave with justice and humility, and hope that the punishment will not affect them	(3:8) The faithful are told to wait until the punishment ends	

The table demonstrates clear distinctions between the first two sections. Both contain warnings to the Jewish people, enveloped by warnings and threats directed against the nations of the world. However, in the first section, the bulk of the prophecy is dedicated to describing the sins of Judah and Jerusalem, which are painstakingly listed, while the threats of global destruction are both short and vague. In the second prophecy, though the sins of Jerusalem and Judah are listed, they comprise a much smaller part of the prophecy. Instead, the majority of the text focuses on the specific types of destruction that will befall Judah's neighbors, who are now explicitly named as Philistia, Ammon and Moab, Cush, and Assyria. Similarly, in the first section, the exhortation at the end of the prophecy is active, directed to the entire nation ("Gather together, O nation that has no desire" [2:1]), and presents the listeners with a roadmap that may allow them to avoid the upcoming calamity. In the second section, the nations have been destroyed, yet despite Zephaniah's hope that the people would learn from their example, Judah and Jerusalem stubbornly continue in their corrupt ways. The most Zephaniah can do now is to merely advise his remaining listeners to wait for better times ahead. Only in this second section does Zephaniah begin to refer to "a remnant" that will survive the cataclysm.

It is highly likely that the first prophecy, uttered while the upcoming destruction was still an abstraction (though terrifying), was aimed at the entire nation in the early days of Josiah's reign, and likely provided the impetus for his reforms. The second, darker prophecy ends with the destruction of Judah's neighbors being a *fait accompli* (3:6–7). Zephaniah does not speak to the nation anymore, for they haven't learned. Instead, Zephaniah talks to a remnant that would soon see the total upheaval of the world. Similarly, the resulting third prophecy, which speaks of joyous redemption for Israel and return to Jerusalem, was uttered during the later years of Josiah's reign, as the tottering Assyrian Empire began to fall and Josiah's inability to make long-lasting change among the people became painfully clear.

1:1

Superscription

> The word of the Lord that came to Zephaniah son of Cushi, son of Gedaliah, son of Amariah, son of Hezekiah, in the days of Josiah son of Amon, king of Judah. (1:1)

Like several other prophetic books,[1] Zephaniah begins with a superscription in which the prophet declares that the declaration that will follow is indeed "the word of the Lord." It then provides the genealogy of the prophet and the king who reigned while he prophesied. This book's genealogy is unusual, tracing Zephaniah's lineage back four generations to his great-grandfather, Hezekiah. This raises two questions. First, why provide a lineage of four generations, unique among the books of the prophets? The second, related question is: Is this Hezekiah the famous king who ruled over Judah generations before, so highly regarded that it is said about him that "[none] after him was like him among all the kings of Judah, nor among them that were before him" (II Kings 18:5)? Some commentaries suggest that this is the same Hezekiah, and that this is the rationale for the lengthy genealogy in this verse (see Ibn Ezra, who claims that it is the same person, and

1. See Hos. 1:1, Joel 1:1, Mic. 1:1, and the Septuagint version of Jer. 1:1.

Radak, who says that this may or may not be the same Hezekiah but that even if this is not, the long lineage which lists four generations indicates at the very least that Zephaniah came from a distinguished family). Others disagree with this identification, bringing several different explanations as to why it could not be, or is not necessarily, the same person. One claim is that since Hezekiah is not referred to as the "king of Judah," the reference could not be to King Hezekiah.[2] Another is that the time span between the birth of Hezekiah's oldest son, Manasseh (ca. 710 BCE), and the birth of Josiah (ca. 648 BCE) is too short to allow four full generations. A third is that Hezekiah was a common name in Judah (cf. I Chr. 3:23, Ezra 2:16, Neh. 7:21), so the mention of the name does not necessarily indicate a reference to the renowned king. However, these explanations do not account for the reason for the listing of four generations.

Rabbi Yoel Bin-Nun offers an interesting and important suggestion as to the reason behind the extended lineage. He views the mention of four generations as demonstrating that Zephaniah represented the last link of a prophetic chain that went back to Isaiah, Micah, Hosea, and Amos, who prophesied in the time of Hezekiah. The many allusions and hints to Isaiah's prophecies in Zephaniah's words reinforce this idea. These references and the link to the earlier prophets add legitimacy and authority to the prophet's words, ensuring that his warning of upcoming danger will be taken more seriously, while also providing an optimistic undertone: despite the generations of darkness and persecution under Manasseh's rule, the word of God has survived.

2. Abarbanel advances this claim, asserting that if other kings of Judah, such as Amon and Josiah, who reigned for less time and were less righteous, were referred to with the title "king of Judah," then certainly the text would have referred to Hezekiah, who was exceedingly righteous and reigned for a long period, as such. However, Abarbanel rejects this argument, pointing out that even if it were the same Hezekiah, the text would not have referred to him as king of Judah, as kings in the Bible are not called "king" after their death or if they have abdicated; e.g., once Solomon ascends the throne, the book of Kings no longer refers to David as "king." Only one person can be called king at any one time.

A third and final question about the genealogy mentioned in the superscription is, Why does the text refer to Josiah as the son of Amon?[3] Mentioning Josiah's father reminds us of his evil ways, which according to II Kings was a continuation of the evil and idolatrous reign of Manasseh (II Kings 21:20). As Josiah assumed the throne at the young age of eight years, his religious and political reforms did not begin for at least a decade. Listing Amon here may allude to the time of Zephaniah's original prophecies, a time when a young boy-king sat upon Judah's throne, advised and influenced by his father's courtiers.[4]

3. In other superscriptions, most kings are not identified by their father, except for Jeroboam son of Joash, who is identified as such to distinguish him from the earlier Jeroboam son of Nebat.
4. Suggested by my son Yoshiyahu, who is appropriately named after King Josiah.

1:2–1:18

"The Day of the Lord"

> The day of the Lord is coming. (1:7)

Other prophets said this, but no one saw it so closely or so clearly as Zephaniah.[1] For this reason, a sense of frantic urgency pervades every line of his prophecy. The first chapter describes the upcoming day of the Lord in three phases, as follows:

a. The impending punishment: God declares that He will destroy the world (1:2–3), and then specifies the particular targets in Judah that He will eradicate (1:4–6).
b. Zephaniah announces the upcoming day of the Lord and the cause of its arrival, i.e., the various social sins of which Judah is guilty (1:7–13).

1. A partial list of mentions of "the day of the Lord" includes Is. 13, Jer. 46, Joel 2, Amos 5, Ob. 1, and Mal. 3. Zephaniah's reliance on previous prophecies in crafting his message has led one commentary to declare that "Zephaniah encapsulates in miniature almost the whole range of Old Testament prophecy" (O'Brian, *Nahum*, 89).

c. Finally, Zephaniah emphatically details the day of the Lord, describing the devastation and horrors that will befall Judah and the world as a result of their sins (1:14–18).

Zephaniah begins by stating that God plans to destroy the world:

I will totally destroy everything from off the face of the earth, says the Lord.

> I will totally destroy man and beast; I will totally destroy the birds of the heavens, and the fish of the sea, and the stumbling blocks with the wicked; and I will cut off man from the face of the earth, says the Lord. And I will stretch out My hand over Judah and over all the inhabitants of Jerusalem. And I will cut off from this place the remnant of Baal, the name of the idolatrous priests with the priests; and those who prostrate themselves on the roofs to the host of the heavens, and those who prostrate themselves who swear by the Lord, and swear by Malcam; and those who turn away from following the Lord, and those who did not seek the Lord nor inquired after Him. (1:2–6)

The Hebrew words *asof asef* in verse 2 can be read as "I will gather them up and make a total end of them," or it can be understood as "I will utterly destroy them" (like Jer. 8:13).[2] The words reappear in the next verse – *asef* (I will destroy) man and beast, *asef* (I will destroy) birds and fish. The repetition strengthens the sense that everything will be destroyed; God is, as it were, cataloging those inhabitants of the world that are targets for destruction. The totality of the upcoming destruction echoes the introduction to the Flood story:[3]

---

2. See *Daat Mikra*, and *Mikra LeYisrael* ad loc.
3. Other parallels to the Flood narrative include Zephaniah's utilization of "from off the face of the earth" (Gen. 6:7, 7:4, 8:8), *kol* ("all," "everything"; cf. Gen. 6:17, 7:4, 8:19), and *adama* ("ground"; cf. Gen. 6:7, 20, 7:4, 8, 23, 8:8, 13, 21). A discussion of the parallels can be found in Hayyim Angel's essay "Zephaniah's Use of the Genesis Narratives," *Revealed Texts, Hidden Meanings*, 162–71.

   There is also an aural allusion in the opening words *asof asef* to another section of the Flood narrative: Gen. 8:21. When Noah exits the ark, he offers a thanksgiving sacrifice. The Torah states "And the Lord smelled the pleasant aroma, and the Lord said

Genesis 6:7	Zephaniah 1:3
And the Lord said: "I will blot out *man* whom I have created *from the face of the earth*; both *man and beast*, and creeping thing, and *the birds of the heavens*; for it pains Me that I have made them."	I will totally destroy everything from off *the face of the earth, says the Lord.* I will totally destroy *man and beast*; I will totally destroy *the birds of the heavens*, and the fish of the sea, and the stumbling blocks with the wicked; and I will cut off *man from the face of the earth*, says the Lord.

Another important parallel between Zephaniah and the Flood narrative is the cause. In Genesis, the Torah explicitly blames *ḥamas*, violence, for the impending flood: "For the earth has become full of *ḥamas* because of them, and behold, I am destroying them from the earth" (6:13). Twice, Zephaniah lists *ḥamas* as rampant in Jerusalem, both in 1:9 – "those who fill the houses of their masters with *ḥamas* (violence) and deceit" and in 3:4 – "Her priests have profaned the Sanctuary; they have done violence (*ḥamsu*) to the Torah. Zephaniah arranges his list in inverse order to that of Creation: man, beast, birds, and fish of the sea (cf. Gen. 1:20–27). Creation found its climax in man, who was made in God's image and given the world as his domain to rule over (Gen. 1:28–30). Therefore, while the coming devastation will begin with man, it will ultimately bring down the entire world.[4] Everything in creation that has become a stumbling-block for man will be destroyed, and man himself will be

---

to Himself, 'I will no longer (*osif*) curse the earth because of man, for the imagination of man's heart is evil from his youth, and I will no longer (*osif*) smite all living things as I have done.'" With this aural allusion, Zephaniah may be signaling a reversal of the promise in Genesis.

4. An androcentric understanding of this principle can be found in the Midrash (Genesis Rabba 28:6):

> R. Pinḥas said: This may be compared to a king who was marrying off his son, and who built his *ḥuppa* (wedding canopy), limed it, and decorated it elaborately. The king later became furious with his son and killed him. What did he then do? He entered the *ḥuppa*, shattered the barrels, ripped down the decorations, and tore down the curtains. The king said, "All this, I made only for my son; [now that] my son is lost, this should remain?" Thus, "From man to animal to bird of the heavens," similar to what is stated in Zeph. 1:2.

cut off from the land that sustains him. Here, Zephaniah effectively uses the literary tool called paronomasia, i.e., usage of words similar in sound to achieve a specific effect, here, to emphasize the connection between man and the earth: In Genesis 2:7, man (*adam*) was formed from the land (*adama*); now, man is cut off from the land.

Facing the enormity and the universality of the destruction that Zephaniah describes, some commentaries attempt to minimize and limit its scope. Radak states that 'birds of the heavens and fish of the sea' was [meant as] an exaggeration";[5] similarly, Abarbanel suggests that the imagery is symbolic: "'Birds of the heavens' alludes to kings and aristocrats who rise in flight in their reigns, [while] 'fish of the sea' describes groups of men who engage in immorality and theft [just as the fish do]." The ending of chapter 1 does not support these suggestions. It states that the effects of the day of Lord will be felt globally; as such, Zephaniah also began with a description of the destruction of the entire world. One of the most defining characteristics of Zephaniah's message is that not only are the fates of the Jewish people and of the non-Jews intertwined, but the actions of the Jewish people affect God's relationship with the entire world. The parallels with the Flood narrative reinforce this message. Just as corruption led to the destruction of the entire world in Noah's time, worldwide catastrophe will now come again as a result of the myriad sins of the Jewish people.

Having announced the upcoming destruction, Zephaniah focuses on the fate of Judah and the Jewish people. In the next three verses, God identifies three different groups of people who are deserving of punishment: the overt pagans and idolaters, those who serve both God and other gods (syncretism), and the religiously indifferent. However, they are not the only ones to face divine punishment. Zephaniah announces that "[God] will stretch out [His] hand over Judah, and over *all* the inhabitants of Jerusalem." In the Torah, the image of God "stretching

5. However, Radak continues with an attempt to understand the verse on a literal level:

> But it could be as it sounds, for most birds will not live in the wilderness, but in a settled area where they will find seeds and fruit and blossoms. When one settled area is destroyed, they will go to another settled area... [similarly] the fish of the sea will not multiply in large numbers other than in waters near settled areas. (commentary on 1:3)

out His hand" is a positive one, implying that God is delivering Israel (Ex. 6:6, Deut. 4:34, 5:15, 7:19, 9:29, 26:8). But the positive nature of this imagery changes throughout the Bible. In Isaiah, the image of God "stretching out His hand" becomes a negative one, symbolizing God's punishment (see Is. 5:25, 9:12, 17, 20, 14:26–27),[6] while in Jeremiah, the image serves as a symbol of God's sovereignty over the world at a time of oppression, when Jeremiah recalls better times and prays for them to return (see Jer. 32:17). In Zephaniah the image is most definitely negative: God's outstretched arm conveys the sense that everyone will be punished and there is no escape.

Many commentaries find the idea expressed in Zephaniah, that God will punish the righteous along with the wicked, theologically troubling, advancing explanations which serve to exclude the righteous from the all-inclusive-sounding punishments described in the verses. Ibn Ezra in his commentary on 1:3 attempts to limit the scope of the punishment, writing: "The stumbling blocks will be for the wicked, specifically, and so 'I will totally destroy man' refers to the wicked [only]." Regarding the verse which states that God will cut off "the name of the idolatrous priests (*kemarim*)[7] with the priests (*kohanim*)" (1:4), Rashi, Ibn Ezra, and Radak assert that the word *kohanim* (priests) refers to a variant form of idolatrous worship, thereby claiming that the *kohanim* mentioned are not, in fact, a reference to the righteous Jewish priests. Ibn Caspi and Rabbi Yosef Kara contend that *kohanim* is a reference to the Jewish priests, but that it refers to only those that are either corrupt or serve at the forbidden "high places" (*bamot*). Similarly, when destruction is promised for "those who prostrate themselves who swear by the

6. The Isaiah reference is particularly striking. In Is. 9:11, Isaiah describes the stubbornness of Israel and Samaria, despite the fact that "His anger has not turned away, and *His hand is still outstretched*," yet 9:12 continues, "And the people have not returned to the One who smites it, and the Lord of hosts they have not sought." As a result, the Northern Kingdom was destroyed. By alluding to Isaiah, Zephaniah is hinting broadly that the same fate awaits the Southern Kingdom if Judah does not mend its ways.
7. The word *kemarim* appears in two other places in Tanakh: in Hos. 10:5, referring to priests who officiated at the golden calf in Bethel; and in II Kings 22:5, referring to priests who officiated at rites associated with Baal and other idols, appointed by Manasseh but removed during Josiah's reforms.

Lord, and swear by Malcam," the above commentaries explain the verse to mean that the ones that are worshipping God are in fact the same ones that are also worshipping idols. Rashi proposes that they "make their idols the essence, saying, 'If you do not trust an oath to God, I will swear by the idol,'"[8] while Radak states that their crime is that "sometimes they bow to God and sometimes to... the idol they have crowned upon themselves. They join something else with God, worshipping it." With this behavior, they are repeating the sins of the Israelites in the time of Elijah the prophet, who at the time reprimanded the people, saying: "Until when skipping between two ideas? If the Lord is God, go after Him, and if the Baal, go after him" (I Kings 18:21).

But others argue that these words are meant to be understood as they are written. God will destroy both good and evil priests. The commentaries who espouse this approach punctuate verse 5 into two separate clauses: "those who prostrate themselves who swear by the Lord; and those who swear by Malcam," such that the meaning is that both innocent and guilty suffer.[9] According to these commentaries, Zephaniah's message is that in a time of global upheaval, no one, no matter how righteous, is guaranteed survival. Rabbinic literature already noted this feature of divine justice when discussing the Flood in the time of Noah: "Wherever you find promiscuity (and idolatry), calamity comes upon the world, killing both good and bad alike" (Genesis Rabba 26:5).

Zephaniah mentions many different forms of idolatry that will be cut off. Not unexpectedly, we find many linguistic parallels between the language that Zephaniah uses in his description of the idolatry that

8. Rashi's approach may be supported by the two different prefixes used for the words following the two instances of "those who swear" in v. 5 – *Lashem* and *beMalcam*. Though they may have outwardly sworn fealty to God, internally, their thoughts were directed to the idol.

9. Abarbanel, Malbim, *Daat Mikra* ad loc. Abarbanel writes that Zephaniah "divided the worshippers into different groups. Some bow upon public altars to the hosts of heaven; these are the wicked who worship idolatry openly. *Some bow and swear by God; these are the righteous.* Some do not bow to idols and do not bow to and swear by God... but they swear by their king, to serve the king." In Abarbanel's interpretation, the righteous are a separate group within the list, and yet they face the same fate of destruction as do the others.

is to be wiped out and the language used in II Kings 23 to describe the idolatry that was destroyed as part of King Josiah's reforms:

Zephaniah 1:4–5	**II Kings 23:4–5**
And I will cut off from this place the remnant of Baal, the name of the *idolatrous priests* (*kemarim*) with the priests; and those who prostrate themselves on the roofs to *the host of the heavens.*	And the king commanded…to take out of the Temple of the Lord all the utensils that were made for the *Baal* and for the *ashera*, and for *the entire host of the heaven*, and he burnt them outside Jerusalem…. And he abolished the *idolatrous priests* (*kemarim*) whom the kings of Judah had appointed… and those who burnt incense to the *Baal*, to the sun, to the moon, and to the constellations, and *to all the host of heaven.*

The list of the many different figures and practices associated with idolatry that Zephaniah mentions is extensive. It includes the "remnant of Baal" worshippers who remained in Judah, the priests of idolatry, the people who worshipped "the host of heaven," i.e., the sun, moon, stars, and planets, a practice which was sometimes performed on the idolaters' rooftops.[10] Additionally, those people who tried to maintain dual loyalty, worshipping both God and pagan gods, were also targets of God's wrath. Zephaniah also mentions those who swore by "Malcam." Some understand this word to be referring to the idolatrous practice of Molech, which was apparently a source of fascination and temptation for the Jewish people. The practice is first mentioned by name and prohibited in the Torah in Leviticus and Deuteronomy, and it is also specifically mentioned as being a target of Josiah's cleansing reforms (see II Kings 23:10). Others, including the ancient Latin and Syriac translations, vocalize "Malcam" as "Milcom," the god of Ammon. This idol was a source of temptation for Israel in the time of the Judges (Judges 10:6), and is directly mentioned as being among the idols that turned

10. See Deut. 4:19, II Kings 21:3, 5, 23:4–5, and Jer. 19:13 for instances of this practice.

Solomon's heart away from God (I Kings 11:5). However, for several centuries afterward, a state of enmity existed between the Jewish people and Ammon, sometimes resulting in large-scale warfare between the two. It is therefore unlikely that Israel would have adopted the worship of their enemy's idol during this time.[11] An interesting suggestion in identifying "Malcam" is found in Radak and Abarbanel. They suggest that the object of Israel's worship was not an idol named Malcam, but rather their king (the Hebrew word "Malcam" is a conjunction of *melekh shelahem*), indicating that some people had elevated the state above their religion as their primary source of loyalty.

Finally, Zephaniah describes how God would also direct His wrath toward those who turn away from Him; and those who do not seek Him or inquire after Him. The Tanakh uses the term "to turn away from," *nisogim*, to describe faithless behavior, whether toward people or God;[12] in the *nifal* verb form (passive), it implies willful action, and Isaiah equates it with the worst levels of dishonesty and oppression (see Is. 59:13). The Hebrew verbs meaning "to seek" (which has the Hebrew root B-K-S) and "to inquire" (which has the Hebrew root D-R-S) occur elsewhere in the Tanakh in the context of turning to God for help when trouble occurs (see Deut. 4:29, II Chr. 20:3, 4). Here, Zephaniah is castigating the people for their failure to reach out to Him during their period of difficulty.

In the next verses, Zephaniah uses a very dramatic and clever metaphor to describe the approaching day of the Lord: a great sacrifice:

> Be silent before the Lord God, for the day of the Lord is near. For the Lord has prepared a sacrifice; He has invited His guests. And it shall be on the day of the Lord's sacrificial slaughter, that I will visit upon the princes, and upon the king's sons, and upon all those who wear gentile garb. And I will visit upon everyone who leaps over the threshold, [and] those who fill the houses of their masters with violence and deceit. And it shall come to pass on that day, says the Lord; a sound of a cry from the Fish Gate,

11. See II Chr. 20, Is. 11:14.
12. Jer. 38:22, Ps. 53:4.

> and a wail from the second gate, and great destruction from the hills. Wail, you inhabitants of Maktesh, for the entire people of Canaan is cut off; all those laden with silver have been cut off. And it shall come to pass at that time, that I will search Jerusalem with candles, and I will visit upon the men who are settled on their lees, who say in their heart, "The Lord shall do neither good nor harm." And their wealth shall become a booty, and their houses a desolation, and they shall build houses and not dwell in them, and plant vineyards and not drink their wine. (1:7–13)

Here, silence is requested of the people; they are in God's presence, the day of God is near, is hosted by God Himself, and is to be attended by God's guests. The word *hass*, here translated "be silent," a term in the command form, can mean either "silence" or "remove"; it echoes two previous appearances in Amos that both describe the totality of the approaching destruction. In the first it says:

> And it shall be, if ten men are left in one house, they shall die. And his kinsman and the one who saved him from burning shall carry him to take out bones from the house, and he shall say to [the one] who is in the end of the house, "Are there any more with you?" and he shall say, "There is none." And he shall say, "*Hass*." (6:9–10)

And the second says: "And the songs of the temple shall be wailings in that day, says the Lord God; corpses shall increase; everywhere "Cast away, *hass*!" (8:3). Assuming Zephaniah's audience was familiar with the warnings of the earlier prophet Amos, Zephaniah's allusions to language used in Amos, and specifically his use of the phrase "the day of the Lord," would have caused the people to associate the phrase with the dreadful warnings that Amos conveyed:

> Woe to those who desire the day of the Lord. Why would you have the day of the Lord? It is darkness, and not light.... Is not the day of the Lord darkness and not light, even very dark, with no brightness in it? (5:18–20)

In its original context, the offering described here, *zevaḥ*, was a fellowship offering, a festive affair attended by many guests before God.[13] In this context, however, it becomes clear from the next verse that instead of being God's honored guests at the sacrificial feast, the Jewish people are the sacrifice. Like Ahab's supporters who responded to Jehu's invitation to worship idolatry (II Kings 10:18–28), the invited guests become the victims. Instead of the word *zevaḥ* denoting a sacrifice, the word now assumes its second, more primal meaning: slaughter. On "the day of the Lord" there will be a slaughter of people.

The phrase "the Lord has prepared (*hekhin*, which has the root K-V-N) a sacrifice (*zevaḥ*)" is also a lexical rarity. This is the only time that the word *hekhin* appears together with the word *zevaḥ*. In the Tanakh, the word "prepare" appears only twenty times with the Lord as the subject. Of these, half refer to the establishment of an everlasting dynasty, mostly in connection with David. For example, "then I will raise up your seed that shall proceed from your body after you, and I will establish (*vahakhinoti*) his kingdom" (II Sam. 7:12).[14] With this uncommon wording, Zephaniah may be alluding to the end of the Davidic dynasty, which, though once assumed to be everlasting, will in fact end with the upcoming destruction.

In the next three subsections (1:8–9, 1:10–11, and 1:12–18), Zephaniah describes what will happen on "that day," and there are many echoes of Amos in the language he uses. Each subsection identifies different targets of God's anger, and each begins with a temporal marker: verse 8 with "And it shall be on the day of the Lord's sacrificial slaughter," verse 10 with "And it shall come to pass on that day," and verse 12 with "And it shall come to pass at that time." Each group receives a separate warning, with three warnings that begin in the divine first person, with the word *ufakadeti*.[15] The first targets of God's anger will be the officials,

13. Examples of the *zevaḥ* as a group offering in Tanakh include I Sam. 9:22, II Sam. 15:11, I Kings 1:9–10, 24–25; cf. Deut. 12:18, 33:19.
14. The other occurrences are: I Sam. 13:13, II Sam. 5:12, I Kings 2:24, Ps. 89:3, I Chr. 14:2, 17:11, 22:10, 28:7, II Chr. 17:5.
15. Greg King in *The Message of Zephaniah* notes that Zephaniah uses the same word as do Hosea and Isaiah when quoting the Lord's first-person announcement of His planned judgment: the verb *ufakadeti* (Zeph. 1:8, 9, 12; see Is. 13:11, Hos. 1:4, 2:15, 4:9).

courtiers, and members of Judah's elite (the king himself is noticeably absent from the list, reinforcing the idea that Zephaniah uttered this prophecy in Josiah's time). What did the leaders and the elite do to deserve the divine wrath? Zephaniah first points to their foreign clothing. What was the essence of this sin? Rashi believes these were special garments made for pagan performances, while Ibn Ezra and Abarbanel maintain that the upper class wore more expensive fashions to distinguish themselves from the common people in a display of arrogance. Radak makes several interesting suggestions as to the exact nature of the transgression with regard to the clothing, spanning from actual sins like robbery and idolatry to religious hypocrisy:

> My father explained that when [the rich] saw someone under their control wearing attractive clothing, they stole it from him and wore it themselves...others explain it as clothes worn for idolatry...and some explain that they [the upper class tried to] present themselves as ascetics and pious people, and wore foreign clothes unlike the rest of the nation so that they would be recognized as ascetics, but [ultimately] their ways were wicked.

In verse 9, the second verse of the first subsection, Zephaniah continues listing the targets of God's upcoming wrath; this time the target is everyone who "leaps over the threshold." Rashi quotes the explanation of the *Targum Yonatan* that the Jewish people in Zephaniah's time had perpetuated a custom that began among the priests of Philistine deity Dagon, when their idol, presumably a statue of Dagon, fell on the threshold, i.e., on a podium, in front of the Ark of the Lord, which had been stolen by the Philistines and taken to the temple of Dagon in Ashdod. This incident resulted in a new custom: "to this day neither the priests of Dagon nor any others who enter Dagon's temple at Ashdod step on the threshold" (I Sam. 5:1–5). Radak's comments on this verse continue the themes he developed on the earlier verse with regard to the nature of the sins with

---

He continues to say that "this word connotes the Lord's personal visit or intervention... [and that] it is the single word that most clearly expresses the essence of Zephaniah's proclamation regarding the Day of the Lord" (p. 215).

regard to clothing, commenting here that skipping over the threshold meant "a sudden rushing into houses to steal the property of strangers." Accordingly, the target here is the servants of the upper class, who serve their master by violently extorting treasures from their dependents.

The words "violence" and "deceit" (*ḥamas, mirma*) which appear one after the other in verse 9 also appear together in two other places in the Tanakh, with significant overtones for Zephaniah's audience. In Micah, chapter 6, the prophet condemns the Kingdom of Israel in his lawsuit against them, declaring their eventual destruction: "Will I declare [you] innocent with scales of wickedness or with a bag of deceitful (*ḥamas*) weights? For the wealthy thereof are full of violence (*remiya*)" (Mic. 6:11–12), while in Psalms, chapter 55, David prays that the wicked will receive their due punishments: "Destroy, O Lord, divide their tongue, for I have seen violence (*ḥamas*) and strife in the city.... Destruction is within it, and blows and deceit (*mirma*) do not move out of its square" (Ps. 55:10, 12).

In the second subsection, Zephaniah continues his assault on Judah's wealthy inhabitants. He describes how God's judgment will cause a great lament which will come from all the sections of Jerusalem. Although inhabitants of all parts of the city will wail, those who will suffer most will be the city's greedy merchants. Zephaniah specifies two districts of commercial activity, the Fish Gate in Jerusalem's northern wall and the Second Quarter northwest of the Temple, where the wailing will be loudest,[16] so loud, in fact, that even Jerusalem's hills will tremor.

16. The Fish Gate was the gate in the north of the city through which the fishermen normally entered the city with their haul (II Chr. 33:14, Neh. 3:3, 12:39). Enemies, like Nebuchadnezzar in 586 BCE, likely entered Jerusalem through this gate, as his invasion route came from the north. Here is Abarbanel's understanding of the city's architecture:

> Jerusalem had three walls [dividing it]. In the first [outer section] lived all of the craftsmen and farmers. In the second [the middle section] lived the nobility and sages and prophets and upper class; regarding this it says of Huldah, "She lived... in the *mishneh*," for her house was in the second wall. In the third wall was the Temple Mount. [Therefore] the prophet said, "A voice of screaming from the Fish Gate" regarding the first wall, where the masses and craftsmen and trappers were located, whom Zephaniah had compared to fish earlier (1:3). "And wailing from the *mishneh*" refers to the second wall. "And great destruction from the hills" refers to the third wall, the Temple Mount, where the devastation was tremendous.

Zephaniah tells the merchants to cry out (v. 11), which ideally would lead them to cry out in prayer and repentance, but Zephaniah indicates that they will be mourning only their lost wealth ("Wail... for the entire people of Canaan is cut off; all those laden with silver have been cut off"). Ibn Ezra and others understand the term "people of Canaan" in verse 11 as a synonym for "merchants" (see Is. 23:8, Job 40:30, Prov. 31:24), while Rashi explains the verse to mean that the Judeans behaved immorally like Canaanites. Abarbanel argues that the metaphor is meant to compare the fate of Judah with that of the Canaanites that they displaced: Just as the Canaanites were cast out of the land due to the severity of their sins, so too the Jewish people will be cast out as well.

In the final subsection, Zephaniah describes the looting of Jerusalem. God's judgment is severe and the resulting destruction is thorough. Zephaniah describes how God will take a lamp and search meticulously among the inhabitants. He doesn't state immediately what God is looking for, but the next verse makes it clear. The invaders will seek out every corner of Jerusalem and carry away its treasures. In this way, God will punish those whose greed, self-satisfaction, and apostasy had developed into a complacent indifference. In verse 12, Zephaniah compares the people to wine that sat for too long, becoming too sweet and over-fermented, with their lees (i.e., the excess dead yeast) accumulating on the bottom of the barrel. Jerusalem's inhabitants had led an apostate and corrupt lifestyle for so long that they had become comfortable and apathetic to genuine spirituality. Even worse, their extreme complacency and indifference had led them to believe that God Himself had become complacent and indifferent as well. It is this sense of comfort that Zephaniah wishes to disturb. Though the people didn't realize it and continued to live as if nothing could disturb their daily routine, the day of the Lord was quickly approaching. The curses of the Bible (see Deut. 28:15–68)

While we have translated *mishneh* as the second gate, Rashi translates it as the Bird Gate, explaining that this gate was called *mishneh* because it was second in importance to the Fish Gate. Ibn Ezra interprets it as the place where the king's assistant lived (Joseph is also commonly identified as Pharaoh's *mishneh lamelekh*; see Gen. 41:43). Radak suggests, based on the episode of Huldah the prophetess in II Kings 22, that this was the location of the city's main house of study (the root S-N-H can also mean "learn").

were quickly becoming reality. They would build houses – but would not be able to live in them; they would plant vineyards – but would not be able to drink their wine. Once again, Zephaniah echoes one of Amos's curses: "Therefore, because you have trodden on poor, and the burden of grain you take from him, houses of hewn stone you have built but you shall not dwell therein, precious vineyards you have planted, but you shall not drink their wine" (Amos 5:11), which was derived from the curses section in Deuteronomy 28: "You will betroth a woman, but another man will lie with her. You will build a house, but you will not live in it. You will plant a vineyard, but you will not redeem it[s fruits]" (Deut. 28:30). The context of the verse in Amos is significant. The verse appears as part of the prophet's lamentation for the Northern Kingdom, whose shortcomings included corruption along with the people's belief in their own invulnerability. Just like Israel had been a century before, Judah is now guilty of these exact same shortcomings, and would soon suffer the same fate.

In verses 14–18, Zephaniah finally describes the actual "day of the Lord":

> The great day of the Lord is near; it is near and hastens greatly, the sound of the day of the Lord, wherein the mighty man cries bitterly. That day is a day of wrath; a day of trouble and distress; a day of ruin and desolation; a day of darkness and gloom; a day of clouds and thick darkness; a day of shofar and alarm against the fortified cities and against the high towers. And I will bring distress upon men, and they shall walk like the blind, for they have sinned against the Lord. And their blood shall be shed like dust, and their flesh like dung. Neither their silver nor their gold will be able to save them on the day of the Lord's wrath. And with the fire of His passion the entire land shall be consumed; for an end, yea, a sudden end, He shall make of all the inhabitants of the land. (1:14–18)

Introducing it as a "day of wrath," he continues with five pairs of synonymous metaphors, drawing heavily upon earlier prophetic descriptions of an upcoming apocalypse. Noticeable is his borrowing of Job's comparison of the fate that awaits the righteous to a desolate wasteland (*shoa umesoa*, "destruction and desolation" [Job 30:3, 38:27]).[17] Most noticeable in this section are the parallels with the prophet Joel's description of "the day of the Lord":

Zephaniah 1:14–18	**Joel 2:1–2, 11**
The great day of the Lord is near; it is near and hastens greatly, the sound of the day of the Lord, wherein the mighty man cries bitterly. That day is a day of wrath; a day of trouble and distress; a day of ruin and desolation; *a day of darkness and gloom; a day of clouds and thick darkness*; a day of *shofar* and alarm against the fortified cities and against the high towers ... for an end, yea, a sudden end, He shall make of *all the inhabitants of the land*	Blow you *the shofar* in Zion, and sound an alarm in My holy mountain; let *all the inhabitants of the land* tremble; for the day of the Lord comes, *for it is near; a day of darkness and gloom, a day of clouds and thick darkness...* And the Lord utters His voice before His army; for His camp is very great, for he is mighty that executes His word; for *great is the day of the Lord* and very terrible; and who can abide it?

However, Zephaniah does more than recycle ancient threats. Transforming previous prophecies into perfect poetry, Zephaniah inserts new ideas that were not mentioned previously. The effect of the repeated trope "the day," with additional misfortunes added after every repetition, is staggering.[18] He then turns to the consequence that the day will have upon those affected. God speaks first: "I will bring distress upon men, and they shall walk like the blind," but then Zephaniah's voice reappears: "for

17. This term for destruction, *shoa*, has entered modern Hebrew as the word used to refer to the Holocaust of European Jewry during World War II.

18. The commentaries debate the exact meaning and nuance of each of these repetitive descriptions. Rashi suggests that the purpose is to describe the accumulation of troubles and sorrows upon the Jewish people, as each adjective is more severe than the previous one (Radak explains the phenomenon in a similar manner, claiming that it is the way of the Tanakh to repeat words for emphasis). Malbim interprets this as referring to the different stages and effects of the upcoming invasion, and concludes his commentary on chapter 1 with the suggestion that these terrifying portrayals of absolute destruction were rhetorical flourishes added by Zephaniah in order to frighten the people and cause them to repent.

they have sinned against the Lord." The alternation blurs the distinction between God and prophet, suggesting that the listener should understand that the two are indivisible when it comes to the accuracy of the message. Zephaniah references his previous critique of the wealthy in verse 18, noting mockingly that their wealth cannot defend them in times of trouble. He sums up the entire passage by returning to the original motif of worldwide destruction with which he began his prophecy: "He shall make [an end] of *all the inhabitants of the land*."[19]

19. The theme of universality is emphasized again by the word "all." The word "all" appears, in various permutations, twenty-three times throughout the book, reinforcing the scope of the totality of God's destruction in the opening chapters and the breadth of the redemption at the book's end.

2:1–2:3

Zephaniah Calls for Repentance

Having described the upcoming horror of the day of the Lord to his listeners, Zephaniah now reveals to them what they must do in order to have a chance of survival:

> Gather yourselves together! Gather together, O nation that has no desire, before the decree is born, as chaff that passes; before the fierce anger of the Lord comes upon you; before the day of the Lord's anger comes upon you. Seek the Lord, all you humble of the earth who executed His judgment; Seek righteousness, seek humility! Perhaps you will be concealed on the day of the Lord's wrath. (2:1–3)

In these verses, Zephaniah again walks in Joel's path. When Joel described the cataclysm, he concluded:

> Yet even now, says the Lord, turn ye unto Me with all your heart, and with fasting, and with weeping, and with lamentation. And rend your heart, and not your garments, and turn unto the Lord your God; for He is gracious and compassionate, long-suffering, and abundant in

> mercy, and He repents of the evil. Who knows whether He will not turn and repent, and leave a blessing behind Him? (2:12–14)

Like Joel, Zephaniah is hoping that the fear that he has aroused among his listeners will become the springboard for meaningful change.

Zephaniah uses imagery taken from the procedure for separating straw from chaff, i.e., taking good from bad. The command to gather is repeated twice with a variation on the same word (*hitkosheshu vakoshu*), which is related to the word for straw (*kash*). In verse 2, he warns the people against being like the chaff, the worthless part of the harvest that is easily and quickly blown away. As such, Zephaniah's metaphor for the upcoming judgment is the act of winnowing: Just as one throws into the wind the straw left over from the threshing to divide the straw from the chaff, so too, when the wind of judgment will blow through the nation, the people will be separated into the righteous (straw) and the wicked (chaff). The command to gather (*hitkosheshu vakoshu*) is repeated, first in the reflexive form and then in the imperative. With regard to this repetition, Radak quotes the following rabbinic homily: "Seek out your blemishes and then seek out the blemishes of others, and eradicate them. And so the Sages said from this verse, 'Decorate (i.e., make honest) yourself, and then decorate (i.e., make honest) others" (Bava Batra 60b).

That the people are "strawlike" is reinforced by the description of the people as *lo nikhsaf*. The word *nikhsaf* can either mean "desire for," or it can mean "worthless/shameless." Rashi understands it to mean that the people have lost their desire for spiritual improvement; others suggest that it means that the Jewish people are not desired by the nations, i.e., that like straw, they have become without worth.

The second verse has three statements designed to encourage the people to repent. Each of the statements begins with the word "before" (*biterem*). The desired effect is to extend the possibility of hope even to the certainty of the judgment. At this point, a proper response by the people will not be enough to completely prevent the threatened destruction, but it may delay it or lessen its severity.[1] The verse's syntax is difficult:

1. Radak connects this to the words that Huldah the prophetess told Josiah when he began his program of reforms:

the verse contains no main clause or verb. By repeating the word *biterem* and the phrase "the Lord's anger," Zephaniah wishes to express a sense of urgency and warn that the decree will soon come to pass.

Based on this tiny glimmer of hope, Zephaniah entreats his audience to change. He echoes two prophets of the previous century, Micah and Amos. Micah summarized Judaism as requiring one "to do justice, to love loving-kindness, and to walk humbly with your God" (Mic. 6:8). Meanwhile, Amos entreated the people "Seek good and not evil in order that you live, and so the Lord God of hosts shall be with you, as you said" (Amos 5:14). Zephaniah concluded his list of the guilty factions of Judah with reference to "those who did not seek the Lord nor inquire after Him" (1:6). Now he repeats the command "Seek" (*bakkeshu*) three times. Zephaniah's instructions do not distinguish between Jew and gentile. Just as the upcoming destruction is not limited to Israel but will have universal ramifications, so too, the behaviors that may serve to protect the people and mitigate the destruction are also universally applicable. Zephaniah's message is that the traits of righteousness and humility, and the ability to attain them through repentance, are not limited solely to the Jewish people, but are open and available to all.

At the same time, like Joel and Amos before him, Zephaniah makes no guarantees that his listeners will survive, even if they repent and act with humility and righteousness. Amos stated that if the people "hate evil and love good, and establish justice in the gate; *perhaps* the Lord God of hosts will be gracious to the remnant of Joseph" (5:15). Zephaniah is similarly noncommittal. Since the decree of "the day of the Lord" had already begun, there is no chance of it being completely recalled or annulled.[2] The best that Zephaniah can offer his listeners in verse 3

"You will take shelter; in that you will not die by the sword with the rest." He did not promise to save them from exile, though, for that decree had already been issued in the days of Manasseh, as it is written, and as it was told to King Josiah, "You will be gathered to your ancestors in peace and your eyes will not see all of the evil I will bring upon this place" (II Kings 22:20).

2. Abarbanel explains that the sins of the people were so overwhelming that any attempt to avoid punishment entirely would be completely pointless. Instead, he suggests that Zephaniah is trying to spur the people of Judah and Jerusalem to action. They had sinned greatly for such a long time that even if they were to seek righteousness and

here is that if they repent, they will be able to find some form of shelter during the upcoming storm. The Talmud relates how this verse caused R. Ami to break down in tears: R. Ami would cry when he reached this verse, saying, "They will do of this [be humble and righteous], and still, 'Perhaps?'" (Ḥagiga 4b).[3]

humility now, it would not make sense that their transgressions would be entirely forgiven without their suffering any punishment, as God cannot ignore [sins] entirely. Therefore, Zephaniah said, "Perhaps you will be concealed," meaning, the people should understand as an unalterable fact that destructive anger has already emerged from before God, and the assault has begun. Should they return to God now, it may not help, as once permission has been given to the destroyer to destroy, he does not distinguish [between the righteous and the evildoers]. But Zephaniah wants them to know that their repentance may still allow them to find shelter on the day of rage, and God will spill His rage upon the rest of the nations. The word "perhaps" in "perhaps you will be concealed" was not meant to negate the efficacy of repentance, but to express that the people may take shelter and be concealed, and therefore evil would either not affect them at all, or at least affect them less severely.

3. For further discussion of the lack of guarantee in prophetic promises, see Hayyim Angel, "The Uncertainty Principle of Repentance in the Books of Jonah and Joel," in *Revealed Texts, Hidden Meanings*, 148–61.

2:4–2:15

Judging the Nations

The second section of the book, as outlined in the introduction to Zephaniah, contains the greater part of chapter 2 and the opening verses of chapter 3. Zephaniah returns to the theme of worldwide destruction, followed by another description of the fate of the Jewish people, and concludes with another direction toward the righteous. He devotes much more attention to the fate of the nations than he did in chapter 1. He calls out those countries and peoples that surrounded the tiny country of Judah and allied themselves with the Assyrian oppressors. Zephaniah then turns to the Jewish people and asks: Have you learned from the example that God has made of them? Do you understand everything that happens in history? Do you take note of what is happening? Are you inspired to improve your ways? Finally, Zephaniah tells his listeners that they are to wait as the day of the Lord is coming.[1]

1. Of the names of the nations and the places that Zephaniah lists in chapter 2, eight of them appear in the listing of Ham's descendants in Gen. 10:6–20 (Gaza, Canaan, Philistines, Sodom, Gomorrah, Cush, Assyria, and Nineveh). In Genesis, they are juxtaposed with the descendants of the two other sons, those who were not cursed by Noah. Zephaniah's listing of them may intend to hint that the divine curse is now being fulfilled.

The prophecy against the nations begins by mentioning the nation to Judah's west, the Philistines (2:4–7). He then moves to the east, naming Moab and Ammon (2:8–11),[2] followed by Cush to the south (2:12), and concludes with an account of the destruction that awaits Assyria to the north of Israel (2:13–15).[3] The portrayal of God conquering the four corners of the earth has ancient overtones. In early Mesopotamia, a king was entitled to claim the title "conqueror of the four winds of the earth" only when he returned from a successful military campaign. Zephaniah might have had this custom in mind, and it might be the reason that he turns his attention to Judah and Jerusalem only once he concludes his prophecy against the nations (3:1–7). As was the case in chapter 1, Zephaniah alternates between God's voice and his own, the effect being to increase the weight of the prophet's words.

---

2. Normally, the country of Edom appears alongside its neighbors Ammon and Moab in the prophecies, but here, Edom is absent from the list. Duane Christensen provides an interesting explanation, which I also heard orally from Rabbi Yoel Bin-Nun, as to why Edom is not mentioned here. He posits that the second chapter of Zephaniah provided the theological backing for Josiah's plans for military expansion, which were directed against the Assyrian proxy states in the area. Since Edom was occupied by Egyptian forces at the time, it was left out of the list, as it was not a factor in Josiah's design. See Duane L. Christiansen, "Zephaniah 2:4–15: A Theological Basis for Josiah's Program of Political Expansion," *The Catholic Biblical Quarterly* 46, no. 4 (October 1984), 669–82.
3. There does not appear to be a uniform pattern to the order in which the prophets organize their prophecies against the nations around Israel. For example, Ezekiel completely inverts Zephaniah's geographic order, moving from the east (the Transjordan region, 25:1–14) to the west (the Philistines, 25:15–17), and then from the north (Phoenicia, 25:26–28) to the south (Egypt, 25:29–32). Jeremiah's prophecies against the nations include two lists. He begins with the list of countries that are adjacent to Israel, and goes from south to north (south: Egypt, ch. 46; west: the Philistines, ch. 47; east: countries in the Transjordan region, 48:1–49:22; north: Damascus/Aram, 49:23–27). In the second list, which includes the nations in Mesopotamia, Jeremiah lists the nations in an order that encircles Babylon (first southwest: Kedar and Hazor, 49:28–33; then east: Elam, 49:34–39; and finally concluding with Babylon, northeast, in chs. 50–51). Amos's prophecies also list locations that surround Judah and Israel, with the list of locations crisscrossing the two kingdoms diagonally from the north/northeast (Aram, 1:3–5) to the southwest (the Philistines, 1:6–8), and then from the northwest (Phoenicia, 1:9–10) to the east/southeast (Transjordan, 1:11–2:3).

Zephaniah begins with Judah's perennial enemy to the west, the Philistines:

> For Gaza shall be deserted, and Ashkelon shall become wasteland. Ashdod – at noon they shall drive her out, and Ekron shall be uprooted. Woe to the inhabitants of the seacoast, the nation of Cherethites! The word of the Lord is against you, Canaan land of the Philistines, and I will destroy you so that there shall not be an inhabitant. And the seacoast shall be breakfast nooks for shepherds and sheepfolds. And it shall be a lot for the remnant of the House of Judah, whereupon they shall pasture. In the houses of Ashkelon they shall lie down in the evening, for the Lord their God shall visit upon them and return their captivity. (2:4–7)

Though the prophecy against the Philistines actually begins in verse 4, verse 5 starts with the word *hoi*, "woe," a word which is usually used at the beginning of a new section. The effect of using *hoi* in verse 5 is to separate verse 4 from what follows, and though the audience, subject, and subject matter are different, verse 4 is linked to the verses that came before it, where Zephaniah exhorted Israel to repent. Hence, Rashi understands the connection between verses 3 and 4 as one of cause and effect, and explains that Zephaniah's message in verse 4 is relaying a divine promise: "For, if you will do so [seek righteousness and humility as prescribed in verse 3], I will take retribution on your evil neighbors: Philistia, Ammon, and Moab" (Rashi on 2:4).

The historical enmity between the Philistines and Israel in the biblical period spans many centuries. Many scholars identify the Philistines as the "sea peoples" that wreaked havoc on the ancient eastern Mediterranean during the late Bronze Age (thirteenth century BCE). Historians suggest that the Philistines migrated from Caphtor (Hebrew for Crete and the Aegean region; see Amos 9:7, Jer. 47:4) during this time period, settling on Israel's southwestern coast. There was a Philistine presence in Canaan in the days of the patriarchs (Gen. 21:32). They were a constant threat to Jewish sovereignty in the land during the time of the judges, and reached the zenith of their power in the time of Saul (I Sam. 4:1–11, 7:1–14, chs. 13–14). King David decisively defeated them at the beginning of his reign (II Sam. 5:17–25, I Chr. 20:4–5); but the remaining members of the nation remained a constant thorn in the Israelites' side (I Kings 15:27–28, 16:15–19, II Chr. 21:16–17, Is. 9:12, 14:28–32, Amos 1:6–8). Though they became vassals to Assyria in the eighth century, they still enjoyed a modicum of independence, and the central Philistine cities mentioned in verse 4 remained active centers of commercial activity. Ekron became the manufacturing center where olive oil was produced for the entire Assyrian Empire, and the port cities of Gaza, Ashkelon, and Ashdod provided commercial hubs for Assyria to reach the Mediterranean. Even the prophets of Judah's final days found it necessary to include the nation and its cities in their condemnations (Jer. 47:1–7, Ezek. 25:15–17). Detailing the final downfall and destruction of their historical rivals and enemies, Zephaniah's words would undoubtedly have affected his listeners, providing them with a measure of consolation and hope.

Zephaniah (like Micah before him)[4] engages in clever puns in his prophecies against the Philistine cities. With the first and last cities, he puns the name of the city with its judgment: "For Gaza shall be deserted (*Azza azuva*)... and Ekron shall be uprooted (*Ekron te'aker*)" (2:4), while with the intervening two cities mentioned in this verse there is a play on the sounds of their names that highlights their upcoming destruction. The destruction of these four cities represents the total destruction of the Philistine territory.[5] Likewise, the mention of their specific fates symbolizes the totality of the upcoming defeat the Philistines would suffer: not just defeat but also destruction, deportation, and being forced to abandon their cities. Another interesting idea suggested by commentaries with regard to the words used to describe the

4. Speaking out against the coastal cities of Judah, Micah engaged in a lengthy series of puns based on their names, which are difficult to convey in the English translation: "Don't speak about it (*al taggidu*) in Gat... in the houses of Aphrah, wallow in the dust (*afar*)... the houses of Achzib shall be a dried-up spring (*akhzav*)... I will yet bring the possessor (*hayoresh*) to you, O inhabitant of Mareshah" (Mic. 1:10–15).
5. The Tanakh normally lists five major Philistine cities. Why did Zephaniah mention only four? Perhaps it was in order to preserve literary parallelism, or perhaps the fifth Philistine city, Gat, had already been subjected to Judahite rule under Uzziah and Hezekiah and did not subsequently regain its independence; see II Kings 18:8 and II Chr. 26:6.

cities' fates is that they are words that could also be construed as connoting the four worst fates that could befall a woman in ancient times: abandonment, widowhood, divorce, and childlessness.[6] Cities in biblical Hebrew were often personified as women; it is not unlikely that Zephaniah might have chosen words with a double entendre since the conditions mentioned are fates with which the people were definitely familiar and hearing them would have caused them to feel unnerved.

Verses 6 and 7 state that once destroyed, the abandoned coast would be repopulated by the remnant of the House of Judah, who would shepherd their flocks there. Archaeology has revealed that after the Assyrian invasions of the late eighth century, most Jewish inhabitants of Judah moved inward, away from the Philistine cities and the sea, and repopulated the destroyed cities that dotted the Judean hills around Jerusalem. Now, as Josiah managed to strengthen his hold on the country and its surrounding areas, the opportunity arose for them to return to their ancestral inheritances.[7]

In the next subsection of the prophecy, Zephaniah moves from the west to the east and focuses his prophecy on Ammon and Moab, two countries who had enriched themselves at Judah and Israel's expense thanks to their alliance with the Assyrians. Israel's tribes on the eastern bank of the Jordan River were severely weakened due to the Assyrian invasions, and their lands were ultimately annexed by Ammon and Moab. As Zephaniah states, "They aggrandized themselves on their [Israel's] border" (2:8):

> I heard the taunts of Moab and the jeers of the children of Ammon, who taunted My people, and they aggrandized themselves on their border. Therefore, as I live,-says the Lord of hosts, the

6. L. Zalcman, "Ambiguity and Assonance at Zephaniah II 4," VT 36 (1986): 365–71. See also Robert Gordis, "A Rising Tide of Misery: A Note on Zephaniah II 4," VT 37 (1987): 487–90.
7. *Daat Mikra* suggests a different perspective to the final line of Zephaniah's oracle against the Philistines. Unlike our approach, which sees the prophecy fulfilled in Josiah's time, *Daat Mikra* suggests that the words in these verses carried an added measure of consolation for the Jewish people. Unlike the other nations that, once exiled, would not return to their land, the Jewish people would be exiled but would also return.

> God of Israel: For Moab shall be like Sodom, and the children of Ammon like Gomorrah; a rattling of nettles, and a salt mine, and desolation forever. The remnant of My people shall plunder them, and the remnant of My nation shall inherit them. They shall have this instead of their haughtiness, for they taunted and aggrandized themselves over the people of the Lord of hosts. The Lord shall be feared by them, for He weakened all the gods of the earth. And every man shall prostrate himself to Him from his place, all the isles of the nations. (2:8–11)

Like the Philistines, Ammon and Moab were longtime antagonists of Israel. Though God commanded the Jewish people to leave the Ammonites alone during their wanderings in the desert (Deut. 2:19), and Israel did its utmost to avoid conflict with the Moabites, the two countries joined together to hire Balaam to curse Israel (Num. 22–25), an event which was still seared into the people's consciousness centuries later (Mic. 6). Both nations harassed the Israelites in the days of the judges (Judges 3:12–30, 11:1–40), forcing both Saul and David to fight against them (I Sam. 11:1–11, 14:47, II Sam. 8:2, 10:1–19, chs. 11–12, I Chr. 20:1–3). When King Solomon reigned, he had both Moabite and Ammonite women in his harem, leading to his spiritual undoing (I Kings 11:1, 5, 7, 33). After Solomon, Israel would skirmish frequently with these two nations (see II Kings 1:1, 3:1–27, II Chr. 20:1–30, 24:26, 26:8, 27:5), and prophets who came before Zephaniah regularly denounced them (Is. 15:1–16:14, 25:10–12, Amos 1:13–15, 2:1–5). Like Isaiah before him (Is. 16:6, 25:10–11), Zephaniah condemns Ammon and Moab for both their pride and their continued blaspheming insults and taunts against God and His people (see also Jer. 48:26–27, 49:1).[8] He predicts that these two nations,

---

8. Rabbinic thought suggests that this reprehensible behavior on the part of Ammon and Moab continued until the destruction of the First Temple. The Midrash describes how "during the invasion of Jerusalem by the foreign nations, Ammonites and Moabites joined with them. [As the Temple was being looted], they entered the Holy of Holies, and took the cherubs and placed them in a cage, and paraded with them through the streets of Jerusalem. As they did so, they mocked Israel, saying, "Didn't the Jewish people claim that they do not worship idols? See what they were doing!" *Pesikta DeRav Kahana* 19:1. Rashi's commentary here also places the taunting at the time of the exile from Jerusalem, when the First Temple was destroyed:

allied together in wickedness, will suffer the same fate as another infamous pair – Sodom and Gomorrah. Being intimately familiar with the deserted, salty wasteland that encompassed their borders, Moab and Ammon would undoubtedly understand the reference to the destruction of Sodom and Gomorrah.[9] The prophet states that their pride will be replaced by shame, as they watch their lands being repopulated by the returning Jewish people and God's power being acknowledged from all ends of the earth.

Zephaniah then turns his attention to the south: "You, too, Cushim – they are the slain of My sword" (2:12). In one short verse, he describes the downfall of Cush (Ethiopia) upon the sword. The mention of Cush, as opposed to Egypt, as the representative of Judah's southern enemy is surprising: Historically, after the Cushites invaded Egypt in the eighth century BCE, the monarchs of the Kingdom of Cush also served as the pharaohs of the twenty-fifth dynasty of Egypt. They ruled over Egypt for more than half a century (ca. 715–655 BCE), until their defeat at the hands of the Assyrian invaders at Memphis in 671 BCE and at Thebes in 663 BCE, when they were forced to abandon their hold on the throne. But by Zephaniah's time, a new, native Egyptian dynasty, i.e., the twenty-sixth dynasty, had risen, with Pharaoh Psamtik I (ca. 663–609 BCE) at its head. If so, why does the text mention Cush, the previous ruling dynasty in Egypt, as opposed to the current one? Based on the first word of the verse, *gam*, both *Metzudat David* and Malbim suggest that the sin of the Cushim was similar to that of Ammon and Moab above: they had either mocked the Jewish people or rejoiced at Israel's downfall. Some scholars suggest that Zephaniah's mention of Cush was solely for literary purposes, to maintain the geographical balance (west-east,

---

> When [the people of] Israel were being led into exile toward the land of the Chaldeans, and they were passing through the lands of Ammon and Moab. They [Ammon and Moab] would see Israel weeping, sighing, and lamenting, and they would taunt them, saying, "Why are you suffering? Aren't you going [back] to your father's house? Your fathers dwelt on the other side of the river in earlier times."

9. Rashi says that the ultimate punishment of Ammon and Moab fits their crime: Just as they taunted the Jewish people for their ancestry, Zephaniah notes that their punishment will also be connected to their roots: "For Moab shall be like Sodom: You, too, shall return to your previous dwelling. Was not your father, Lot, from Sodom?"

south-north) mentioned above, while others suggest that Cush is used as a synonym for Egypt (see Ezek. 30).

Zephaniah's fourth and final message, in verses 13–15, is directed at Judah's oppressor to the north – Assyria:

> And He shall incline His hand on the north, and destroy Assyria and make Nineveh desolate wasteland like the desert. And flocks shall lie down in its midst, all the beasts of the nations. Also, both the pelican and the owl shall lodge in its lintels. Their voice shall sing in the window; desolation in the doorpost – for the cedar work has been destroyed. This is the joyful city, dwelling securely, saying to herself, "I am, and there is none besides me." How did it become desolate, a resting place for the beasts? Yea, everyone who passes by her shall hiss and wave his hand. (2:13–15)

Like Nahum before him, Zephaniah pronounces the upcoming downfall of the world's sole superpower.[10] But unlike Nahum, who prophesied at the height of the Assyrian Empire's reign, Zephaniah likely prophesied during the latter days of Ashurbanipal, the last unchallenged king of the Assyrian dynasty, when weak leadership and imperial overreach meant that the demise of the Assyrian Empire would have been a more imaginable scenario, and therefore a more relatable one for Zephaniah's audience. Verses 4–10 had spoken of the Philistine cities, which had allied themselves with Assyria for the purpose of monetary gain, and would metaphorically become, upon their destruction, the widowed and abandoned wives, with no children to carry on their legacy. Those verses also mentioned the twin countries of Moab and Ammon, who had mocked Israel and Israel's God, and were now to become vast desert wastelands like the twin cities of Sodom and Gomorrah. In this brief vision of verses 13–15, Zephaniah's usage of picturesque language is at its height: Zephaniah invites the listener to visualize a scene in which wild animals run unencumbered through the boulevards and gateways

10. Indeed, some of the wording and many of the images that Zephaniah uses are taken directly from Nahum.

of what was once the world's most impressive city,[11] an image of a desolated landscape in which the only sound disturbing the eerie silence among the rubble and ruins of palaces and gardens is the hooting of wild birds. Nineveh, once carefree and self-assured, the same Nineveh that had once declared: "I am – that is all there is" (v. 15), is to be totally devoid of inhabitants, with only the occasional passerby remaining to shake his hand at the debris.

11. When the Talmud wished to portray the total desolation of Jerusalem and the Temple Mount after the defeat of the rebellion against Rome in 70 CE, it drew on this imagery of wild animals (specifically foxes) running among the ruins of the *Beit HaMikdash* (Makkot 23b–24a).

3:1–3:8

Jerusalem Will Not Escape

Woe to her who is rebellious and defiled – the oppressive city. She did not obey, she did not accept reproof. She did not trust in the Lord. She did not draw near to her God. Her princes in her midst are roaring lions; her judges, wolves of the evening. They did not leave over the bones for morning. Her prophets are unstable, treacherous people. Her priests have profaned the Sanctuary; they have removed the Torah. The Lord is just in her midst; He commits no injustice. Every morning He brings His judgment to light. It does not fail. But the one who commits injustice knows no shame. I have cut off nations; their towers have become desolate. I have destroyed their streets so that no one passes by. Their cities have become waste so that there is no man – so that there is no inhabitant. I said, "Surely you will fear Me, you will accept reproof, and her dwelling shall not be cut off, all that I ordained upon her." But they arose early and corrupted all their deeds. Therefore, wait for Me, says the Lord, for the day that I will rise up to meet [with you]. For it is My judgment to assemble nations, to gather kingdoms, to pour out My fury upon them; yea, all the kindling of My wrath, for with the fire of My jealousy all the earth shall be consumed. (3:1–8)

Having graphically portrayed the devastation that awaits the surrounding nations, Zephaniah now turns back to warn the Jewish people that a similar fate awaits them. Amos did the same at the beginning of his book, but unlike Amos, Zephaniah's focus on the larger world is not a simple rhetorical device to draw his listeners in before condemning them. Just as he focused his pronouncement against Assyria on Nineveh, Zephaniah's pronouncement against Judah centers on Jerusalem. The two cities are linked through the repetition of the word "city" (in 2:15 and 3:1), so that they become indistinguishable from one another. Indeed, verse 1 does not identify Jerusalem as its subject immediately, and without the "woe" pronouncement, it could easily have been read as a continuation of the last chapter's prophecy against Nineveh. Only in the middle of verse 2, when Zephaniah attacks the city's failure to trust in God and correct its rebellious ways, would it become clear to Zephaniah's listeners that he was talking about Jerusalem. They had undoubtedly reveled in the news of Nineveh's impending downfall; but now they would, to their shock and dismay, discover that in God's eyes, Jerusalem was no different, not with regard to behavior, and not with regard to fate. Again, as in the first prophecy (1:2–2:3), the fates of Israel and the nations are intertwined.[1]

In verse 1, Zephaniah uses three adjectives to describe the city: rebellious, defiled, and oppressive. In verses 2–4, he explains and amplifies each of the terms:

1. The first three adjectives in verse 1 can be interpreted in two ways, as positive descriptions or as negative ones. The approach we have chosen to follow in our commentary is to view them as negative, but Malbim interprets the words of v. 1, *mora venigala*, as positive descriptions, meaning "awesome and redeemed," and believes that the rebuke of Jerusalem begins only in v. 2, where he suggests that Jerusalem ignored two forms of rebuke – both an appeal to its better self ("she did not listen") as well as threats of punishment ("she did not accept reproof"). He understands ch. 3 as describing a brief period in time, under Josiah's reign, when Assyrian power had waned but Babylonia had yet to rise. It could have been a perfect time for redemption, Malbim suggests, had the people been ready. Unfortunately, the Jewish people missed their moment. As such, according to Malbim, the rosy descriptions of redemption that Zephaniah describes in the final section of the chapter will have to wait for a more distant messianic future.

Woe Jerusalem	
Verse 1: Jerusalem is a ...	Verses 2–4 explain
rebellious city	She did not obey, she did not accept reproof. (v. 2)
defiled city	Her priests have profaned the Sanctuary; they have removed the Torah. (v. 4)
oppressive city	Her princes in her midst are roaring lions; her judges, wolves of the evening. They did not leave over the bones for morning. (v. 3)

With regard to the first charge, that of rebelliousness, the accusation is not a new one, and the Hebrew root for "rebellious" (M-R-H) almost always appears when Israel rebels against God or the Torah[2] (see Is. 3:8: "Jerusalem certainly stumbles, Judah falls, for their words and actions offend the Lord, they rebel (*lamrot*) against his royal authority"; and see also Is. 63:10, Jer. 4:17, 5:23, Ezek. 20:8, 13, 21). The theme of rebelliousness, as identified by the use of the root M-R-H, appears in different guises throughout the books of the prophets. Isaiah equates the people's rebelliousness with their need to provoke God (Is. 3:8), while Jeremiah declares that their rebelliousness stems from their lack of fear (Jer. 5:23). In Zephaniah, the people's rebellion is expressed as their refusal to heed reproof. This includes reproof that may have been delivered directly, by God's messengers, or indirectly, through the political upheavals that surrounded them: With so many nations having fallen around them, including the Philistines to their west, the Egyptians to their south, Ammon and Moab to the east, and finally their brothers, the Kingdom of Israel, to the north, the people should have understood that something was awry and that they too should take stock of their behavior and engage in serious self-reflection.

2. The appearance of the extra *alef* in the word here is unusual. Ibn Ezra and *Daat Mikra* here note that the letters *alef* and *heh* are often interchangeable, and they bring examples. But the extra *alef* may also serve to allude to additional meanings, including "disgusting" (see Nahum 3:6) or "fearful."

Zephaniah returns to the theme with which he opened chapter 1: the intertwined crimes of social inequity and religious corruption. Verse 3 describes how the civil leadership oppresses the people; verse 4 explains how Jerusalem became defiled due to the corruption of the priests and prophets. Physically, the people suffer as Judah's princes and judges squeeze the people dry of all they have, like lions and wolves who attack and leave nothing behind, not even "the bones for morning."[3] Malbim notes that the metaphoric usage of the two predators, lions and wolves of the evening, reflect the two manners in which Jerusalem's corrupt leadership oppressed its populace. The politicians (the princes) openly flaunted their power, like lions that hunt in the open. The judges took their bribes quietly and privately, like wolves that go out in the dusk, when they are difficult to see. Spiritually, corruption permeated Jerusalem's religious leadership, those most responsible for the spiritual and moral fiber of the populace. The false prophets do not deliver the divine message; the priests, responsible for the purity of the *Beit HaMikdash* and of the Torah (see I Chr. 23:28), distort it for their own purposes instead, causing Torah to be forgotten.[4]

In lambasting Jerusalem's leadership and their corrupt behavior, Zephaniah draws heavily on Micah's denunciations from the previous century, and in doing so alludes to the judgment with which Micah threatened the leadership of his time, that "Zion shall be plowed as a field; Jerusalem shall become heaps." The parallels can be seen clearly in the following chart:

3. Zephaniah's description of the leadership echoes Micah's words a century before. He had described Judah's leadership then as those who "eat the flesh of my people, and flay their skin from off them, and break their bones; yea, they chop them in pieces, as that which is in the pot, and as flesh within the cauldron" (3:1–4). Like Zephaniah, Micah also fought against the dual predicament of corrupt civil and religious leadership, and his prophecy regularly alternates between the two themes (see Mic. 2–3).
4. Ezekiel (22:26) amplifies Zephaniah's charges, pointing out that in his day, the situation is much worse, as the priests willfully profane all that is sacred.

Zephaniah 3:1–5	Micah 3:9–12
Woe to her who is rebellious and defiled – the oppressive city. She did not obey, she did not accept reproof. She did not trust in the Lord. She did not draw near to her God. Her princes in her midst are roaring lions; *her judges*, wolves of the evening. They did not leave over the bones for morning. *Her prophets* are unstable, treacherous people. *Her priests* have profaned the Sanctuary; they have removed the Torah. The Lord is just *in her midst*; He commits no *injustice*. Every morning He brings His *judgment* to light. It does not fail. But the one who commits injustice knows no shame.	Listen now to this, you heads of the House of Jacob and you rulers of the House of Israel, who condemn *justice* and pervert all that is straight. Each one builds Zion with blood and Jerusalem with *injustice*. Its heads *judge* for bribes, and its *priests* teach for a price; and *its prophets* divine for money, and they rely on the Lord, saying, "Is not the Lord *in our midst*? No evil shall befall us." *Therefore, because of you, Zion shall be plowed as a field; Jerusalem shall become heaps, and the Temple Mount like the high places of a forest.*

Zephaniah reminds his listeners that God is ultimately Judah's leader (3:5–7). Judah's leadership is corrupt, but the Lord is righteous. Jerusalem's judges left no evil undone by morning (v. 3 – *lo garmu laboker*), but God's justice shines forth with every new morning's beginning – *baboker mishpato yiten laor*. The comparison is made explicit within the verse itself – God knows no wickedness (*avla*), but the wicked (*aval*) know no shame. Zephaniah's laments echo those of his contemporary Jeremiah, who cried out "Woe unto the shepherds that destroy and scatter the sheep of My pasture!… For both prophet and priest are ungodly; in My house have I found their wickedness, says the Lord" (Jer. 23:1–11). Unlike Jeremiah, though, who predicted the return of a righteous strand of David's line to lead the people (23:5–6), Zephaniah is content to have God alone at the helm. This difference may reflect the influence of the different kings under which each prophet prophesied. Jeremiah worked in tandem with the righteous Josiah, whose piety gave hope that a king could reign with justice; Zephaniah's later prophecy (especially chapter 3) appears to have been uttered when the wicked Jehoiakim ruled, near the time of the Babylonian invasion, when repentance was no longer an option and it was only a matter of time until Judah would fall.[5]

Zephaniah concludes by reminding his listeners that God has already destroyed other nations. Verses 6–7, which detail the destruction of other nations, lend support to the later dating of the second half of the book (Nineveh was destroyed in 612 BCE), and also give additional insight into the nature of God's actions. The neighboring countries were punished for their behavior and accordingly, they were destroyed. God held up the fate of the other nations as an example and a warning sign for the Jewish people, hopeful that they would recognize and internalize that destruction is the only eventuality for those who do not repent, and that this realization would stir the people to action and repentance. At the beginning Jerusalem "hearkened not to the voice, she *received* not *correction*" (v. 2). After hearing of the destruction of the other nations, Zephaniah, speaking the words of God, had hoped with regard to the people: "Surely you will fear me, you will *receive correction*" But sadly, the people had become so thoroughly corrupt in their deeds that they awoke early to commit evil (see v. 7). Zephaniah concludes his second prophecy with a direction to his righteous listeners. He describes God's "verdict to assemble nations, to gather kingdoms, to pour out My fury upon them" (3:8). The words "assemble" and "gather" appear together in three other prophecies: in Micah 2:12, 4:6, and in Isaiah 11:12. In all of those, the object of God's gathering and assembling is the remnant of the Jewish people, who will now live peacefully in their land. In Zephaniah, however, it is not the righteous few being gathered for salvation, but rather the nations being gathered for destruction. For the righteous few, Zephaniah can only ask them to wait for better times. In the Tanakh, waiting for the Lord always brings blessings (see Is. 8:17, 30:18, 64:3, and Ps. 33:20). Here, however, it is the stark contrast with the ending of his first speech that stands out. In 2:3,

5. The dichotomy between prophecies that express hope for the future and those that urge acceptance of and submission to the upcoming cataclysm can be found within Jeremiah as well (cf. Jer. 25).

Zephaniah called upon his listeners to actively improve themselves and others through the pursuit of justice and humility. Now that he has despaired of that happening, all the prophet dares to ask from his listeners is to passively wait out the storm.

3:9–3:20

Ending with Hope

For then, I will convert the peoples to a pure language that all of them call in the name of the Lord, to worship Him of one accord. From the other side of the rivers of Ethiopia, My supplicants, the community of My scattered ones – they shall bring Me an offering. On that day you shall not be ashamed of all your deeds [with] which you rebelled against Me, for then I will remove from your midst those who rejoice in your pride, and you shall no longer continue to be haughty on My holy mount. And I will leave over in your midst a humble and poor people, and they shall take shelter in the name of the Lord. The remnant of Israel shall neither commit injustice nor speak lies; neither shall deceitful speech be found in their mouth, for they shall graze and lie down, with no one to cause them to shudder.

Sing, O daughter of Zion! Shout, O Israel! Rejoice and jubilate wholeheartedly, O daughter of Jerusalem! The Lord has removed your afflictions; He has cast out your enemy. The King of Israel, the Lord, is in your midst – you shall no longer fear evil. On that day it shall be said to Jerusalem, "Have no fear! O Zion, let your hands not be slack. The Lord your God is in your midst – a Mighty One who will save. He will rejoice over you

> with joy. He will be silent in His love. He will jubilate over you with song." Those who are removed from the appointed season I have destroyed. They were of you – it was a burden of shame upon her. Behold, I wreak destruction upon all those who afflict you at that time. And I will save the one who limps, and I will gather the stray one, and I will make them a praise and a name throughout all the land where they suffered shame. At that time I will bring them, and at [that] time I will gather you, for I will make you a name and a praise among all the peoples of the earth when I restore your captivities before your eyes, said the Lord. (3:9–20)

The conclusion of Zephaniah's prophecy, verses 9–20, clearly constitute a distinctive unit, which can be divided into two sections, verses 9–13 and 14–20. The sections are linked through repeated words and similar themes, including "on that day" (vv. 11, 16), "shame" (vv. 11, 19), and "shudder/fear" (vv. 13, 16). The opening words "For then" signal a major change in time, as well as a change in the focus of Zephaniah's prophecy: whereas before the focus was punishment, now it is redemption. As with his other prophecies, Zephaniah begins with a universal prophecy: God promises to give the people of the world "pure language" that will speak truth, rather than the "unclean lips" of the Jewish people of which Isaiah spoke (see Is. 6:5), which presumably uttered lies and deceit (Is. 6:5–7). In Genesis 11, the people of the earth were punished by being scattered, and their unified language was confused such that they could not understand one another. Zephaniah alludes to this incident, prophesying that when redemption arrives the ancient curse of Babel will be reversed and all people of the earth will be reunited with clear speech.[6] As proof of their newfound recognition of God, the nations of the world will bring gifts and offerings to Jerusalem. According to many commentaries (see, e.g., Malbim), the gift that the nations are bringing is the Jewish people itself, as prophesied in Isaiah: "They will

6. Another possible allusion to the Babel story is found in the description of Israel as "daughter of My dispersed (*bat putzi*)." The word for "dispersed" comes from the same root as the word used to describe the scattering of the nations of the world as a result of the building of the Tower of Babel (Gen. 11:4, 8).

bring back all your countrymen from all the nations as an offering to the Lord (*minḥa Lashem*). They will bring them on horses, in chariots, in wagons, on mules, and on camels to My holy hill Jerusalem, says the Lord, just as the Israelites bring offerings to the Lord's Temple in ritually pure containers" (66:20). They will return even from the "rivers of Cush," with Cush either representing the ends of the earth (see Est. 1:1, where Ahasuerus's empire is described as extending from Hodu to Cush) or serving as a synecdoche, i.e., a figure of speech where a part represents the whole, meaning that the scattered ones will return from all parts of the world. In verse 11, Zephaniah turns again to directly address the Jewish people, who are spoken about in second person now, not in third person. The words "for then" at the beginning of verse 9 marked a change in focus from punishment to redemption; in verse 11, the opening phrase, "on that day," symbolizes another shift in focus, from the universal (the people of the world) to the particular (the Jewish people), and reiterates that on that day, no feeling of shame shall accompany the people, for the haughty and the proud will have been removed, leaving behind a humble, destitute remnant which will become a symbol of honesty and righteousness among the nations.

Based on the assurances that Zephaniah gave the people in the first half of this prophecy, he now directly instructs the people to rejoice in their redemption, and declares that God Himself will rejoice in their redemption. The parallel of the people's joy and God's joy is apparent in the chiastic structure that contrasts Judah's future rejoicing over being saved with God's equally strong rejoicing for His people, as reflected in His commitment to protect them in the future as well:

A. *Sing* (*ronni*), O daughter of Zion!
B. *Shout*, O Israel!
C. *Rejoice* (*simḥi*) and *jubilate* wholeheartedly, O daughter of Jerusalem!
D. The Lord has removed your afflictions; He has cast out your enemy.
E. The King of Israel, *the Lord, is in your midst* (*bekirbekh*).
F. You shall no longer *fear* evil.
G. *On that day* it shall be said to Jerusalem,

F1. Have no *fear*! O Zion, let your hands not be slack.
E1. *The Lord* your God *is in your midst* (*bekirbekh*).
D1. A Mighty One who *will save*.
C1. He *will rejoice* over you with joy (*besimḥa*).
B1. He *will be silent* in His love.
A1. He *will jubilate* over you with song (*rinna*).

Zephaniah gives four simple instructions to the people of Israel: sing for joy, shout aloud, rejoice, and be glad. In response, God will also rejoice and jubilate with song. Verse 17 states that in His love, He will remain silent, or He will silence. To what does this silence refer? Rashi and other commentaries suggest that the meaning of this is that once the people are redeemed, God will cover up, i.e., silence, their future sins, because of His deep love for His people. Throughout the Bible, the relationship between God and the Jewish people is often described as being based on *ḥesed*, even when the metaphor of husband and wife is being used to describe the relationship between them (Hos. 2:21–23). But here, Zephaniah chooses to use the word *ahava*, which conjures images of the Bible's most passionate relationships and love stories: Jacob's love for Rachel (Gen. 29:20), Michal's love for David (I Sam. 18:28), Jonathan's love for David and vice versa (I Sam. 18:3, II Sam. 1:26), and the psalmist's love of Torah (Ps. 119:97). It is this deep love that will cause God to break forth in joyful singing in Zephaniah (3:17). Verse 16, which introduces God's love and joyful singing, begins with the words "on that day." The return to this phrase is meaningful, serving as a stark contrast to the phrase "the day of the Lord" that occupied Zephaniah in the first chapter. There, the "day" referred to was one of darkness and destruction. By contrast, the "day" in 3:16, positioned at the center of the chiasm and at the climax of Zephaniah's message, is one of love, light, and redemption.

Zephaniah concludes with three final verses that, on the surface, seem to mainly provide further rationale for the fourfold command to rejoice in verse 14. Read on a deeper level, one can discern that these verses contain Zephaniah's final literary artifice: Whereas at the beginning of chapter 3, Zephaniah spoke on God's behalf, and God was referred to in the third person (until 3:6), now, like at the beginning of

Zephaniah (1:2), God speaks in the first person, and speaks directly to the people. Eight times in verses 18–20 does God say, "I will," "I am going to," or "When I." But in sharp contrast to the beginning of the book, when God spoke in first person and stated that He would personally destroy the world, now God offers the world reassurance that He will personally gather up those who have been driven away and return them to Jerusalem, so they can participate in the celebration of the holidays and festivals. A clever wordplay is used to emphasize this contrast: the original threat was *asof asef* (1:2), which meant "I will destroy everything" – now God promises *asafti,* meaning "I will gather." The final verse includes a final, additional shift in Zephaniah's focus: He does not end his prophecy with a focus only on the redemption of the Jewish captives and their return to Israel. Instead, Zephaniah once again looks outward to the entire world, describing how the return of the Jewish people will affect the nations of the world and bring them to praise God.

Conclusion

From Destruction to Deliverance

Our commentary on Zephaniah is much shorter than the commentary on the other books explored in this study. This is in large part due to the clarity of his message, which can be distilled into two words – *yom Hashem*, "the day of the Lord." His message is not analogous to Nahum's exuberant celebration over the defeat of a hated and wicked enemy, nor is it analogous to the style of the theological questions raised by Habakkuk as he attempts to contend with knowledge that the downfall of the Assyrian enemy means the coming of an even greater and more deadly foe. Zephaniah avoids both extremes. His message to the people is simple: the day of reckoning is near. There is a brief window of opportunity for change, but it will not last forever. Without quick action, the brief glimmer of light will darken, and redemption will have to wait.

At the same time, complex religious ideas serve as the underpinnings of his ideas. Zephaniah's portrayals of "the day of the Lord" are among the darkest in all of Tanakh, yet his descriptions of the eventual redemption jump off the page with excitement and passion. In Zephaniah, judgment and deliverance are not irreconcilable opposites that cannot coexist; rather they are two simultaneous aspects of God's ultimate purpose and plan. A surviving remnant will see both the darkest of days as well as the great redemption. That remnant will return to their land, and they will dwell in security and worship in gladness. But Zephaniah does not limit his vision to Israel alone. Humanity will also undergo upheavals, as ancient empires fall and the world order crumbles. Zephaniah alludes several times to stories from the book of Genesis; through these allusions he suggests that the effects of the Flood and the Tower of Babel will be reversed, and the nations of the world will assume their place as partners in serving God. This is the breadth and depth of Zephaniah's vision – the ability to see both immediate threat and dangers while simultaneously maintaining his gaze toward the horizon, where the ultimate redemption for the Jewish people as well as the deliverance of the entire world lies.

Epilogue

Living deep in the Judean hills, the shepherd Amos could not have known about the birth of a young baby named Nabopolassar thousands of miles away. Nor could Amos imagine that young Nabopolassar would grow up to join the army and overthrow Assyrian rule: by 612 BCE, Babylonia would sack the capital city of Nineveh and defeat the once-invincible Assyrian Empire. The cruel Assyrian oppressor would disappear, only to be replaced by an even more brutal oppressor with the era of Babylonian domination. Ultimately, Nabopolassar's son Nebuchadnezzar would burn Solomon's Temple to the ground, and exile the people of Judah to the rivers of Babylon.

Between these two peaks of darkness, a fleeting ray of light would shine on Amos and the Jewish people. Manasseh's dark reign of evil would end. Though his son Amon would attempt to continue in his father's wicked ways, his brief reign would be cut short when his own servants assassinated him, installing his young grandson Josiah in his place. Within a decade, the young boy would lead a movement of return to Torah on a scale unseen in Jewish history. He encouraged the people to renew their covenant with God, to commit themselves to worshipping God exclusively, and to perform justice and kindness. During this brief respite, prophets once again began to speak. Courageous voices arose, calling for fidelity and faith, warning of dangers that lay ahead, but always providing hope.

Among these prophets were Nahum, Habakkuk, and Zephaniah. Their messages were short, but their influence was everlasting. To listeners who despaired and worried that God had forgotten His people, Nahum revealed that even the evil Assyrian oppressor, who was seemingly invincible, would soon face divine reckoning. Even the mighty Assyrian capital, the city of Nineveh, would be destroyed for eternity. Just beyond the deceptive and short-lived period of calm, both physical and spiritual dangers awaited the Jewish people. Habakkuk accurately foresaw the challenges that would arise. Courageously, he stood before God and challenged Him on the people's behalf. Finally, during the brief respite from oppression, Zephaniah also foresaw the coming cataclysm. At a time of national security and confidence, he made a valiant attempt to convince the people to abandon their sinful ways, so that they could be spared when "the day of the Lord" arrived. Ultimately, King Josiah took to heart the essence of their messages – the message that there was still hope for Jerusalem and her people and that salvation was still possible. Together, king and prophet gave instruction and provided hope to a weary people. They reminded them that despite the seemingly insurmountable darkness that had come before them and that was predicted to return in the near future, those who held onto faith would see lights in the valley.

Selected Bibliography

Biblical Texts and Commentaries

Achituv, Shmuel. *Mikra LeYisrael: Nahum, Habakkuk, Zephaniah* (Hebrew). Tel Aviv: Am Oved, 2006.

Achtemeier, Elizabeth Rice. *Nahum–Malachi: Interpretation: A Bible Commentary for Teaching and Preaching.* Nashville: John Knox, 1986.

Baker, David W. *Nahum, Habakkuk and Zephaniah: An Introduction and Commentary.* Tyndale Old Testament Commentaries series. Leicester, UK, and Downers Grove, IL: Inter-Varsity Press, 1988.

Berlin, Adele. *Zephaniah: A New Translation with Introduction and Commentary.* The Anchor Bible. New Haven: Yale University Press, 1994.

Boleh, Menachem. *Daat Mikra: Trei Asar,* vol. 2 (Hebrew). Jerusalem: Mossad HaRav Kook, 1990.

O'Brien, Julia Myers. *Nahum, Habakkuk, Zephaniah, Haggai, Zechariah, Malachi.* Abingdon Old Testament Commentaries (AOTC). Nashville: Abingdon Press, 2004.

Patterson, Richard. *Nahum, Habakkuk, Zephaniah.* Wycliffe Exegetical Commentary. Chicago: Moody Press, 1991.

Smith, Ralph L. *Micah-Malachi.* Word Biblical Commentary. Waco, TX: Word Books, 1984.

Sweeney, Marvin A. *The Twelve Prophets, Volume 2: Micah, Nahum, Habakkuk, Zephaniah, Haggai, Zechariah, Malachi.* Berit Olam: Studies in Hebrew Narrative and Poetry. Collegeville, MN: The Liturgical Press, 2000.

General Commentaries

Alter, Robert, and Frank Kermode. *The Literary Guide to the Bible.* Cambridge, MA: Harvard University, 1987.

Angel, Hayyim. *Revealed Texts, Hidden Meanings: Finding the Religious Significance in Tanakh.* Jersey City: Ktav Publishing, 2009.

———. *Vision from the Prophet and Counsel from the Elders: A Survey of Nevi'im and Ketuvim.* Jersey City: Ktav Publishing and OU Press, 2013.

———. *Peshat Isn't So Simple: Essays on Developing a Religious Methodology to Bible Study.* Jersey City: Ktav Publishing, 2014.

Anglim, Simon. *Fighting Techniques of the Ancient World 3000 BCE–500 CE.* New York: Amber Books, 2013.

Christensen, Duane L. "The Acrostic of Nahum Reconsidered." *Zeitschrift für die alttestamentliche Wissenschaft* 87 (1975): 25.

———. "Zephaniah 2:4–15: A Theological Basis for Josiah's Program of Political Expansion." *Catholic Biblical Quarterly* 46 (1984): 669–82.

Cline, Eric H. and Mark W. Graham. *Ancient Empires: From Mesopotamia to the Rise of Islam.* Cambridge, UK: Cambridge University Press, 2011.

Dorsey, David A. *The Literary Structure of the Old Testament: A Commentary on Genesis to Malachi.* Grand Rapids, MI: Baker Book House, 1999.

Floyd, Michael H. "The Chimerical Acrostic of Nahum 1:1–10." *Journal of Biblical Literature* 113 (1994): 421–37.

Heschel, Abraham J. *The Prophets.* New York: Harper & Row, 1962.

House, Paul R. *Zephaniah: A Prophetic Drama.* Sheffield: Sheffield Academic, 1989.

Johnston, Gordon H. "Nahum's Rhetorical Allusions to Neo-Assyrian Treaty Curses," *Bibliotheca Sacra* 158, no. 632 (October–December 2001): 415–36.

Kagan, Jeremy, *The Jewish Self.* New York: Feldheim, 1998.

King, Greg A. "The Message of Zephaniah: An Urgent Echo." *Andrews University Seminary Studies* 32, no. 2 (Autumn 1996): 211–22.

Lau, Binyamin. *Eight Prophets* (Hebrew). Rishon LeZion: Yediot Aharonot Publishing, 2016.

Maier, Walter A. *The Book of Nahum: A Commentary* (reprint). James Family Publishers, 1977.

O'Brien, Julia Myers. *Nahum.* Readings: A New Biblical Commentary. Sheffield Academic Press, 2002.

———. *Challenging Prophetic Metaphor.* Louisville: Westminster Press, 2008.

Patterson, Richard D. and Michael E. Travers. "Literary Analysis and Unity of Nahum," *Grace Theological Journal* 9.1 (1988): 55–58.

_____ . "A Literary Look at Nahum, Habakkuk, and Zephaniah," *Grace Theological Journal* 11.1 (Spring 1990): 17–27.

Podhoretz, Norman. *The Prophets: Who They Were, What They Are.* New York: The Free Press, 2002.

Ryken, Leyland. *Words of Delight: A Literary Introduction to the Bible.*

Smith, Gary V. *Prophets as Preachers.* Nashville: Holman Bible Publishers, 1994.

Sweeney, Marvin A. "Zephaniah: A Paradigm for the Study of the Prophetic Books." *Currents in Research: Biblical Studies* 7 (1999): 119–46.

Weinberg, Yaakov. *Fundamentals and Faith.* Jerusalem: Targum Press, 1991.

Selected Historical Sources

Heater Jr., Homer, 2014. "The Rise of the Neo-Babylonian (Chaldean) Empire," available online at https://bible.org/seriespage/19-rise-neo-babylonian-chaldean-empire.

Lendering, Jona. "Babylon Empire," available online at http://www.livius.org/articles/place/babylonian-empire/.

Mark, Joshua J. "Assyria," entry in the *Ancient History Encyclopedia*, available online at http://www.ancient.eu/assyria/.

Riddle, A. D., 2015. "Neo-Assyrian Kings and Biblical History," posted at http://blog.bibleplaces.com/2015/04/neo-assyrian-kings-and-biblical-history.html.

Roux, Georges, 1992. *Ancient Iraq*. London: Penguin Books. "The House of Sargon II," available online at http://www.gatewaystobabylon.com/introduction/assyriankings.htm.

Unattributed. "A Brief Overview of Assyrian History: From Early Beginnings to Sargon II," available online at http://www.gatewaystobabylon.com/introduction/overviewassyria.htm.

Other books in the Maggid Studies in Tanakh series:

Genesis: From Creation to Covenant
Zvi Grumet

Joshua: The Challenge of the Promised Land
Michael Hattin

Judges: The Perils of Possession (forthcoming)
Michael Hattin

I Kings: Torn in Two
Alex Israel

II Kings: In a Whirlwind
Alex Israel

Isaiah
Yoel Bin-Nun and Binyamin Lau

Jeremiah: The Fate of a Prophet
Binyamin Lau

Ezekiel (forthcoming)
Tova Ganzel

Jonah: The Reluctant Prophet
Erica Brown

Haggai, Zechariah, and Malachi:
Prophecy in an Age of Uncertainty
Hayyim Angel

Ruth: From Alienation to Monarchy
Yael Ziegler

Esther: Power, Fate, and Fragility in Exile
Erica Brown

Nehemiah: Statesman and Sage
Dov S. Zakheim

The fonts used in this book are from the Arno family

Maggid Books
The best of contemporary Jewish thought from
Koren Publishers Jerusalem Ltd.